CHINESE GOVERNMENT

Yang Fengchun

Foreign Languages Press

First Edition   2004

Home Page:
http://www.flp.com.cn
E-mail Addresses:
info@flp.com.cn
sales@flp.com.cn

ISBN 7-119-03285-2
© Foreign Languages Press, Beijing, China, 2004
Published by Foreign Languages Press
24 Baiwanzhuang Road, Beijing 100037, China
Distributed by China International Book Trading Corporation
35 Chegongzhuang Xilu, Beijing 100044, China
P.O. Box 399, Beijing, China
Printed in the People's Republic of China

CONTENTS

Chapter One

THE NATURE OF THE CHINESE GOVERNMENT

Section 1 The Nature of the Socialist State

I. The General Nature and Tasks of the State

According to the Marxist-Leninist theory on the state, all states and governments have a class nature. It is a tool of the ruling class with which it exercises its rule. Friedrich Engels said, "The state is no more than a machine for the rule of one class over another."[1] Vladimir Lenin said, "The state is a machine for maintaining the rule of one class over another."[2] Therefore, in the view point of Marxism-Leninism, the state has never been a public organization of power in the general sense, but "a special public organization of power." It has a distinct class nature, a definite mission and a special form of existence. This is even true of the "proletarian" state, which is established and developed according to Marxist-Leninist theory.

According to the general theory of Marxist political science, the state has the following nature and characteristics:

First, the state is the tool of those who own the means of production to exercise rule over others. Therefore, the different ownerships of the means of production in a class society will determine the attribution of the political power of the state and the relationship between the rulers and ruled in a particular society.

Second, the social form of existence of the state is as the "superficial mediator" of irreconcilable conflicts among different classes for state power. That is, the state in normal conditions appears as the impartial public authority usually keeping aloof from society. This aloofness often conceals the class nature of the state. As determined by the class nature of

1

the state, the impartiality of the state and its neutrality as a "mediator" are inevitably greatly limited.

Third, in order to perform its function of political rule in safeguarding the interests of the ruling class, the state must at the same time perform the function of political administration over the entire society. "Political rule everywhere is based on the performance of certain social functions, and political rule can be maintained only when it performs this social function."[3] Although the conflict of interests in a class society is irreconcilable, there is, after all, a given, routine and constant requirement for the state to function in a way that keeps society in existence, which entails increasingly gathering resources for exercising political rule over society. In fact, in the history of the political life of humanity, there has never been a state which entirely and purely relies on political rule without improving necessary administrative services for the entire society.

Fourth, the state is a "special apparatus for the systematic application of force and the subjugation of people by force"[4]. As the conflict of class interests is unavoidable and economic resources are limited, the ruling class must rely on violence to undermine the claims and struggles of other classes for their interests, in order to defend its economic interests. Therefore, no matter how much the state denies it, its violent character cannot be eliminated. The state has systematic tools of violence and specific targets of violence. As the major tool of class rule, the state uses violence to safeguard the interests of the ruling class. In reality, the Marxist theory of the state puts special stress on the violent character of the state. An understanding of this is not only necessary for understanding the essence of the state forms of the exploiting classes, but also for enabling the socialist state to rely on the strength of the state machine to perform its own mission in a better way.

II. The Nature and Tasks of the Socialist State

The socialist state is a new type of state established by the proletarian representatives of the advanced productive forces, who rule in the interests of the proletariat and the broad masses of the working people after the extinction of the capitalist state.[5] As the historical mission of the proletariat is to eliminate all class differences and social inequalities, and create the conditions to finally achieve the extinction of the state, the socialist state is a state based on class rule before the state withers away, that is, before the dictatorship of the proletariat withers away.

Since it is a state based on class rule, the socialist state also inevitably has the general nature of a state based on class rule. But, because it is different from all states throughout history which have been ruled by exploiting classes, the socialist state has some new characteristics.

First, because it takes the common interests of the proletariat and the broad masses of the working people formed on the basis of the public ownership of the means of production as the economic and interest foundation of the state, the socialist state, by nature, is the state form with which the proletariat and the other working people exercise political rule, and the proletariat and other working people own the means of production, thereby forming the political and economic interest relations of the whole society.

Second, the socialist state assumes broader and more comprehensive responsibilities. Because the public ownership of the means of production is the foundation of the system of ownership of the economic interests of society, many functions of social management arising from the public ownership of the means of production emerge as required. Moreover, as the proletariat and the other working people constitute the majority of the people in society, the general responsibilities of social management of the socialist state are, by comparison, massive and heavy.

Third, the socialist state is still one that exercises its rule by means of violence. As the socialist state is the final state of class dictatorship in human history, and assumes the mission of eliminating classes, it inevitably has the function of oppression and suppression by violence common to all states based on class rule. The socialist state still needs to suppress some members of the society so as to force the entire society to comply to the rule of the state.

Fourth, as the socialist state is a new type of state entirely different from all other states ruled by exploiting classes in history, and represents the demands of the new social classes and forces, it requires the establishment of a new political form at the level of state rule and political administration, thus giving expression to its new political characteristics. The political attribute of the socialist state, in the first place, calls for establishing the leading position of the proletarian party institutionally and politically. The leading position of the proletarian party is unshakable. This is not only determined by the class characteristics of the proletariat, but also by the inseparability from the state of the proletarian interests formed on the basis of public ownership of the means of production.

Fifth, as the socialist state is established on the basis of Marxist-Leninist theory, Marxism-Leninism is thus the guiding principle of the socialist state. The history of the Communist movement over the world shows that without Marxist-Leninist theory there would not be the practice of socialism and communism. Therefore, if it is divorced from the theoretical guidance of Marxism-Leninism, the socialist state will lose its foundation and soul. If it abandons Marxist-Leninist principles, the socialist state shall not be a genuine socialist state.

Section 2   The Nature of the Chinese Government

The government of the People's Republic of China was established by the victorious Communist Party of China (CPC) in 1949, after protracted domestic class struggles and civil war. The nature of the CPC as a proletarian political party determines the nature of the socialist state of the People's Republic of China.

I. The CPC Is China's Ruling Party

Party politics in modern states is, generally speaking, divided into the party politics of the capitalist state and the party politics of the proletarian state. In a capitalist state, because the bourgeoisie, which holds state power, cannot represent the fundamental interests and demands of the entire society, in which there are irreconcilable conflicts of interest among the different groups of people, it is difficult to form a single party that represents the interests and demands of all people. As a result, there are more than one parties that represent the respective interests and demands of the different interest groups, thus giving rise to the multi-party system and the political arrangement in which the different parties hold state power in turn. Therefore, by nature, the modern multi-party system is linked to the divisions and conflicts of interest among different social groups in a capitalist society and is simply a political arrangement for the ruling class to keep these conflicts of interest under control.

Party politics in the socialist state is totally different from that in the capitalist state. Because a proletarian political party, fundamentally speaking, represents the interests of the greatest majority of society, therefore, the integration and coordination of the interests and demands of the whole society, which can never be achieved in capitalist society, becomes a reality in a socialist society. Because the interests of the entire society are integrated, the interest representation function of the proletarian party is concentrated in the representation of the interests of the entire society by the proletarian party. Because there is no interest difference of dividing social groups that contradict and conflict with each other, fundamentally speaking, there is no need for other political parties to represent and reflect the interests and demands of the different social groups in the socialist state. Hence, in a socialist state, the proletarian party, which represents in a concentrated form the fundamental and common interests and demands of the entire society, becomes the sole ruling party. The multi-party system of the capitalist society thus loses the foundation and necessity to exist in the socialist state.

Moreover, there is a major difference between a proletarian party and a bourgeois party in political goals. In other words, the proletarian party is a political party that is most completely free from narrow limitations of class interest. Its interests lie not only in emancipating itself, but also in emancipating mankind and finally achieving communism. The reason why the proletarian party has the ability to assume this mission is that it has scientifically grasped the fundamental laws of development of human society, and can lead the whole people to achieve the ideal communist society step by step. To achieve this goal, transformation of the old society is unavoidable. The process of transforming the old society is a process of readjusting and reshaping the existing pattern of interests. In this process, if the proletarian party cannot transcend the general interest limitations in society, it will be unable to fulfill this task. In fact, the advanced character of the proletarian party dictates that it not only has no special interests of its own to pursue, but also, because of the universality and fundamentality of its interest representation, it has the obligation not to share political leadership with other political parties. By contrast, because it is limited by its particular class interest, the political goal of a bourgeois party is usually limited to the interests of its own class or group, which means that it can never assume the mission of emancipating mankind. Therefore, in order to alleviate the conflicts of interest among the different groups, the different parties have no choice but to hold power in turn. The difference of political goal naturally gives the proletarian party greater, more authoritative and freer space for political activities than other political parties. It doesn't have to follow the rules as well as usual practices and values that the bourgeois political parties are accustomed to.

The position obtained by the CPC as the sole ruling party is linked to the tradition of the Chinese society and its own unique historical position. The traditional Chinese society did not have the democratic tradition that is taken for granted in a Western society and the foundation for the division of social interests. Therefore, politics of strength or power politics has a deep root in the Chinese society. It is unimaginable for any political force to gain political rule without having corresponding strength as its backing. One of the political consequences of this tradition is that any political movement originating from the common interests and demands of the ordinary members of society, in fact, can succeed only by resorting to violent revolution if it intends to be able to actually influence state politics. Otherwise, it will come to no avail because it has no realistic way to produce any actual political influence for lack of a foundation of strength. This tradition and law of politics resulted in a deep-rooted political culture of having blind faith in violence and coercion, and objectively stifled the formation of any potential political forces. The CPC grew up under such circumstances and culture. The Chinese communists had a profound knowledge of the Chinese tradition and political and cultural mentality, and in their protracted revolutionary struggles never had they put faith blindly in the so-called legal struggle and parliamentary road or any other means that brought about changes in a Western society, but from the very beginning, adhered to the principle of "political power growing out of the barrel of a gun," waged armed struggle, feared no bloodshed or sacrifices, advanced wave upon wave, and finally won state power. The process in which the CPC gradually grew from a tiny and weak party to a strong one, finally overthrowing the "legal" government, was also a process in which it won the trust of the whole people. The trust the people placed on the CPC led to the collapse of the "legal" government of the Kuomintang and at the same time excluded any other political forces from possibly sharing the leadership of the Chinese government. In fact, there was no other political force in Chinese society that could rival in strength the CPC in the Chinese political and cultural environments. Therefore, once the CPC obtained the leadership of the Chinese government by relying on its own strength, its position as the sole ruling party was established.

Therefore, the CPC will remain as the sole ruling party in China, and this reflects the fundamental nature of the party politics of the socialist society and is in keeping with the political goals of the proletarian party as well as the peculiar Chinese traditional political and cultural mindset.

II. The People's Democratic Dictatorship

The theory of Marxism concerning the state holds that every state has its given class attribute. The class attribute of the socialist state is the dictatorship of the proletariat. In China, the dictatorship of the proletariat is expressed as the people's democratic dictatorship.[6]

The people's democratic dictatorship is the quintessence of the class nature of the Chinese government. That is, it defines the standings of the different classes vis-a-vis state power and their mutual relations: "Our dictatorship is the people's democratic dictatorship led by the working class and based on the worker-peasant alliance. That is to say, democracy operates within the ranks of the people, while the working class, uniting with all others enjoying civil rights, and in the first place with the peasantry, enforces dictatorship over the reactionary classes and elements and all those who resist socialist transformation and oppose socialist construction."[7] The people's democratic dictatorship means "the combination of .... democracy for the people and dictatorship over the reactionaries."[8] The people's democratic dictatorship shows that the political standings of the different members of society are different in China: To the members of society with specific capacities and under specific circumstances, some can enjoy democratic rights, but some can only be put under dictatorship. This difference of political standing and political capacity of the members of society is entirely determined by the historical mission of the CPC and the nature of the proletarian dictatorship of the Chinese government.

In concrete terms, the nature of the people's democratic dictatorship determines the different positions of the different social classes, strata and groups in the political life of the state. Within the framework of the people's democratic dictatorship, generally speaking, the composition of the "people" is different in different periods, but the working class, the peasantry, the petty bourgeoisie, the national bourgeoisie and the patriotic democrats who have abandoned the reactionary classes belong to the camp of the people. They represent 95% of the national population. The peasantry, which forms an alliance with the working class, has become an important component of the people's camp, next only to the working class, which takes the leading position.[9] In the early years following the founding of the People's Republic of China, the members of society who were not counted as belonging to the category of the "people" were mainly remnant military and political personnel of the Kuomintang, members of the bureaucratic comprador bourgeoisie, elements colluding with imperialism, elements opposing the Communist Party of China, and saboteurs of economic construction. Later, landlords, rich peasants, counter-revolutionaries, bad elements, "Rightists" opposing the Communist Party of China, and "all social forces and groups who resist the socialist revolution and are hostile to and sabotage the socialist construction,"[10] were included within the scope of the "enemies of the people," constituting, all together, about 5% of the population.[11] Not only were they were deprived of democratic rights, but their activities were invariably put under surveillance. In the subsequent socialist period, although large-scale class struggles no longer existed, small-scale class struggles have continued and will continue to exist for a fairly long period of time. There were and will still be hostile elements who oppose the Communist Party of China, socialism and the government, and all sorts of criminals. Therefore, there were, are and will be "enemies," and it is still necessary to wage struggles against the "attempts of the counter-revolutionary classes, groups and individuals to oppose the revolution and restore their political power,"[12] and the dictatorship over enemies must be maintained. From the angle of methodology, while enforcing the people's democratic dictatorship, it is necessary to correctly distinguish and handle the two types of contradictions that differ in nature, namely, those between ourselves and the enemy, and those among the people, when the relationship between democracy and dictatorship is handled. Different methods are employed to resolve the two different types of contradictions: The method of democracy is only applied to those among the people, while the method of dictatorship is used to deal with the enemy.[13] The contradictions among the people refer mainly to the different types of contradictions arising among the people themselves, between the people and the government, between the CPC and the people, among the organizations at different levels, and between the governors and the governed. These contradictions are non-antagonistic. Their resolution does not mean that one aspect of a contradiction is eliminated by the other. They can exist together and can be resolved by the method of unity — criticism — unity.

The contradictions between ourselves and the enemy are antagonistic. The existence of one aspect of this type of contradiction is conditioned by the elimination of the other. Their relationship is one of life and death. Only the method of dictatorship is applicable to its resolution. However, according to Marxist philosophy, these two types of contradiction, which differ in nature, can transform themselves into each other under given conditions: If a contradiction among the people is not properly handled, it can be transformed into a contradiction between ourselves and the enemy, while a contradiction between ourselves and the enemy can also be transformed into a contradiction among the people under given conditions. As a matter of fact, this methodology for handling democracy and dictatorship has the characteristics of a high degree of flexibility and uncertainty at the same time. For example, how does one judge the nature of a contradiction? Once a contradiction is manifested in social life, it often has a variety of characteristics and factors, making it difficult to identify which ones determine the nature of a concrete contradiction. Again, under what conditions and in the presence of what characteristics can it be decided that the nature of a contradiction has changed. It is precisely the difficulty and uncertainty in handling contradictions that have played into the hands of political extremists, and led to such aberrations as the "cultural revolution" (1966-1976), during which extremist elements intentionally confused the two types of contradictions, which differ in nature, wantonly extended the scope of the state's dictatorial power, and finally provided an opportunity for the minority to attack and persecute the majority. At the same time, the complexity and flexibility of the methodology left a window of opportunity for "rule-by-man" politics.

At the present stage, the stress on the theory and practice of the people's democratic dictatorship is somewhat different from what it was in the past, and especially following the experience of the "cultural revolution." The extremist dictatorship enforced during the "cultural revolution" not only worsened the relations among the ordinary members of society, it also brought great harm to the leading cadres of the CPC at all levels, weakening the Party's ability to run the state. In view of this, Deng Xiaoping advocated strengthening democracy and the legal system to remedy the mistakes made by the CPC in the practice of democracy in the past.[14] He said that the root cause of the mistakes in promoting democracy lay in the over-emphasis on dictatorship and the failure to guarantee the realization of the people's democratic rights. "We did not consciously and systematically build the systems to guarantee the people's democratic rights. The legal system was not complete, and we did not attach enough importance to it. Privileges were restricted, criticized and attacked for some time, but they were revived later."[15] As the scope of dictatorship was too broad and the scope of attack was too big during the ultra-"Left" dictatorship period of the "cultural revolution," Deng Xiaoping demanded that the government "strictly differentiate the two types of contradictions that differ in nature, broaden the scope of education and reduce the scope of attack."[16] It can be said that prior to the Deng Xiaoping era, the function of the people's democratic dictatorship was strengthened too much, and not enough play was given to the function of democracy. Deng Xiaoping's emphasis on the aspect of democracy in the framework of the people's democratic dictatorship is one way that his reform and opening policy differed from the policies of the Mao Zedong era.

However, the people's democratic dictatorship is of crucial significance to the CPC and the socialist nature of the Chinese government. Although democracy is being promoted to some degree to atone for the mistakes made by the ultra-"Left" politics, it does not at all mean any weakening of dictatorship in the system of people's democratic dictatorship. While advocating the promotion of democracy and the legal system, Deng Xiaoping also put special emphasis on strengthening dictatorship over "hostile forces." Deng Xiaoping believed that in the era of reform and opening, hostile forces will step up political, ideological and cultural infiltration, subversion and attempts at peaceful evolution, as well as social activities intended to change and overthrow the socialist system and the leadership of the CPC, and sow "distrust in the socialist and communist cause and the leadership of the Communist Party."[17] This will "affect the destiny and future of the Communist Party and the nation."[18] Therefore, Deng Xiaoping said, resolute blows must be dealt at erroneous ideas, conduct and activities that threaten the leadership of the CPC and the socialist system. It can be seen that the function of "dictatorship" in the people's democratic dictatorship still plays an important role in safeguarding the leadership of the state by the CPC and the socialist system.

III. The People's Congress System

The principle of all state authority emanating from the people is one followed in almost all modern countries, including China. According to the current Constitution, "All power in the People's Republic of China belongs to the people" (Article 2). State authority in the People's Republic of China belongs to the people and the people are masters of the state.

The people's congress system is a system by which the people wield and exercise their state authority. For any modern nation, how to organize the "people" who are great in number and differ in interests into a political subject who can actually wield and exercise state power is a great challenge. There are different political and legal arrangements in the different political systems and different states. In the capitalist state, because of the complicated and diverse interests of the members of society, it is impossible to simplify and unify the interests and demands of the people into a simple representative system. Therefore, a representative system is usually used to organize and express the interests and demands of the "people." In the arrangement of the representative system, the "people" choose their representatives through their votes. Once the representatives win the confidence of the "people," they get the right to exercise their power independently. As there are obvious relationships of giving and receiving power between the voters and the representatives, the various interests and demands of the "people" are expressed directly and in a concrete way to form representative politics. Moreover, as the representatives can directly or indirectly make decisions on state policies, direct relations can be established between the "people" and the state authority. It can thus be said that the political practice of all state authority emanating from the people in the capitalist countries via the representative system is the sole political arrangement for the "people" to exercise state authority where pluralistic interests are present.

There is no difference between the principle of all state authority emanating from the people practiced by the Chinese government and that practiced in the capitalist countries, but there is a great difference in how the "people" wield and exercise "state authority." As the People's Republic of China is a state led by a proletarian party and exercises the people's democratic dictatorship, the whole people have common interests to pursue, and there are no essentially irreconcilable conflicts of interests among the various social strata and groups. Therefore, the fundamental interests of society are harmonious. Because of the identity of the fundamental interests, presentation of the interests and demands of the "people" is fully guaranteed, as the CPC represents the pursuit of the common interests of society. Therefore, there is no need in China for a number of "representatives" who belong to different social strata and groups to pursue the essential or fundamental interests of the "people." Therefore, the Chinese government has the conditions and foundation for exercising state authority in a way different from that in the capitalist countries. These conditions and foundation determine the rationality of introducing the people's congress system by the Chinese government.

This is a political system totally different from the representative system practiced in the capitalist countries. It reflects and represents in a more fundamental and broader way the interests and demands of the people. This system, first of all, is not characterized by the sharing of power in form, but takes as its goal the pursuit of the most fundamental interests of the whole people, and exercises the supreme state power directly through the more representative "people's deputies" instead of representatives under the leadership of the ruling party, thus achieving the political goal of having the people become masters of the nation. Second, in the era of party politics, this system has created the conditions for the CPC to be involved in and give leadership to the political life of the nation. Different from the capitalist multi-party system, party politics in China takes the Communist Party of China's position as the sole ruling party as its nucleus. Therefore, there is no political competition among different political parties for the ruling party position, as commonly seen in the politics of the capitalist countries with the representative system as its basic form. Therefore, the people's congress system in China does not have the position and role of the parliament in the multi-party system. However, this does not mean that the Chinese government system does not have the nature of party politics. As a matter of fact, the Chinese governmental system is still a system of party politics and the CPC, as a political party, must also inevitably face the question of how it reflects the nature of a political party, how it achieves its political purposes and goals, and in what form it gets involved in the political life of the state in the situation of not facing party competition. The people's congress system, which both represents the interests of the "people" and has the position of supreme exerciser of state authority, legitimizes the role of the CPC as the sole ruling party.

The implementation of the people's congress system in China also demonstrates the importance of the interests of the specific social strata and groups, to a certain extent, to the overall interests of society and the perfection of state politics. Fundamentally speaking, although the people's congress system operates on the basis of the identity of the fundamental interests of society, there are pursuits of different and specific interests among the "people." Sometimes, the local and specific interests and demands cannot be all and fully expressed and reflected in the general political arrangements of the state. If the imperfections cannot be remedied properly, the government will inevitably neglect or sacrifice the interests of some of the members of society while pursuing the overall interests of society. This is obviously detrimental to mobilizing the enthusiasm of the people and guaranteeing the due interests of all members of society. Therefore, it is of great importance to adopt an appropriate form to ensure that the interests and demands of these members of society are conveyed and understood. The establishment of the people's congress system and the guarantee that all people have their own representatives to represent and convey their interests and demands can help to achieve this goal to the maximum extent. The inclusion of the specific interests and demands of the members of society embodied in the people's congress system helps all members of society obtain full opportunities and conditions to achieve their own interests. The realization of the interests of all members of society to the maximum extent is an inextricable part of the principle of all state authority emanating from the people, which reflects the fact that all power belongs to the people and that the people are the masters of the state.

The necessity of instituting the people's congress system in China is also linked with the theory of the relationship between the CPC and the people. The CPC represents and embodies the fundamental interests and pursuits of the whole people, but it is not the "people," nor the Chinese government. There is a gap between the CPC and the people and between the CPC and the government. The representation of the interests of the people by the CPC is finally embodied in the will of the state and the policies of the government. If it is only the wish of the CPC and is not transformed into the will of the state and the policies of the government, the CPC will be unable to use the tools of the resources of the state and government policies to actually materialize the interests of the people, and in no way will the interests of the people be satisfied. Therefore, as the CPC is not the government, and it cannot perform the functions of the government, the representation of the interests of the people by the CPC must be turned through certain channels and links into acts of the state and policies of the government. It is obvious that there must be a place where the will of the CPC can be transformed so that the opinions of the Party are raised to the level of the will of the state and the policies of the government. This place is no other but the people's congress. On the other hand, although the CPC can represent the interests of the people fundamentally, according to the principle of all state authority emanating from the people, the representation of the interests of the people by the CPC must be accepted and supported by the people. Only in this way can the political purpose of the CPC have the nature of representing the interests of the people. It is thus clear that the institution of the people's congress system is the most realistic and feasible way to ensure that the CPC wins the favor and support of the people, and thereby achieves its political perfection.

The people's congress system also helps to improve the relations among state organs, and provides a channel for the people's supervision over state organs. Although the socialist state has many advantages, there still arise problems regarding relations among state organs and between government functionaries and the people in the sphere of the political life of the state. The authority of the state organs must have their source, and their interrelations must be coordinated by appropriate institutions and through appropriate channels. Superficially, as the sole ruling party the CPC represents the common interests of the whole people and it can become the appropriate guarantor of the state authority and coordinator of the relations between state organs. However, as the People's Republic of China follows the principle of all state authority emanating from the people, and the party and the government administration are separated to a certain extent, it is impossible for the CPC to become the guarantor of the power of all state organs and coordinator of their mutual relations legally and formally. Therefore, it is necessary to set up a state institution to grant the due power to the state organs on behalf of the people and judge whether the working staff of those organs are trusted by the people. Whether there is such a state institution becomes an important measure to judge the degree of perfection of the institutional building of the Chinese government. Judging from its operation, the existence of such a state institution, first of all, can ensure the setting up of state organs as stipulated in the Constitution, and grant power to them; second, it can serve as an indispensable buffer link between the ruling party and the actual realization of the interests of the people so that all state organs can assume the necessary responsibilities of the government; third, if a state organ or organs cannot perform its or their duties properly, and their personnel fail to fulfill their obligations as "civil servants," such a state organ can provide a real place and the proper conditions for conveying the wishes of the people, and taking actions against such an organ or organs and the personnel involved. Therefore, the establishment of the people's congress system is of positive significance for the perfection and legalization of the Chinese governmental system.

IV. The System of Multi-Party Cooperation and Political Consultation

All governmental and political systems make efforts to tap and increase the sources of their political legality. Under normal conditions, an important source of legality is the number of members of society represented by the government or political system by which such representation functions, and the institutionalization of the relevant rules.

So far as the Chinese government is concerned, although the nature of the CPC and the socialist nature of the state have fundamentally resolved the question of the legality of the Chinese government, the further increase of political resources still helps to strengthen the foundation for the legality of the Chinese government. Because the CPC represents the interests of the greatest majority of the people, at least in theory, the interests and goals of the CPC and the great majority of the people are identical. Therefore, there is no need for other political representatives to represent and give expression to the interests of the greatest majority of the people in society. But while it is true that this situation has laid the theoretical basis for the position of the CPC as the sole ruling party, it has also set limits to the further increase of political resources. There are two aspects to such limits: One, there are still various social strata and groups in society, and their interests are fundamentally identical to those of the greatest majority of people. But, under certain circumstances, they still have their own demands that cannot be represented by the CPC. Hence, these strata and groups and their demands show that part of the political resources are still aloof from the system. If these resources can be properly integrated, the basis for legality will be extended. If these resources cannot be integrated, the foundation of legality of the leadership of the CPC will be weakened. Two, the CPC's position as the sole ruling party is apt to encourage excessive totalitarianism and even a personality cult, which will, in the end, bring harm to the CPC leadership itself. Therefore, how to further increase the political resources to integrate the non-organizational members of society and transform them into positive factors needed by actual politics becomes the political prerequisite for the existence and development of the non-communist parties. And how to show the political existence of the non-communist parties and ensure their communication and linkage with the CPC so as to achieve the political value of their actual existence is key to whether the CPC achieves the integration of all political resources, increases its legality and coordinates its relations with the non-communist parties. Therefore, the function and practical usefulness of the non-communist parties constitute the foundation for multi-party cooperation while the actual ways of linkage between the CPC and the non-communist parties constitutes the main content of the political consultation system. It is not hard to see that the multi-party cooperation and political consultation system forms a component part of the united front of the CPC at different levels and in different aspects.

The united front nature of the multi-party cooperation and political consultation system determines that the multi-party cooperation system led by the CPC is fundamentally different from the multi-party system or from the one-party system, that is, there is neither multi-party competition on equal terms for state power under the multi-party system nor one-party monopoly over state power, but co-existence of multiple parties on the premise of their consent to the CPC's position as the sole ruling party. The fact of co-existence of multiple parties means that there is a certain relationship of political cooperation between the CPC and the non-communist parties and among the non-communist parties on the issue of state power. That is, the CPC is the ruling party of the Chinese government to the non-communist parties, and to the CPC, the non-communist parties are "parties playing a role in state affairs" with the CPC controlling the government. The CPC holds state power and the non-communist parties "participate in and discuss state affairs".

The multi-party cooperation and political consultation system, apart from helping to extend the foundation for the legality of the Chinese government, also has, in theory, the function of supervision and restriction under the condition of the CPC's one-party rule. The mutual supervision and restriction among the parties in the multi-party cooperation system is different from the inter-party relations formed by multi-party competition under the multi-party system, that is, the CPC's position as the ruling party is unshakable while supervision by the parties participating in state affairs is a well-meaning reminder and remedy for the errors made by the ruling party. In other words, criticism from the non-communist parties must be measured against the criterion of whether or not they acknowledge the CPC's leading position and conform to socialist principles.[19]

The reason why supervision of the CPC by the non-communist parties is necessary is that while the long-term one-party ruling position of the CPC has strengthened its leadership, it has also brought to it potential harm. "Once we have won national power, there arises a great danger. A number of people may be corrupted by bourgeois sugar-coated bullets, be carried away by success, engender bureaucratism, be divorced from the masses, and even become individual careerists and betray the masses."[20] It is easy to make a big mistake and bring about a great calamity. "Who is qualified to make a big mistake in China? The Communist Party of China is. The mistakes it makes will have a great impact."[21] Therefore, "if the Party wants to give good leadership, … it must be subject to supervision."[22] Although such supervision comes from multiple sources and channels, and, more fundamentally, from the masses of the people, the non-communist parties which "represent the opinions and demands of one aspect of society, and have a certain amount of political experience and professional knowledge, can often make criticisms and comments to the point."[23] Therefore, advice and criticism from the non-communist parties play a considerable role in helping the CPC appraise itself correctly and rectify its mistakes. Supervision of the CPC by the non-communist parties is not only of great utility to the CPC, but also an important aspect of showing their political existence. Therefore, it can also be said that how far play is given to their supervisory function is an important indicator of the political existence of the non-communist parties.

The system of multi-party cooperation and political consultation is a political system with Chinese characteristics. It has undergone development and changes over a long period of time. In the early 1950s, the system of multi-party cooperation and political consultation was manifested mainly in the cooperation among the political parties, including the CPC, in jointly establishing organs of state power and the coalition government. Later, and especially during the "cultural revolution," the scope of the political activities of the non-communist parties was greatly limited, and even rescinded for a time. Political consultation existed in name only. After the reform and opening began in the late 1970s, the leaders of the CPC again attached importance to the political function of the non-communist parties. The latter resumed their activities and developed their functions. The relations of cooperation between the CPC and the non-communist parties have gradually become institutionalized. At present, the activities and influence of the non-communist parties in the political sphere of the state are manifested mainly in the following aspects:

Leaders of the non-communist parties can hold consultations with the leaders of the CPC on major issues at the annual democratic consultation meeting. If need be, leaders of the CPC may invite leaders of the non-communist parties for advice at any time. The CPC calls a meeting every two months to listen to policy proposals put forward by members of the non-communist parties or to discuss topics. Members of the non-communist parties may submit policy proposals in writing to the Central Committee of the CPC or make appointments with responsible persons of the CPC Central Committee for discussions of major issues.

The CPC guarantees that members of the non-communist parties account for proper percentages of the deputies to the National People's Congress, of the members of the NPC Standing Committee and of the members of the permanent special committees of the NPC.[24] The NPC may employ members of the non-communist parties as advisors or consultants to the NPC special committees. Members of the CPC's leading Party group in the NPC should constantly exchange information, ideas and comments with members of the non-communist parties who hold leading posts in the NPC. The NPC and its Standing Committee should include members of the democratic parties from among its deputies, and employ experts from the non-communist parties to take part in the work when they organize investigation committees on special issues, or special committees organize investigations on related issues.

The CPC and the government make arrangements for members of the non-communist parties to take leading posts in the State Council and other state organs. The United Front Work Department and the Organization Department of the CPC are responsible for the examination and training of candidates recommended by the non-communist parties.

The CPC guarantees that members of the non-communist parties account for given percentages of the members of the standing committee and leading members of the National Committee of the Chinese People's Political Consultative Conference (CPPCC). The special committees of the CPPCC must include members of the non-communist parties. The offices of the CPPCC must have a fixed number of members of the non-communist parties in leading posts. The CPPCC must make arrangements for members of the non-communist parties to visit other countries and take part in international activities.

In brief, since the introduction of the reform and opening-up policies, the CPC has constantly enhanced its understanding of the political importance of the non-communist parties, and continuously increased methods and channels for their members to take part in and discuss state affairs, and make the political existence of the non-communist parties more conspicuous and manageable. On the other hand, although these also brought to light the fact that, although great attention has been paid to the importance of the non-communist parties, there has been no major change in the understanding of the fundamental position and role of the non-communist parties in the political life of the state. That is, the non-communist parties participate in state affairs on the premise that they acknowledge the position of the CPC as the sole ruling party. This understanding means that, under the current conditions in China, the non-communist parties participate in state affairs chiefly at the top level. Therefore, the cooperation and political consultation between the CPC and the non-communist parties are expressed chiefly in the importance attached by the CPC to the participation of the top-level leaders of the non-communist parties in the political activities of the state and the importance of allocating a fixed number of posts to top-level members of the non-communist parties in state organs and offices. But the present model does not show sufficient attention paid to giving full play to the role of the non-communist parties in the political life at the grassroots level.

As the number of members of the non-communist parties and their social representation are limited, compared to other social strata and groups, the degree of participation of the non-communist parties in the political activities of the state is very high. Correspondingly, the representation of the interests and demands of the members of the non-communist parties is also at a high level, and when compared with other social strata and groups, their share of political rights and representation of their interests are unbalanced to some degree. Therefore, while the current system of multi-party cooperation and political consultation places emphasis on the role of the non-communist parties, how to balance the positions of the different social strata and groups in the political life of the state in a rational way is an issue to be solved for the further development and consolidation of the system of multi-party cooperation and political consultation.

Section 3 The Stipulations on and Description of the Basic System of the Chinese Government in the Constitution

The Constitution is the fundamental law of the state. It has supremacy in the political life of the state both in form and in substance. The stipulations for and design of the basic system of the government are important components of the Constitution.

When the People's Republic of China was founded, the basic system of the Chinese government was decided on through discussions among the parties at the political consultation meetings led by the CPC. When the First National People's Congress was convened in 1954, the basic system of the Chinese government was decided on through the making of the Constitution by the supreme people's representative body. The stipulations on the basic system of the Chinese government in the Constitution determined the basic rules concerning the Chinese government and the political life of the state. However, because of ultra-"Left" political influence, the position and importance of the Constitution in the political life of the state were later undermined and affected from time to time, and the Constitution's articles defining the specific state system often became meaningless nonsense and empty words. In recent years, with the better understanding of the importance of managing state affairs according to law, people have been attaching growing importance to the position and role of the Constitution as the supreme rules of the state in political life. Therefore, relatively speaking, the gap between the text of the Constitution and actual political life, to a certain degree and in some specific aspects, has become smaller and smaller, and the Constitution has acquired greater and greater true and practical significance. However, it is undeniable that, because of the incompleteness of the Constitution, a considerable gap still exists between the stipulations of the Constitution and real social and political life, and some of the stipulations still remain as words only. Therefore, the stipulations concerning the basic system of the Chinese government in the current Constitution are genuine and valid in some respects, but have no actual serviceability in other respects.

In specific terms, the stipulations on the Chinese government in the Constitution are mainly as follows:

First, the Constitution clearly provides for the priority and absolute leading position of the CPC in the political life and governmental system in China, the socialist nature of the Chinese state and the overall distribution of political rights on the basis of the nature of the state.

As to the leadership role of the CPC, the Constitution definitely describes the relationship between the CPC and the People's Republic of China as founded by the CPC. Therefore, the CPC was, is and will remain leader of the Chinese people.

On the premise of making clear the leadership position of the CPC, the Constitution states that the People's Republic of China "is a socialist state under the people's democratic dictatorship led by the working class and based on the alliance of workers and peasants." Therefore, the working class is a leading class of the state. The peasant class is the ally of the working class, and is also a leading class of the state. The socialist system is the "basic system" of the People's Republic of China.[25]

The social strata which enjoy political rights also include the patriots who do not belong to the working class or the peasant class, but support socialism and national reunification. Because they are not included in the leading class or the alliance of workers and peasants, it is necessary to establish a special united front organization to bring in these members of society so as to better mobilize them to make contributions to the realization of the long- and immediate-term goals of the state, namely, to consolidate and continue to develop "under the leadership of the Communist Party of China a broad patriotic united front which is composed of the democratic (non-communist) parties and people's organizations and which embraces all socialist working people, all patriots who support socialism and all patriots who stand for the reunification of the motherland."[26]

Regarding the principle of organization of the state organs, the Constitution states that the state organs of the People's Republic of China apply the principle of democratic centralism, that is, the individual being subordinate to the organization, the minority being subordinate to the majority, the lower level being subordinate to the higher level, and local government being subordinate to the central government. The people's congresses at all levels are constituted through elections, and they "decide on the major policies and elect the governments"; that is, the people's congresses elect the administrative, judicial and procuratorial organs of the state.[27]

Second, the Constitution provides for the principles of the legal system.

The distribution of the political rights of the state and the normal operation of political life depend on the building of the legal system and the rise of the level of the legal system. Although China is a state with a socialist nature, is led by a proletarian party and has had no tradition of managing state affairs according to law, the harm done to the whole country, the ruling party and their leaders by the situation in which "there were no laws to go by or the laws were not observed when there were" during the period of ultra-"Left" politics made it clear that workable laws were essential. In order to establish the rules for governing the state according to law, the first priority is to fix the position of the Constitution as the "fundamental law." This means that every individual, political party and public organization "must take the Constitution as the basic standard of conduct,"[28] that is, they must take the Constitution as the basic rules to govern their political life. Second, "no organization or individual is privileged to be above the Constitution or the law." That is, the stipulations on the rights of public organizations and their members in the Constitution are the result of reaching unanimity through consultation among all members of society. Therefore, anything that goes beyond the rights provided for in the Constitution inevitably means a violation of the rights of other public organizations and their members, and will inevitably undermine the existing pattern of the distribution of the rights already attained by society. Third, violation or undermining of the Constitution and the law by any public organization or member is tantamount to indirect violation of other public organizations or members. Such acts must be subject to appropriate punishment, thus guarding against any new possible violation of the Constitution and the law. "All acts in violation of the Constitution and the law must be investigated."[29] It is not difficult to see that although the stipulations on the rights and obligations of the members of society laid down in the Constitution are

not all equal and identical, the establishment of the position of the Constitution as the "fundamental law" is still of great importance. Because,
at least within the scope of the stipulations of the current Constitution,
the acts of all public organizations and their members are restricted by
the Constitution, it is obvious that this helps strengthen the consciousness of the members of society of the stipulations of the Constitution
and their rights.

Corresponding to the position of the Constitution as the "fundamental
law," the power to supervise the enforcement of the Constitution belongs
to the National People's Congress (NPC) and its standing committee, the
supreme organ of state power.[30] For technical reasons, the NPC's regular
power of interpreting the Constitution is delegated to its Standing Committee.[31] However, the NPC can still reverse or negate interpretations made
by the Standing Committee through appropriate channels and methods.

The right to revise the Constitution belongs to the NPC. "Amendments to the Constitution are to be proposed by the Standing Committee
of the National People's Congress or by more than one fifth of the deputies to the National People's Congress and adopted by a vote of more
than two-thirds of all the deputies to the Congress."[32]

Third, the Constitution provides for the position and rights of the citizens in the political life of the state.

That of the citizen is a legal concept. Different from the political concepts of people, masses, etc., the acquirement of the position and the
corresponding rights and obligations of the citizen is not dependent on
any political factor. The citizenship of all members of society itself is the
sure guarantee of their corresponding rights and obligations. As the concept of the citizen is a non-political one, and Chinese society has been
over-politicized for a long time, there is a general lack of understanding
of it among the general public. At the same time, under the influence of
the notion of class struggle, the citizenship of the members of society and
their corresponding rights and obligations, replaced in large degree by
political factors such as the relations between ourselves and the enemy,
political consciousness and political rights, have not had their proper
place, the citizen's rights have not been protected. The result was that
political power was so over-extended that the citizen's rights were often
suppressed at will. All this produced unfortunate consequences. In fact,
from the perspective of the general standards of the Constitution, the
status of the citizen, with its corresponding rights and obligations, consti-

tutes one of the basic elements of the political system of the state, marking the fundamental relations between the state and the citizens, that is, society. In the period of placing emphasis on managing state affairs according to law, improving the awareness of the status of citizens and protecting the rights of citizens should be given priority.

Judging by the text of the Constitution, the current Constitution carries fairly complete stipulations concerning the rights of citizens, and reflects the general situation of citizens' rights in the modern world. The main right of citizens confirmed by the current Constitution is the right of equality. The Constitution stipulates that all citizens of the People's Republic of China are equal before the law.[33] There must be no legal discrimination against any citizen because of his or her political view, economic status, religious belief or other factors. As to the right to vote, all citizens who have reached the age of 18 have the right to vote and stand for election except persons deprived of their political rights according to law.[34] As for political rights, citizens enjoy the rights to "freedom of speech, of the press, of assembly, of association, of procession and of demonstration."[35] They also enjoy the freedom of religious belief.[36]

Besides, the Constitution also stipulates that citizens have the right to criticize, make suggestions to and bring charges against any state organ or functionary: "Citizens have the right to criticize and make suggestions regarding any state organ or functionary. Citizens have the right to make complaints to relevant state organs, or bring charges against or make exposures of any state organ or functionary for violation of the law or dereliction of duty."[37]

Therefore, to sum up, because of the particularity of China's national conditions, the stipulations on the rights of citizens in the Constitution also show certain particularity: Although the stipulations on the rights of citizens in the current Constitution are fairly complete, there are still no definite stipulations in some respects. For example, do the citizens have the freedom of migration? Do the workers have the right to strike (neither the Constitution nor the law have stipulations that the workers do not have the right to strike)? Moreover, the rights that are clearly stipulated in the Constitution but the citizens cannot exercise them in practice for lack of specific regulations, such as the right to associate, must be examined to ensure that the citizens can truly enjoy all the rights provided in the Constitution.

Notes:

[1] *Selected Works of Marx and Engels*, Vol. II (Chinese edition). Beijing: People's Publishing House, 1972, p. 336.

[2] V. I. Lenin: *Collected Works*, Vol. 29. Moscow: Progress Publishers, 1965, p.478.

[3] *Selected Works of Marx and Engels*, Vol. III (Chinese edition). Beijing: People's Publishing House, 1972, p. 219.

[4] V.I.Lenin: *Collected Works*, Vol. 29. Moscow: Progress Publishers, 1965, p. 474.

[5] Wang Puqu, ed.: *The Basics of Political Science*. Beijing: Beijing University Press, February 1995, first edition, p. 246-247.

[6] A confidential circular of the CPC Central Committee to its senior cadres, issued on December 19, 1953, points out: "There is no substantial difference between the dictatorship of the proletariat and the people's democratic dictatorship." Liu Shaoqi stated in his political report to the Eighth National Congress of the CPC on September 15, 1956: "The people's democratic dictatorship in our country at the present stage is, in essence, a form of the dictatorship of the proletariat." (*History of the Political System of the People's Republic of China*, edited by Chen Mingxian, Nankai University Press, 1998, p. 58)

[7] *Selected Works of Mao Tsetung*, Vol. 5. Beijing: Foreign Languages Press, p. 387-388.

[8] *Selected Works of Mao Tsetung*, Vol. 4. Beijing: Foreign Languages Press, p. 418.

[9] Zhou Enlai: "The Characteristics of the Draft of the Common Programme of the People's Consultative Conference," included in *History of the Political System of the People's Republic of China*, edited by Chen Mingxian, Nankai University Press, October 1998, p. 60.

[10] *Selected Writings of Mao Tsetung*, Vol. 2. Beijing: People's Publishing House, 1986, p. 757.

[11] "Speech at the Enlarged Work Conference of the Central Committee of the CPC (January 30, 1962)", included in *Selected Writings of Mao Tsetung* (Vol. 2). Beijing: People's Publishing House, p. 834.

[12] "The Second Batch of Materials Concerning Hu Feng's Anti-Party Group," *People's Daily*, May 24, 1955.

[13] *Selected Works of Mao Tsetung*, Vol. 5. Beijing: Foreign Languages Press, p. 391.

[14] *Selected Works of Deng Xiaoping*, Vol. 2. Beijing: People's Publishing House, October 1994, p. 168.

[15] *Selected Works of Deng Xiaoping*, Vol. 2. Beijing: People's Publishing House, October 1994, p. 332.

[16] *Selected Works of Deng Xiaoping*, Vol. 2. Beijing: People's Publishing House, October 1994, p. 73.

[17] *Selected Works of Deng Xiaoping*, Vol. 3. Beijing: People's Publishing House, October 1994, p. 40.

[18] *Selected Works of Deng Xiaoping*, Vol. 3. Beijing: People's Publishing House, October 1994, p. 45.

[19] Mao Tsetung: "On the Correct Handling of Contradictions among the People," *Selected Works of Mao Tsetung*, Vol. V. Beijing: Foreign Languages Press, pp. 412-414.

[20] Zhou Enlai: "Long-Term Coexistence and Mutual Supervision" (April 24, 1957), see *Selected Works of Zhou Enlai on the United Front*. Beijing: People's Publishing House, December 1984.

[21] Deng Xiaoping: "The Communist Party Must Be Subject to Supervision" (April 8, 1957), see *Selected Works of Deng Xiaoping*, Vol. I. Beijing: People's Publishing House, May 1989, p. 270.

[22] Ditto.

[23] *Selected Works of Li Weihan*. Beijing: People's Publishing House, 1987, p. 323.

[24] Percentages of the members of the non-communist parties of the deputies to the National People's Congress and its Standing Committee: 25.5% and 49.4% (First NPC), 42.2% and 49.4% (Second NPC), 45.1% and 41.7% (Third NPC), 8.3% and 22,7% (Fourth NPC), 14.2% and 21.9% (Fifth NPC), 18.2% and 27.1% (Sixth NPC), 18.2% and 31% (Seventh NPC), 19.2% and 30.3% (Eighth NPC), and 15.44% (Ninth NPC).

[25] Article 1, Chapter One of the *Constitution of the People's Republic of China*. Beijing: Foreign Languages Press, fourth edition, 1999.

[26] "Preamble" of the *Constitution of the People's Republic of China*. Beijing: Foreign Languages Press, fourth edition, 1999.

[27] Article 1, Chapter One of the *Constitution of the People's Republic of China*. Beijing: Foreign Languages Press, fourth edition, 1999.

[28] "Preamble" of the *Constitution of the People's Republic of China*. Beijing: Foreign Languages Press, fourth edition, 1999.

[29] Article 5, Chapter One of the *Constitution of the People's Republic of China*. Beijing: Foreign Languages Press, fourth edition, 1999.

[30] Article 62 and Article 67, Section I, Chapter Three of the *Constitution of the People's Republic of China*. Beijing: Foreign Languages Press, fourth edition, 1999.

[31] Article 67, Section I, Chapter Three of the *Constitution of the People's Republic of China*. Beijing: Foreign Languages Press, fourth edition, 1999.

[32] Article 64, Section I, Chapter Three of the *Constitution of the People's Republic of China*. Beijing: Foreign Languages Press, fourth edition, 1999.

[33] Article 33, Chapter Two of the *Constitution of the People's Republic of China*. Beijing: Foreign Languages Press, fourth edition, 1999.

[34] Article 34, Chapter Two of the *Constitution of the People's Republic of China*. Beijing: Foreign Languages Press, fourth edition, 1999.

[35] Article 35, Chapter Two of the *Constitution of the People's Republic of China*. Beijing: Foreign Languages Press, fourth edition, 1999.

[36] Article 36, Chapter Two of the *Constitution of the People's Republic of China.* Beijing: Foreign Languages Press, fourth edition, 1999.

[37] Article 41, Chapter Two of the *Constitution of the People's Republic of China.* Beijing: Foreign Languages Press, fourth edition, 1999.

Chapter Two

THE RULING PARTY AND THE PARTIES PARTICIPATING IN STATE AFFAIRS IN CHINA

Section 1 The Communist Party of China

The Communist Party of China (CPC) was set up in 1921. It overthrew the Kuomintang government by means of armed struggle, and founded the People's Republic of China (PRC) in 1949. Since then, the CPC has been the sole ruling Party in the Chinese government. It now has more than 66 million members and about 3.5 million organizations at the grassroots level, and has set up formal (elected) or informal (appointed) organizations in the Chinese government at all levels.

I. The Political and Organizational Principles of the CPC

The CPC is a modern type of political Party. Party politics is the primary form of organization and administration of the modern state. This is no exception in the socialist state. However, as the CPC is a political Party of a Marxist-Leninist nature, this determines the fact that it is not only fundamentally different from the bourgeois political parties in the West, but is distinctly different from them in its organization, inner-Party relations, relations with society, and the qualities of individual Party members, which form its distinct characteristics.

1. Democratic Centralism Is the Supreme Principle in Inner-Party Relations

How to handle inner-Party relations is an important aspect to distinguish different types of political parties. The CPC attaches particular importance to the principle of democratic centralism, that is, centralism on the basis of democracy and democracy under centralized guidance. Democratic centralism is the fundamental organizational principle of the CPC, and also its fundamental organizational system.

Democratic centralism, as "centralism on the basis of democracy and democracy under centralized guidance," comprises both democracy and centralism. It reflects the relations between the leaders of the Party and the led, the relations between the organizations at the higher levels and those at the lower ones, the relations between the individual members and the Party as a whole, and the relations between the Party's Central Committee and the local organizations at all levels and the masses of the Party members.[1] Its essence is the relationship between democracy and centralism. Because this relationship "reflects the contradiction between objective facts and reflects the structure of the Party's contradictions,"[2] it is necessary to correctly understand the meaning of "democracy" and "centralism." In the abstract sense, "democracy" in the sense of democratic centralism itself depends on the nature of the proletarian Party. That is, according to Marxist theory, the organization of the proletarian Party is entirely democratic itself, and this alone blocks the way of any conspirator seeking dictatorship. Because of the advanced nature of the proletarian Party, the proletarian democracy advocated by the proletarian Party, developed and enlarged on an unprecedented scale, is no other but democracy for the majority of the people, namely, the exploited masses. Hence, Marxism holds that the proletarian Party enjoys the broadest basis for democracy. "Democracy" under democratic centralism is different from bourgeois absolute democracy. It does not mean inner-Party anarchism in any circumstances. "Democracy" in the true sense should mean that all Party organs must be elected, must report on their work to the Party members, and can be replaced by the Party members. As to the work style of the Party organs, the leading Party organs and the organizations at higher levels should pay greater attention to following the Party principle of democracy, holding more discussions and more meetings, and obeying the decisions of the majority when dealing with Party members and organizations at lower levels. Thus, "democracy" in the sense of democratic centralism has nothing in common with traditional bourgeois democracy.

Mao Zedong said, "What is centralism? First of all, it means centralizing correct opinions. On the basis of centralizing correct opinions, common understanding, centralized planning, centralized command and

centralized action are achieved."[3] In actual practice, "centralization" means
the correctness of the Party achieved through the concrete activities of
the leadership provided by the leading organs of the Party; it is finally
embodied in the discipline of the organization and activities of the Party
as understood and approved by the highest leading group of the Party.
In Liu Shaoqi's words, "centralism" means "all meetings of the Party
are called by the leading organs, all meetings proceed under leadership,
all decisions and rules are made after full preparations and deliberation,
and all elections have lists of carefully considered candidates. The
whole Party has a centralized Party constitution and unified discipline
which all Party members must observe, and has a centralized leading
organ which all Party members must obey."[4] Centralism requires "absolute and unconditional obedience". But does this "absolute obedience"
conflict with the demands and substance of "democracy"? According to
Marxist-Leninist theory, "absolute centralism" not only is not undemocratic, but, on the contrary, is genuine "democracy" and "democracy" at
a higher level. To prove this point, Liu Shaoqi said, "Absolute, unconditional obedience is not undemocratic. On the contrary, it is perfectly
democratic. However, extreme liberalistic ideas are undemocratic, because
they want the whole Party to obey a part of it, and want the majority to
obey the minority."[5] It can be seen that there exists a complicated relationship of dialectical unity between "democracy" and "centralism" in the
democratic centralism, and correctly understanding and grasping this relationship is important in judging the political qualities of a Marxist Party.

Democratic centralism is of great importance to the CPC. It is a matter of whether full play can be given to the role of the Party, and whether
the Party's cause will succeed or fail. At the same time, it is a question of
whether the Party's nature will change. Deng Xiaoping once said, "...
especially if we fail to practise democratic centralism satisfactorily, the
Party, the state, socialism, the cadres and everyone may degenerate."[6]
First of all, democratic centralism can enhance the fighting capacity of
the Party. The formation of the Party's fighting capacity is closely related
to the degree of perfection of the Party's organization. Attaching importance to organizational capacity is a distinct characteristic of Marxism-
Leninism. Lenin once said that an individual proletarian is powerless, but
millions of proletarians are all-powerful. He also said that in the struggle
for political power, the proletariat has no other weapon than organization.
The more perfect the organization is, the greater the fighting capacity of

the organization. Democratic centralism is an important method of building a powerful organization, and can greatly raise the degree of perfection of the Party's organization. When the Party's organization is perfect, the Party's capacity will be greatly expanded. Second, democratic centralism can guarantee the ideological unity of the CPC. The reason why the proletariat can be an invincible force is that its ideological unity, formed on the basis of Marxism, is consolidated by the physical unity of the organization. The CPC is a Marxist-Leninist Party. But, it is far from enough for it just to be armed with Marxism-Leninism ideologically. Its ideological unity must be based on and guaranteed by its unity of the organization and, relatively speaking, the unity of the organization is even more important. As a matter of fact, democratic centralism has often been the chief weapon used to oppose and defeat all sorts of influences of non-Marxist-Leninist thinking in the history of the CPC. Third, democratic centralism can materialize the principle of "democracy under centralized guidance and centralism based on democracy," thus making it possible for the Party to create different political situations in different environments and under different conditions. Because the Party is confronted with different situations in different periods, excessive "democracy" or excessive "centralism" is not appropriate at certain times. "Democracy" or "centralism" must be put under control in good time. "Democracy" or "centralism" will, in the end, be manifested in the Party members' response to the Party's demands and discipline, namely, in the political situation both within and outside the Party reflected in the behavior of the individual Party members. Therefore, democratic centralism, as an organizational principle and discipline, can adjust the balance between "democracy" and "centralism" so as to enable the Party to adapt to the circumstances and the demands of its objectives. The close attention paid to the political situation within and outside the Party has a political, cultural and psychological significance. It is an important task and tool of the Party's leadership to develop from simple political leadership to cultural and psychological leadership. As Mao Zedong put it: "I hope a situation will be created in which we have both unity of will and liveliness, that is, both centralism and democracy, both discipline and freedom."[7] As democratic centralism itself embodies the complicated relationship of dialectical unity, it can achieve goals that seem almost impossible to achieve at the same time, and turn baffling political phenomena into political reality.

2. The Organizational and Disciplinary Norms of Democratic Centralism

The concrete contents of the principle of democratic centralism are clearly defined in the Constitution of the CPC:

First, individual Party members are subordinate to the Party organization, the minority is subordinate to the majority, the lower Party organizations are subordinate to the higher Party organizations, and all the constituent organizations and members of the Party are subordinate to the National Congress and the Central Committee of the Party.

Second, the Party's leading bodies at all levels must be elected, except for the representative organs dispatched by them and the leading Party members' groups in non-Party organizations.

Third, the highest leading body of the Party is the National Congress and the Central Committee elected by it. The leading bodies of local Party organizations are the Party congresses at their respective levels and the Party committees elected by them. Party committees are responsible and report their work to the Party congresses at their respective levels.

Fourth, higher Party organizations shall pay constant attention to the views of lower organizations and the rank-and-file Party members, and solve in good time the problems they raise. Lower Party organizations shall request instructions from and report on their work to higher Party organizations; at the same time, they shall handle, independently and in a responsible manner, matters within their jurisdiction. Higher and lower Party organizations shall exchange information and support and supervise each other. Party organizations at all levels shall enable Party members to be well informed of inner-Party affairs and to have as many opportunities as possible to involve themselves in them.

Fifth, Party committees at all levels practice the system of combining collective leadership with individual responsibility based on division of work. All major issues shall be decided upon by the Party committees after discussion, in accordance with the principle of collective leadership, democratic centralism, individual consultations and decision by meetings. The members of the Party committees shall earnestly perform their respective duties in accordance with the collective decisions and division of work.

Sixth, the Party forbids all forms of personality cult. It is necessary to ensure that the activities of the Party leaders are subject to the supervision of the Party and the people, and at the same time to uphold the prestige of all the leaders who represent the interests of the Party and the people.

The above stipulations provide the principled norms for the Party organizations and all aspects of inner-Party relations. In practical political life, these norms are expressed as a series of organizational and disciplinary restrictions within the Party, with distinct characteristics. The central and most crucial of them is the emphasis on strict inner-Party discipline and opposition to any form of factional activities.

Emphasis on strict inner-Party discipline is an important characteristic differentiating a proletarian Party from a bourgeois Party. In fact, the formulation and implementation of disciplinary requirements, in a certain form and with a certain intensity, are a prerequisite for any organization to survive, but the characteristic strictness of the disciplinary requirements of the proletarian Party is something for any other political Party to emulate. The strict requirements in Party discipline are closely linked with the emphasis the proletarian Party lays on its organization and its illegal status in the long historical course of development, as well as the special forms of activities the Party had adopted in view of its illegal status. Due to the extreme importance of the Party organization, the Party pays special attention to discipline, by which the Party is held together. As Marx said, it is necessary to uphold Party discipline; otherwise, nothing would be accomplished. Lenin said that unconditional centralism and strict discipline of the proletariat are part of the basic requirements for the defeat of the bourgeoisie. He also said that denial of Party spirit and negation of Party discipline amount to complete disarmament of the proletariat, and it will only benefit the bourgeoisie. Mao Zedong said that if discipline is strengthened, revolution is bound to succeed. Now, stress on discipline is still one of the characteristics of the CPC. Deng Xiaoping said, "It won't do without discipline. When we made revolution in the past, we relied on discipline, and conscious discipline."[8] Jiang Zemin said, "All Party members and cadres, and the leading cadres in particular, must strictly observe Party discipline and consciously conform to the Party's line, policies and resolutions in word and action. They must not be allowed to act in their own way."[9]

Democratic centralism also means that no factional activities are allowed in the Party. The Party must have a unity of will, and this is not compatible with the existence of any factional organizations. Centralism relies on unity. If the Party cannot uphold unity, it will be impossible to achieve centralism. Therefore, democratic centralism inherently negates the existence in the Party of any factional or splittist activities detrimental to its solidarity and unity. Moreover, the proletarian Party has a lofty mission, the fulfillment of which makes the Party view any factional and splittist activities as immoral and destructive.

3. The CPC as the Sole Ruling Party in China

The Communist Party's position as the sole leadership over the country is determined by its nature and mission. The task of the proletariat is to overthrow the capitalist system, establish the dictatorship of the proletariat and then achieve the gradual transition to communism. In this process, all classes will be transformed and eliminated, including the proletariat itself. The only force that can transform the proletariat is the Communist Party, and this is determined by the progressive character of the proletariat. Lenin said that only the political Party of the working class, namely, the Communist Party, can unite, educate and organize the vanguard of the proletariat, ridding the proletariat of the recurrence of any bad traditions and habits. Only the Communist Party can unite the diverse tendencies within the proletariat, and enable it to focus on the goal of the emancipation of the whole of society. When Mao Zedong analyzed the conditions of all social strata in China, he said, "Of all the social strata and political groupings in semi-colonial China, the proletariat and the Communist Party are the ones most free from narrow-mindedness and selfishness, are politically the most far-sighted, the best organized.... Hence, only the proletariat and the Communist Party can lead the peasantry, the urban petty bourgeoisie and the bourgeoisie...."[10]

As the Communist Party is naturally endowed with the qualifications and ability to lead all classes in society, in socialist countries only it can be the ruling party. Moreover, as it allows no factional activities, it is thus the sole ruling party. In concrete political practice of different countries, the ruling party position of the Communist Party can be somewhat different, its leadership over state power, however, is all alike. In China, the sole ruling party position of the Chinese Communist Party is embodied in the system of multi-party cooperation under the leadership of the CPC.

4. Emphasis on the Role of the Revolutionaries and Leaders

Emphasis on the importance of professional revolutionaries in the wartime years and Party leaders in peace-time circumstances in politics and organizational affairs is one of the characteristics of the Communist Party. Because the Communist Party is a revolutionary party that takes it as its task to overthrow the existing regime and achieve communism, it mainly engages in "illegal" underground activities before seizing political power, which are highly dangerous and call for the spirit of fearing no hardships and sacrifice. This necessitates the emergence of a number of professional revolutionaries being devoted heart and soul to the Party's cause and fearing no danger and sacrifice, and being armed with certain political and organization ability. For their advantages in the spirit of devotion, lofty personality, knowledge and ability, they would naturally become of the core of the Party, and the organization formed by these professional revolutionaries would eventually turn into the policy-making organ within the Party.

After the Communist Party seizes political power, the surroundings in which the professional revolutionaries operate change, but the importance of the revolutionaries to the Party's leadership remains the same. Therefore, Lenin laid special emphasis on the importance of the leaders to the Party's cause. He said that no revolutionary movement could last long if there was not an organization of leaders that remains stable and maintains continuity. He also said that the greater the number of people who were spontaneously involved in the struggles…, the more urgently the organization was needed, and the stronger it needed to be. In other words, the role of the professional revolutionaries is not at all weakened or affected because the revolutionary situation changes for the better. On the contrary, the better the situation of the revolution and the more masses take part, the more important and obvious is the role of these leaders.

Who are these leaders? After the Communist Party wins state power, the leadership should be composed of the most prestigious, most influential and most experienced people among the professional revolutionaries. Under normal circumstances, they form a stable group inside the Party and hold the leadership of the Party, which leads and influences the entire society. In most cases, at least in modern civilized countries, the class leadership is exercised through its political Party, and the political Party is usually presided over by a fairly stable group composed of the most prestigious, most influential and most experienced people, who are selected to hold the most important posts and are called leaders. As an authoritative policy-making group, such a group is not large under normal conditions. It should have about a dozen people. In addition to the limited size of the leaders' group, the requirements for the qualities of the members of the leaders' group and the degree of coordination among them are also very high. This not only makes a clear distinction between the leaders and the ordinary Party members and masses, but also offers the power and rationale for the selection of leaders and judgment of the candidates for membership of this group.

As the emphasis on leaders in Lenin's theory may give rise to such aberrations as personality cult in an ultra-"Left" political environment, the CPC reformulated a set of principles guiding inner-Party relations after the end of the "cultural revolution," putting stress on the importance and role of the system of collective leadership combined with division of work and individual responsibility in the organization and life of the Party. That is, under normal conditions, "major issues must be discussed collectively. When a decision is made, everyone strictly follows the principle of the minority being subordinate to the majority, one person one vote .... It's not the First Secretary's words that count .... Matters that are decided collectively should be handled separately, with each person assuming his or her own responsibility. They should not shift responsibility onto each other .... There should also be a head of a collective leadership. The first secretaries of the Party committees at all levels should assume the primary responsibility."[11] At the highest level of the leadership of the CPC, the collective leadership system is embodied in the system of combining "the leading collective and leading core," with due emphasis on the role of the "leading core." The theory of the "leading core" is the main content and one characteristic of Deng Xiaoping Theory and is Deng Xiaoping's creation. According to his interpretation of the evolution of the leadership system of the CPC, the "leading core" is a homologous concept to "leading collective," but it is an individual, not a collective. Deng Xiaoping held that the success of the revolution and construction efforts of the CPC is inseparable from the correct leadership of the Party at the highest level. Since the Zunyi Meeting[12], there has always been a leading collective at the highest level of the leadership of the CPC, and also a "leading core" in the leading collective. Therefore, he said, the history of the CPC proves that "a collective leadership must have a core; without a core, no leadership can be strong enough."[13] He also said that every Party member should "make an effort to maintain the core...."[14] The system of combining the "leading collective and leading core" is the way to exercise collective leadership under normal conditions. But when major issues and differences arise in the Party, the leading collective must obey the final verdict made by the leading core of the Party. It can be clearly seen that strong emphasis on the role of the leader is still the most important political and organizational idea of the CPC and Deng Xiaoping Theory, and this idea essentially reflects the nature and task of the Communist Party.

II. The Organization of the CPC

At present, the CPC has more than 66 million members and some 3.5 million grassroots organizations. The primary organizations are "militant bastions of the Party in the basic units of society, where all the Party's work proceeds and which serve as the foundation of its fighting capacity."[15]

1. The National Congress and Conference of the CPC

The National Congress and Local Congresses

The national congress and local congresses at all levels are the organs of power of the Party organizations at the corresponding levels. The highest organ of leadership of the CPC is the National Congress of the Party and the Central Committee it elects. The local organs of leadership of the Party are the local congresses of the Party and the committees they elect. The committees of the Party at all levels are responsible and report on their work to the congresses at the respective levels.

The National Congress of the Party is held once every five years and convened by the Central Committee. It may be convened before the normally scheduled date if the Central Committee deems it necessary or if more than one-third of the organizations at the provincial level so request. Except in extraordinary circumstances, the National Congress may not be postponed.

The functions and powers of the National Congress of the Party include: (1) Hearing and examining the reports of the Central Committee; (2) Hearing and examining the reports of the Central Committee for Discipline Inspection; (3) Discussing and deciding on major questions concerning the Party; (4) Revising the Constitution of the Party; (5) Electing the Central Committee; and (6) Electing the Central Committee for Discipline Inspection. However, because the National Congresses and their delegates are non-permanent, the functions and powers of the National Congress and its delegates exist only during the session. Once the National Congress is not in session, its functions and powers naturally disappear.

At present, there are no stipulations whatsoever in the Constitution of the Party or the published documents of the CPC on the qualifications of or requirements for the delegates to the National Congress and the National Conference, their rights and duties, the distribution of the quotas of the delegates or rules for the distribution. In particular, there are no stipulations on the responsibilities and rights of the delegates. Under the system of non-permanent tenure, the delegates may be regarded more as component parts of the Congress than as political figures who have clear rights and obligations, and have close connections with the organizations of the Party in given localities or units. Therefore, the current Constitution of the Party provides only for the general procedures and principles for elections: The list of candidates shall be fully deliberated and discussed by the Party organizations and members. It may be decided by direct competitive election, in which more candidates are nominated than the actual number of delegates to be elected or by choosing candidates through preliminary election. In either case, the election of the delegates should be conducted by secret ballot. In practice, the distribution of the quotas of the delegates to the National Congress and the election procedure are usually decided by the previous Central Committee, under the guidance of which the election of delegates is held by the various electoral units. The electoral units are the local congresses at the provincial level and the Party congresses or conferences of the organs directly under the Central Committee of the Party, the central state organs, the People's Liberation Army and the Armed Police Force. Therefore, the constituents of the National Party Congress are not only the local Party organizations, as the Party organizations of the various organs under the Party Central Committee, the central government and the armed forces also make up for a fairly large percentage.

The number of delegates to the National Congress has been relatively stable since the Eleventh National Congress — between 1,500 and 2,000 — although the number of Party members they represent has multiplied. Following is a table showing the numbers of delegates to the National Congresses since the Eleventh, and the numbers of Party members they represented:

	Time Convened	Number of Delegates	Number of Party Members Repre-sented (million)
11th National Congress	August 12-18, 1977	1,510	35
12th National Congress	September 1-11, 1982	1,600 (alternate delegates: 149)	39.65
13th National Congress	October 25-November 1, 1987	1,936 (specially invited delegates: 61)	46
14th National Congress	October 12-18, 1992	1,989 (specially invited delegates: 46)	51
15th National Congress	September 12-18, 1997	2,048 (specially invited delegates: 60)	58
16th National Congress	November 8-14, 2002	2,114 (specially invited delegates: 40)	66

The local congresses at all levels are the leading organs of the Party at their respective levels, and they are composed of the delegates elected to them. The *Regulations on the Work of Election of the Local Organizations of the Communist Party of China* enacted in 1993 prescribes in detail the procedures and measures for the election of delegates to the local congresses at all levels: The number of delegates is decided by the plenary session of the committees that convene the meetings, and is submitted to the committees of the Party at the next-higher levels for approval. The number of delegates to the congress of a province, autonomous region, municipality directly under the Central Government is, in general, 400-800; 300-500 for a city that is divided into districts, and 200-400 for a county or city not divided into districts. The distribution of the quotas of delegates is also decided by the same committees; the candidates for the delegates to the provincial congresses should include no less than 25% professional technological workers and "advanced and model personages"; the difference between the number of candidates and that of delegates to be elected should be no less than 20%; the formal candidates shall be screened and decided by the electoral units, and then elected by the electoral units; a candidate is elected only when he or she wins votes from more than half of the people present who have the right to elect. The result of the election is submitted to the corresponding committee that convenes the congress for examination and approval. The credentials of a delegate are valid after being endorsed at the congress or at a meeting of the presidium of the congress.

The functions and powers of the local Party congresses at all levels are: to hear and examine the reports of the Party committees and the commissions for discipline inspection at the corresponding levels; to discuss and decide on major issues in given areas; and to elect the Party committees and commissions for discipline inspection at the corresponding levels. The local congresses at all levels are held once every five years and convened by the Party committees at the corresponding levels. In extraordinary circumstances, they may be held before or after their normally scheduled dates upon approval by the Party committees at the next higher level.

National and Local Conferences of the CPC

The Central Committee and the local committees of the CPC at all levels may convene conferences when necessary. The number of delegates to the conferences and the procedure for the selection of delegates are to be determined by the corresponding committees.

The functions and powers of the National Conference of the Party are as follows: to discuss and make decisions on major issues; and to replace members and elect additional members of the Central Committee and the Central Commission for Discipline Inspection. The number of Central Committee members and alternate members to be replaced or newly elected shall not exceed one-fifth of the total number of members and alternate members of the Central Committee elected by the National Party Congress.

The local committees of the Party at all levels may convene conferences when necessary to discuss and make decisions on major urgent issues, and the number of delegates to the congresses and the procedure for the selection of delegates are to be determined by the corresponding committees.

Why is the conference system established in addition to the congress system? It has something to do with the nature of the procedure for the selection of the delegates. In the usual practice of the CPC, if the delegates are elected, the meeting they attend is called a congress, and if the delegates are not elected but selected by other means, the meeting is called a conference. Therefore, the form of the conference can often give the corresponding committees that convene and preside over the meetings more flexibility and better control. In the history of the international communist movement, the conference was often used to handle tough organizational issues and major questions of policy adjustment.

The difference between a congress and a conference also lies in the fact that a conference is not the highest leading organ of the Party at the corresponding level, and is convened under the leadership of the Party committee at the same level. Also, the resolutions adopted at the conference are subject to approval by the Party committee at the same level, although some must be submitted to the Party committee at the next higher level for approval.

Since the Seventh National Congress, the CPC only held two national conferences. One was the conference on the question of the "Gao (Gang)-Rao (Shushi) Anti-Party Alliance," convened March 21-31, 1955, and the other was the conference on lowering the average age of cadres, convened September 18-23, 1985. In accordance with the decision of the Party Central Committee , the 1985 conference was attended by 992 delegates, including 343 members and alternate members of the Party Central Committee, 161 members of the Central Advisory Commission, 127 members of the Central Commission for Discipline Inspection, 35 chief leading officials of the localities at the provincial level, PLA military area commands, Central Party and state departments and mass organizations, and 326 representatives of ordinary Party members. The difference from the congress was that regardless of their status, all the delegates had the right to vote at the conference. Also at this conference, 91 members and alternate members of the Central Committee, 56 members of the Central Advisory Commission, and 31 members of the Central Commission for Discipline Inspection were newly elected. In fact, on the day following the closing of the conference, the new Central Committee, Central Advisory Commission and Central Commission for Discipline Inspection were convened, and a large number of new members were appointed to important posts.

2. The Central Committee of the CPC

The Central Committee is the highest leading organ of the CPC when the National Congress is not in session. The Central Committee is elected for a term of five years. When the next National Congress is convened before or after its normally scheduled date, the term of the Central Committee shall be correspondingly shortened or extended.

Members and Alternate Members of the Central Committee

The members of the Central Committee are elected by the National Congress. The Central Committee is made up of members and alternate members. Vacancies on the Central Committee shall be filled by its alternate members in the order of the number of votes by which they have been elected. Members and alternate members of the Central Committee must have a Party standing of five years or more. Judging from the angle of their rights and obligations, there is a big difference between the members and the alternate members. The members have the right to elect and the right to vote, while the alternate members have no right to elect or to vote. Although the alternate members have the right to fill vacancies on the Central Committee, because of the large number of alternate members and the limited number of vacancies, most of the alternate members find it impossible to become full members with the right to elect and the right to vote. Therefore, the alternate membership indicates more of a person's political position in the Party than his or her actual political rights.

Since the 13th National Congress, the members and alternate members of the Central Committee have been elected in the following manner: On the basis of the nomination by the local Party organizations at the provincial level and Party organizations in the departments of the Central Committee and central government and the major units of the PLA, the Political Bureau of the previous Central Committee submits a suggested list of preliminary nominees for the candidates to the Presidium of the National Congress. After the list is passed by the Presidium after examination, it is submitted to the various delegations for "deliberation." On the basis of comments and remarks from the delegations, the Presidium determines the list of preliminary nominees for the candidates, and then the delegates to the National Congress select the final list of candidates in a primary election by differential voting. After the final list of candidates is prepared on the basis of the primary election, the National Congress elects the members and alternate members of the Central Committee by secret ballot. As the current Constitution does not state whether the members and alternate members of the Central Committee have to be elected by equivalent election or competitive election and whether a primary election should be held, it is still unknown at present whether the current primary competitive election will be adopted by future National Congresses.

The numbers of members and alternate members of the Central

Committee is decided by the National Congress. They are different for the different Central Committees (See following table).

	Members	Alternate Members
11th National Committee	201	132
12th National Committee	210	138
13th National Committee	175	110
14th National Committee	189	130
15th National Committee	193	151
16th National Committee	198	158

From the above table, one may notice that, while the number of members of the Central Committee has remained basically stable, the number of alternate members has tended to increase gradually.

The Importance of the Central Committee

Because the National Congress adopts a non-permanent tenure system, the importance of the Central Committee becomes all the more prominent when the National Congress is not in session. The importance of the Central Committee is manifested in the following aspects:

First, the Central Committee and its working departments carry out the decisions of the National Congress, direct the work of the whole Party and represent the Party in its external relations when the National Congress is not in session.

Second, the members of the Central Committee include almost all the important political figures in the country.

Third, the Central Committee is an organ that decides other important leading organs, and is the final organ that grants political legality to the supreme political leaders.

Fourth, as the Central Committee adopts a permanent tenure system and a committee system, it is the most easy and effective way to convene a meeting of the Central Committee if any important policy question or political question calls for support in the name of the whole Party when the National Congress is not in session.

The Constitution of the Party stipulates that the Central Committee of the Party meets in plenary session at least once a year, and such sessions are convened by its Political Bureau. Because the Central Committee enjoys an important position and plays an important role, and because of the lessons learned from the abuse of and trampling on the Central Committee during the ultra-"Left" political campaigns, the question of how to further strengthen and improve its meetings and systems has drawn widespread attention in recent years, namely, how to guarantee the number of meetings provided for in the Constitution of the Party and to give better play to the role of collective leadership of the Central Committee on this basis. The annual plenary session of the Central Committee has been virtually guaranteed (the Political Bureau of the Central Committee of the 13th National Congress decided to increase the number of plenary sessions of the Central Committee from once to twice a year). However, the question of how to give better play to the role of collective leadership of the Central Committee has not yet been properly solved.

3. The Political Bureau of the Central Committee and Its Standing Committee

Although the Central Committee practices the permanent tenure system, it is not a permanent organ. Therefore, it is necessary to set up a permanent organ that can perform the functions and powers of the Central Committee when the latter is not in session. The Political Bureau of the Central Committee and its Standing Committee are such organs. The Political Bureau of the Central Committee and its Standing Committee are elected by the plenary session of the Central Committee, and exercise the functions and powers of the Central Committee when the latter is not in session. Because they are permanent organs, the Political Bureau of the Central Committee and its Standing Committee are the *de facto* top leading organs of the Party for most of the time. Beginning with the 12th National Congress of the CPC, the Standing Committee of the Political Bureau of the Central Committee has become the leading core of the regular work of the Central Committee .

The supreme leading position of the Political Bureau of the Central Committee and its Standing Committee is also manifested in the fact that they give concrete leadership to the various departments of the Central Committee. The Central Committee has several departments that are subject to the leadership of the top organ of the Central Committee. As the Central Committee is not a permanent organ and practices the committee system, it is, in fact, unable to give concrete leadership to these departments. However, the work of these departments embodies the overall leadership of the CPC over the nation, and the leadership over these departments is of great significance.

As the Standing Committee of the Political Bureau of the Central Committee is elected mutually from among the members of the Political Bureau, it holds more centralized and more important power, as well as greater and timelier information. Therefore, how to straighten out the relations between the Standing Committee of the Political Bureau and the Political Bureau itself merits attention. The Political Bureau of the Central Committee of the 13th National Congress stipulated that the Standing Committee of the Political Bureau of the Central Committee should reports on its work to the Political Bureau on a regular basis, and the Political Bureau reports on its work to the Central Committee at regular intervals.

Although the Political Bureau is elected by the Central Committee, it also exerts certain influence over the Central Committee, as is mainly manifested in the fact that the Political Bureau of the Central Committee convenes and presides over the plenary session of the Central Committee. The current Constitution of the Party stipulates that only the Political Bureau of the Central Committee has the right to convene a plenary session of the Central Committee. Therefore, the right of the Political Bureau of the Central Committee to convene and to preside over the plenary session of the Central Committee is of vital significance to the relationship between the Political Bureau of the Central Committee and the Central Committee itself.

The Political Bureau of the Central Committee has a membership of around 20. It has two to four alternate members, and its Standing Committee has seven to nine members. The members of the Political Bureau of Central Committee and its Standing Committee are elected by the plenary session of the Central Committee. The usual practice is that the members of the Political Bureau of the Central Committee and its Standing Committee are all members of the Central Committee, but the Constitution of the Party provides for no definite restriction on this.

4. The General Secretary of the Central Committee of the CPC

The general secretary of the CPC Central Committee enjoys the highest political position in the CPC, and he or she is the top leader of the Central Committee. He or she is responsible for convening the meetings of the Political Bureau and its Standing Committee, and presides over the work of the Secretariat of the Party Central Committee. The general secretary must be a member of the Standing Committee of the Political Bureau and is elected by the plenary session of the Central Committee. The current Constitution of the Party does not have a stipulation on the tenure of office of the general secretary.

After the Seventh National Congress, the highest political position of the Central Committee of the CPC had rested in the chairman of the Central Committee until 1982. The general secretary, as the highest political position of the Central Committee of the CPC, began at the 12th National Congress of the Communist Party. During this period, the Constitution adopted by the Eighth National Congress of the Party stipulated to establish the position of general secretary, but the general secretary at that time was only the general secretary of the Secretariat under the leadership of the Political Bureau of the Central Committee and its Standing Committee, not the top leader of the Central Committee of the CPC. The status of the general secretary established by the Fifth Plenary Session of the 11th Central Committee of the Party was the same as that of the general secretary established by the Eighth National Congress. If you consider the change in the light of the political environments of that time, you would find that the change of the highest political position of the Central Committee of the CPC from chairman to general secretary was not merely a change of the title, but implied some change in the rules governing the system of work. It can be said that the system of chairman practiced between 1949 and 1982 was inseparable from the personal political position and influence of Mao Zedong. In Mao Zedong's era, the position of the chairman of the Central Committee was taken by Mao Zedong himself. After his death, it was taken by the successor he had chosen. The coexistence of the positions of the general secretary and the chairman was linked with the intention to reduce the absolute influence of the highest political position of the Party and divide power properly. At present, because the Party has established only the general secretary, therefore, whether the position of the general secretary still has the implications of dividing the power and striking balance awaits further observation.

5. The Secretariat of the Central Committee

Since 1949, the Secretariat of the Central Committee may be the organ that has witnessed the biggest change in the status and functions among all organs of the Central Committee of the CPC. The Secretariat established in accordance with the Constitution of the Party adopted by the Seventh National Congress was elected by the Central Committee. It presided over the day-to-day work of the Central Committee. In fact, it was equivalent to the Standing Committee of the Political Bureau (there was no Standing Committee of the Political Bureau at that time). The Secretariat set up by the Party's Eighth National Congress was a working organ handling the day-to-day work of the Central Committee under the leadership of the Political Bureau and its Standing Committee. Members of the Secretariat were elected by the Plenary Session of the Central Committee. The Constitutions of the Party adopted at the Ninth, Tenth and 11th national congresses abolished the establishment of the Secretariat. The Fifth Plenary Session of the 11th Central Committee and the 12th National Congress of the Party restored the Secretariat, with its members being elected by the Plenary Sessions of the Central Committee. It handled the day-to-day work of the Central Committee under the Political Bureau of the Central Committee and its Standing Committee, and its status and functions were virtually similar to those prescribed in the Constitution of the Party adopted by the Eighth National Congress. The Constitution adopted by the 13th National Congress made a major adjustment to the status and functions of the Secretariat: The Secretariat was a working body of the Political Bureau of the Central Committee and its Standing Committee, and its members were nominated by the Standing Committee of the Political Bureau and approved by the Plenary Session of the Central Committee. Since then, this system has remained unchanged.

From the development and changes of the secretariat system since 1949, it can be seen that the status and functions of the Secretariat experienced two stages of development. Before 1956, the Secretariat was in fact a permanent organ of the Political Bureau and it enjoyed the highest status then. Afterwards, the status of the Secretariat, due to the division of labor between the so-called "frontline" and "rear-line" of the top leaders of the Central Committee, was reduced to the status of a day-to-day working organ of the Political Bureau of the Central Committee. This situation remained unchanged until the end of the "cultural revolution." The second stage started after the end of the "cultural revolution." During this period, between its restoration in 1980 and 1987, the status of the

Secretariat was lowered considerably as compared with the Secretariat established according to the stipulations of the Constitution of the Party adopted by the Seventh National Congress. But, as its members were still elected by the Plenary Session of the Central Committee, the Secretariat still enjoyed a fairly high political standing among all organs of the Central Committee. After 1987, the status of the Secretariat was further lowered. The fundamental difference between the current Secretariat and the past ones lies in that the current Secretariat does not hold the power of making policies, and it only acts as a working organ of the Political Bureau of the Central Committee and its Standing Committee, while the past secretariats had both the powers of making policies and handling day-to-day affairs or the Party Central Committee.

The Secretariat is usually made up of five to seven members.

6. The Central Military Commission

The Central Military Commission is the highest military leading organ of the Central Committee of the CPC. The members of the commission are not elected but decided on by the Central Committee. The Central Military Commission has one chairman, and a few vice chairmen, standing members and members.

The highest leading organ of the People's Liberation Army in the war years was the Central Military Commission of the Party. In April 1949, in the situation when the Party was about to seize national power, the Revolutionary Military Commission of the Central Committee of the CPC was renamed as "the People's Revolutionary Military Commission of China" in its external affairs. After the People's Republic of China was founded, the People's Revolutionary Military Commission of the Central People's Government was the highest commanding organ and highest headquarters of the People's Liberation Army in accordance with the stipulations of the Common Program, but it was still called the "Central Military Commission" for short in its external affairs. After it was established, the commission replaced the function of the Central Military Commission of the CPC and there was no military commission in the Central Committee of the CPC. However, there was little difference between the Central People's Revolutionary Military Commission and the Military Commission of the Central Committee of the CPC. In the People's Revolutionary Military Commission established subsequently, its Chairman was Mao

Zedong, and all its vice-chairmen but one and other members were all the most important political and military leaders of the CPC. However, from the founding of the People's Republic of China to 1954, as there was no military commanding organ inside the CPC, the People's Revolutionary Military Commission, at least in form, remained as the highest military commanding organ within the framework of the government.

In September 1954, the Political Bureau of the Central Committee decided to re-establish the Military Commission of the Central Committee of the CPC. It was responsible to direct military work under the leadership of the Political Bureau and Secretariat of the Central Committee. At the same time, the Constitution of the People's Republic of China, adopted by the First National People's Congress that was just concluded, stipulated that the chairman of the People's Republic of China command the armed forces of the whole country and take the chairmanship of the National Defense Council. The coexistence of the highest military commanding organs of the government and the Party remained until 1975. During these years, Mao Zedong and Liu Shaoqi, respectively, served as the chairman of the People's Republic of China and concurrently the chairman of the National Defense Council. But, only Mao Zedong served as the chairman of the Military Commission of the Central Committee of the CPC. The Constitution of the People's Republic of China adopted in 1975 and 1978 stipulated that the chairman of the Central Committee of the CPC command the armed forces of the whole country, and there would be no national defense council or military commission under the government. The Central Committee of the CPC decided in September 1982 that the Military Commission of the Central Committee of the CPC be composed of the chairman, vice-chairmen, secretary-general and deputy secretaries-general, and that the secretary-general and deputy secretaries-general form the standing council of the Military Commission to handle the day-to-day work of the commission. There has been no secretary-general since 1993, and the Standing Council of the Central Military Commission was composed of the vice-chairmen and members of the commission and presided over by a vice-chairman.

In December 1982, the Constitution revised and adopted by the Fifth Session of the Fifth National People's Congress stipulated that the Central Military Commission of the People's Republic of China would be set up to lead the armed forces of the whole country. The Sixth National People's Congress convened in the following year set up the Central

Military Commission of the State. The newly established Central Military Commission of the State, like the Central Military Commission of the Party, is also called "Central Military Commission" for short. The functions and members of the two commissions are entirely the same. This system has continued until today.

7. The Organ for Discipline Inspection

The organ for discipline inspection of the Party was an organ set up in correspondence with the central and local committees of the Party at all levels to be responsible for discipline supervision in the Party. At the central level is the Central Commission for Discipline Inspection. It carries out its work under the leadership of the Central Committee, and the local commissions for discipline inspection at all levels carry out their work under the dual leadership of the Party committees at the corresponding levels and the commissions for discipline inspection at the next-higher level. The commissions for discipline inspection at all levels serve a term of the same duration as the Party committees at the corresponding levels.

The first discipline inspection organ of the CPC was set up in November 1949. Called the Central Commission for Discipline Inspection, it was composed of eleven members. In accordance with the "Provisions on the Organizational Setup and Scope of Work of the Central Commission for Discipline Inspection" promulgated by the Central Committee of the CPC on February 24, 1955, it was the assistant of the Party Central Committee in enforcing Party discipline and its principal responsibility was to ensure that the Party organizations at all levels carry out the Party's line and policies in a better way and combat bureaucratism. In March 1955, the National Conference of the CPC made a decision to dismantle the discipline inspection organ and set up supervisory commissions at all levels. The conference also elected the Central Supervisory Commission. Made up of 15 members, the commission's principal duty was to enforce Party discipline and oppose all violations of laws and discipline by Party members. The Constitution of the Party adopted by the Eighth National Congress further clarified the status, functions and powers of the commission. It stipulated that the commission would be elected by the Central Committee. The Constitution of the Party adopted by the Ninth National Congress and the Tenth National Congress dismantled the Central Supervisory Commission and made no stipulation for the establishment of a substitute organ. The Constitution of the Party adopted by the 11th National Congress stipulated that a discipline inspection organ be re-established and that the Central Commission for Discipline Inspection would be elected by the Central Committee. The Constitution of the Party adopted by the 12th National Congress stipulated that the Central Commission for Discipline Inspection would be elected by the National Congress. The Central Commission for Discipline Inspection elected by the 15th National Congress was made up of 121 members and its Standing Committee was made up of 18 members.

In accordance with the stipulations of the Party Constitution, the Central Commission for Discipline Inspection is elected by the National Congress, and the local commissions for discipline inspection at all levels and the primary commissions for discipline inspection are elected by the local congresses at all levels and the primary congresses. The Central Commission for Discipline Inspection elects its standing committee, secretary and deputy secretaries at its plenary session and reports the results of the election to the Central Committee for approval. The local commissions for discipline inspection elect their standing committees, secretaries and deputy secretaries at their plenary sessions, and the results of the elections are subject to endorsement by the Party committees at the corresponding levels and be reported to the Party committees at the next higher levels for approval. It is up to the Party committees at the next higher level to decide whether a primary Party committee should set up a commission for discipline inspection or simply appoint discipline inspection commissioner. A Party general branch committee or a branch committee shall have discipline inspection commissioners.[16]

The Party Constitution also stipulates that the Central Commission for Discipline Inspection can accredit discipline inspection groups or commissioners to Party or state organs at the central level. The leaders of the discipline inspection groups or discipline inspection commissioners may attend relevant meetings of the leading Party organizations in the said organs as non-voting participants. The leading Party organizations in the organs concerned must support their work.[17]

The main tasks of the discipline inspection commissions are to uphold the Constitution and other statues of the Party, to check up on the implementation of the line, principles, policies and decisions of the Party, to assist the respective Party committees in improving the Party's style of work, and in organizing and coordinating the work against corruption, to provide regular education to Party members on their duty to observe Party discipline, to supervise the exercise of power by Party members holding leading positions, to examine and deal with relatively important or complicated cases of violation of the Constitution and other statutes of the Party, to decide on or rescind disciplinary measures against Party members involved in such cases, and to deal with complaints and appeals made by Party members.[18]

The competence of the discipline inspection organs in carrying out their tasks is subject to different limits for different cases: they must report to the Party committees at the corresponding levels on the results of their handling of cases of special importance or complexity, as well as the problems encountered. If a commission for discipline inspection at any level discovers a violation of Party discipline by a member of the Party committee at the corresponding level, it may make a preliminary verification in advance. If it is necessary to put the case on file, it should report to the Party committee at the corresponding level for approval. If a member of the standing committee of a Party committee is involved, it should first report it to the Party committee at the corresponding level, and then to the commission for discipline inspection at the next higher level for approval. Higher commissions for discipline inspection have the power to examine the work of the lower commissions, and to approve or modify their decisions concerning any case. If decisions so modified have already been ratified by the Party committee at the corresponding level, the modification must be approved by the next higher Party committee. If a local or a primary commission for discipline inspection does not agree with a decision made by the Party committee at the corresponding level in dealing with a case, it may demand that the commission at the next higher level reexamine the case. If a local or primary commission discovers a case of violation of Party discipline by the Party committee at the corresponding level or by its members, and if that Party committee fails to deal with the case properly or at all, it has the right to appeal to the higher commission for assistance in dealing with such a case.[19]

8. The Local and Primary Organizations

The CPC sets up Party congresses, Party committees and standing committees, and commissions for discipline inspection in all administrative regions, namely, the provinces, autonomous regions, municipalities directly under the central government, cities that are divided into districts, autonomous prefectures, counties, autonomous counties, cities that are not divided into districts, and districts directly under municipal governments.

Local Party Committees and Standing Committees at All Levels

The local Party committees at all levels are the local leading organs of the Party when the local Party congresses at the corresponding levels are not in session. They are elected by the local Party congresses at the corresponding levels for a term of five years. The number of members and alternate members of the local Party committees at various levels is determined by the Party committees at the next higher levels.

When the Party congresses of the given localities are not in session, the local Party committees are responsible to carry out the directives of the Party Central Committee and the higher Party organizations as well as the decisions of the Party congresses at the corresponding levels, direct work in their own localities and report on their work to the next-higher Party committees at regular intervals. The local Party committees meet in plenary session at least twice a year.

The members and alternate members of the Party committees of the provinces, autonomous regions, municipalities directly under the Central Government, cities divided into districts, and autonomous prefectures must have a Party standing of five years or more. The members and alternate members of the Party committees of the counties, autonomous counties, cities not divided into districts and municipal districts must have a Party standing of three years or more.

Local Party committees at various levels elect, at their plenary sessions, their standing committees, secretaries, and deputy secretaries, and report the results of the election to the next higher Party committees for approval. The standing committees of local Party committees at various levels are the local day-to-day or permanent leading organs at the corresponding levels. They exercise the functions and powers of the local Party committees when the latter are not in session. They continue to handle the day-to-day work when the next Party congresses at their levels are in session, until the new standing committees are elected.

The Primary Organizations

Primary organizations of the Party are established in enterprises, rural areas, government departments, schools, scientific research institutes, urban communities, companies of the People's Liberation Army and other units at the primary level, where there are at least three full Party members. The forms of primary organizations are primary Party committees, Committees of the general branches or Party branches. A primary Party committee is elected by a general membership meeting or a delegate meeting. The committee of a general Party branch or a Party branch is elected by a general membership meeting. A primary Party committee is elected for a term of three to five years while a general Party branch committee or a Party branch committee is elected for a term of two or three years. The results of the election of a secretary and deputy secretaries by a primary Party committee, general Party branch committee or branch committee shall be reported to the higher Party organizations for approval.

The primary organizations hold an important position in the organizational setup of the CPC. They are "military bastions" of the Party in the basic units of society, where "all the Party's work proceeds and which serve as the foundation of its fighting capacity."[20] Their basic tasks are to organize and lead Party members, expand Party organizations, and educate and supervise Party members and any working personnel. As the various primary organizations are in different concrete environments, their specific tasks are also different. In recent years, because of the reform measures adopted, the functions of the primary organizations are also changing. However, generally speaking, the primary organizations of the Communist Party still preserve the position of leading core in the basic organizations of society.

9. Leading Party Members' Groups

The current Constitution of the Party stipulates that a leading Party members' group shall be formed in the leading body of a central or local state organ, people's organization, economic or cultural institution, or other non-Party units. That is, in order to guarantee the implementation of the intentions and specific policies of the CPC, all state organs, government departments, social organizations and other institutions must have leading Party members' groups playing the role of the core of leadership and directly accredited by the higher Party committees and at the same time directly under the corresponding Party committees. The main tasks of the leading Party members' Groups are to see to it that the Party's line, principles and policies are implemented, discuss and decide on matters of major importance in their own units, manage affairs concerning cadres properly, unite with non-Party cadres and the masses in fulfilling the tasks assigned by the Party and state, and guide the work of the Party organizations of the units and those directly under them. In other words, while performing the rights and duties laid down in the Constitution of the country and the other statutes, any state organ, people's organization, economic organization, cultural organization and other non-Party organization must accept the leadership of the leading Party members' group. The leadership of the leading Party members' group over the state organs and units, apart from the policy-making, is embodied in the fact that the establishment of the leading Party members' group further strengthens the organization and leadership of Party members in these organizations and units, thus enhancing the Party's influence in state organs and various types of social organizations.

As the leading Party members' group is an representative organ of the higher Party committee, the members of the group don't have to be elected by Party members in the corresponding organ or unit. Instead, they are appointed by the Party organization that approves the establishment of the leading Party members' group. Moreover, the members of a leading Party members' group are, in general, Party members who hold leading positions in the related state organ or social organization. In this way, a direct relationship of leadership is established between the specific state organ or social organization on the one hand and the leading organ of the Party on the other. The leading Party members' group has a secretary and, if necessary, deputy secretaries.

The establishment of the leading Party members' group in the leading body of a state organ, people's organization, economic organization, cultural organization and other non-Party organization has been one of the methods of leadership used by the CPC over a long period of time. It has played an important role in strengthening its leadership. The general tendency shows that there has been little change in this method. The only exception was that the Constitution adopted by the 13th National Congress of the Party stipulated for the abolishment of the leading Party members' group in the leading bodies of the central and local state organs, people's organizations, economic organizations, cultural organizations and other non-Party organizations, which was meant to meet the need of separating the functions of the Party from those of the government. However, the Constitution adopted by the 14th National Congress made a revision and reinstated the leading Party members' group system.

10. Representative Organs of the Party

The Constitution of the Party stipulates that local committees of the Party at provincial level may dispatch representative organs and establish prefectural committees or Party organizations analogous to them. A profectural Party committee, or an organization analogous to it, is a representative organ dispatched by a Party committee at the provincial (autonomous regional) level to a region covering several counties, autonomous counties or cities. It exercises leadership over the work in the given region as authorized by the provincial or autonomous regional Party committee.[21]

In addition to the prefectural committee as stipulated in the Party Constitution, there are, in fact, representative organs at other levels, and their status and duties are similar to that of the prefectural committee.

III. The Leadership of the CPC over the State Affairs and Social Life

The leadership of the CPC over the state and social life is determined by the nature of the CPC itself; it is also determined by the position of the CPC as the sole ruling Party. The current Constitution of the People's Republic of China does not include specific stipulations on the political party system, nor does it have detailed stipulations regarding the position and role of the CPC in government and social life in China. However, the Constitution acknowledges that the People's Republic of China was founded by the CPC, China has made the achievements in its economic construction and social development under the leadership of the CPC, and the people of all ethnic groups in China were led in the past, are led at present and will still be led by the CPC in the future.[22] The Constitution acknowledges and includes the Four Cardinal Principles set by the CPC. Therefore, it can be said that the leadership role of the CPC in the state and social life of China is guaranteed by the Constitution.

The current Constitution of the Communist Party of China defined even more clearly the leadership role of the CPC. It says that the CPC is "the core of leadership for the cause of socialism with Chinese characteristics, and represents the development trend of China's advanced productive forces, the orientation of China's advanced culture and the fundamental interests of the overwhelming majority of the Chinese people."[23]

1. The Nature of the Leadership of the CPC

In accordance with the stipulations of the Constitution of the CPC, the leadership by the CPC is mainly "political, ideological and organizational leadership".[24] Therefore, the Party's leadership over the state and social life in China is comprehensive. In other words, the CPC not only wants to exercise the political leadership over the state power just as all ruling parties do, but also wants to exercise the organizational and ideological leadership over all the social organizations and members of society. In this sense, the leadership by the CPC is not at all similar to that of any other ruling parties.

In specific terms, political leadership means leadership by means of political principles, political orientation and major policy decisions, namely, the line, guiding principles and policies of the Communist Party must be implemented in all aspects of the state politics and social life, thus to guarantee the realization of the political aim of the CPC. In other words, the political leadership by the CPC does not permit, in all aspects of the state politics and the social life, the emergence of anything that goes against the political concept and political aim of the CPC.

The precondition for the CPC to realize its political leadership is, first of all, to ensure the correctness of its own line, principles and policies. The criteria for judgment, fundamentally, lies in whether the line, principles and policies the CPC adopts are conducive to adhering the socialist road, the people's democratic dictatorship, the leadership of the CPC, and Marxism-Leninism, Mao Zedong Thought and Deng Xiaoping Theory. Under the conditions of reform and opening-up, to develop the productive forces and promote the economic development is also one of the criteria for judging whether the Party's political line is correct or not. How to handle well the relationship between the Four Cardinal Principles on the one hand and the reform and opening-up is a question that calls for careful deliberation on the part of the CPC while formulating its political line and exercising its political leadership.

Once the political line of the CPC is determined, it provides a strong guidance to and compulsory restraint over the state and social life, that is to say, political leadership in the general term. The political leadership of the CPC find expression at different levels and in different fields. Sometimes, it is manifested as a common question of political ideology, sometimes a major question of political and economic policy decision, and still sometimes an important question of selecting and appointing the right people to important political and administrative posts. Sometimes, the question occurs inside the CPC, sometimes in the various departments and at different levels of the government, and sometimes it is extended to the various fields of social life.

Ideological leadership is manifested in the fact that the CPC not only wants to convey its political program to the whole society, but also needs to ideologically educate the members of society to ensure that the members of society can accept its concepts and policies ideologically and physiologically. Ideological leadership is the prerequisite and foundation for political and organizational leadership. Without ideological leadership, political leadership may be limited only to the use of political power, and it will make the Party fail to achieve a unity of thinking. Without ideological leadership, organizational leadership may be limited to merely form and procedure, and the Party won't be able to know what people really think, eventually causing the organization to lose its vitality.

By ideological leadership, it means, first of all, that, under the premise of the Four Cardinal Principles, the Party wants to use Marxism-Leninism, Mao Zedong Thought and Deng Xiaoping Theory to command and standardize every aspect of social life so that the whole society can automatically use these thoughts and theories to understand and treat the objective reality and standardize their own conduct. Second, the nature of the Communist Party determines that the CPC must constantly transfuse the advanced thinking and ideology, transform those ideas existing in society that are incompatible with the ideology of the CPC and wage struggles against them, and finally create the correct ideological tendency and orientation for public opinion. Third, because of the complexity and diversity of social life, there is a gap between the ideological and political consciousness of the ordinary members of society on the one hand and the demand from the Four Cardinal Principles put forward by CPC. In real life, the heretical thinking from outside will gradually influence and violate the orthodox thinking. Therefore, another important task of the ideological leadership is to criticize and ward off the influence of the unorthodox thinking.

Organizational leadership is the guarantee for the political leadership and ideological leadership of the CPC. It's hard to imagine political leadership and ideological leadership without the guarantee and support of strong organizational leadership. In fact, if the Party does not hold leadership over the state organs and the various social organizations, its political and ideological leadership would be impossible. Compared with political and ideological leadership, organizational leadership is a more concrete, more practical form of leadership.

The organizational leadership of the CPC is embodied in all aspects of the relations between the Communist Party and the state power, public organizations and social life in general. In terms of state power, the organizational leadership of the CPC over the state organs is embodied mainly in strengthening control and leadership over the Party member cadres in these organs. That is, the CPC can select the best of its cadres to take the leading posts in the state organs. When these people perform their duties functionaries in these organs and hold themselves responsible to the state and the voters, they also perform the duties as Party member cadres of the CPC and hold themselves responsible to the line and policies of the CPC. In this way, the leadership and control of the Communist Party over the state organs are guaranteed. They are chosen and dispatched to take the posts in the state organs and are to ensure the Party's political and ideological leadership in these organs during their tenure of office. Therefore, although the organizations of the CPC are independent from the state organs, and the state organs have their own goals and duties, the CPC, however, can see to it that its line is implemented in these organs through the work of these Party member cadres. The leadership of the CPC over the Party member cadres in the state organs is highly organized. Such organization is manifested in the following aspects. First, in those organs where there are no Party organizations, the CPC directly exercises its organizational leadership over the Party member cadres in these organs by establishing leading Party members' groups of a representative nature. Second, it encourages the Party member cadres in these organs to make further contributions to the Party's cause by making new arrangements for the political life of the cadres. As the system of limited tenure of office is adopted in all state organs, it's impossible for the Party member cadres to hold their posts permanently. Yet, the Party can choose the suitable cadres and appoint them to different new posts according to the needs of the Party.

As to the relations between the CPC and the social organizations, the CPC establishes. Party organizations and exercise direct organizational leadership The Party organizations established in these social organizations are either Party committees directly elected by Party members or leading Party members' groups dispatched directly by higher Party committees.

The Constitution of the Party stipulates: "The Party must conduct its activities within the framework of the Constitution and other laws. It must
see to it that the legislative, judicial and administrative organs of the state
and the economic, cultural and people's organizations work with initiative, independently, and in harmony."[25] Yet, it is also unquestionable that
the organizations of the CPC have crucial authority in all social organizations, the organizational network of Party organizations make up the basic
frameworks of these social organizations and the Party members form the
backbone and basic force in them.

The organizational leadership of the CPC in the every-day social life
is manifested in the following fact. On the one hand, primary Party organizations are established at the grassroots level of the social life and
members of society who meet the criteria of the Party are admitted into
the Party. On the other, the CPC brings all the members of the society
into various social organizations by means of active mobilization of the
public and various kinds of political and organizational activities, thus
making it possible for it to enforce effective leadership over all social
organizations.

2. Style of Leadership of the CPC

The CPC is the ruling Party, and a ruling Party naturally wishes to
convert its political ideas, line and policies into concrete political and
administrative activities and makes full use of its ruling position to rear-
range and allocate the political and material resources in society, so to
form a specific political society. Therefore, how to carry out the political
operation and how to arrange and allocate the political and material resources of the society is closely related to the nature of the ruling Party.
Every ruling Party has its own style of ruling and the ruling style of a ruling Party reflects the nature of the ruling Party.

On the other hand, the ruling position of the CPC is exclusive, and is
created by history. Therefore, its style of ruling is also historical. That is
to say, the specific ruling style of the CPC will change along with the
change of the historical and realistic environments. Over a long period,
the leadership of the Communist Party over the Chinese society has experienced a process of change — from direct political and administrative
control to gradual adoption of a legal system and eventually to ruling the
country by law in the future. At present, the CPC is exercising leadership

over the state power and social life mainly in the following ways:

First, Organizing and Leading Legislative Work and Law Enforcement of the State

In accordance with Marxist theory on the state, law is the embodiment of the will of the ruling class of a state. Therefore, law is also a useful and effective tool of rule by the ruling class. As law has the distinct attribute of a tool, it is of positive value to the leadership of the CPC over the state power and social life. However, law is after all more stable and more non-personified as compared with the specific policies and administrative mandates, therefore, stress on the importance and value of law helps to change the abuses caused by the ultra-"Left" politics. It is even more advantageous to the balance and steady development of the political life, and also, in a degree, restricts the political arbitrariness, and the unrestricted political influence and control of a handful of political leaders. As law and the legal system have the nature of reliability and balance, after the style of political leadership in the form of "military mobilization" and large-scale political movement has become more and more incompatible with the actual social life, the leadership of the CPC over the state power and social life has gradually evolved into the style of leadership by formulating and enforcing law. Organization of and leadership over the legislative work and law enforcement of the state have become an important aspect of the leadership the CPC now exercises over the state power and social life.

The organization of and leadership over legislative work and law enforcement by the CPC includes two aspects. On the one hand, in view of the fact that for a long period of time the CPC had failed to handle the relationship between the Party and law well, after the end of the "cultural revolution" the CPC has more than once stressed that "the Party must conduct its activities within the framework of the Constitution and other laws"[26] and "no organization or individual is privileged to be beyond the Constitution or the law."[27] It has recognized the supreme authority and supreme legal validity of the Constitution as the fundamental law of the state, and tried its best to remedy such malpractices as "placing the Party above the law" and "replacing the law with the Party," thus bringing the CPC within the framework of the Constitution and other laws. On the other hand, in view of the fact that the long-time neglect of legislation led to the situation in which there were no laws to go by, after the end of the "cultural revolution" the CPC has made great efforts to strengthen legislative work and law enforcement and lay due stress on administration by law.

Relative to law enforcement, legislative work is the more important and crucial step of the leadership over the legislative work and law enforcement of the state by the CPC. First, legislation is the means by which the CPC administers the state power and social life, and turns its will of administering the state affairs and society to practical administration of the state power. How well the Party leads and controls the legislative work is vitally important to whether the laws reflect and represent the will of the CPC and whether the CPC can realize its leadership over the state and social life within the framework of law thus established. Second, strengthened efforts in legislation helps change the situation in which there are no laws to go by, gradually improve the system of laws and regulations, turn the rule by man into the rule by law, and hold in check the influence of ultra-"Left" politics. Third, law enforcement is in fact the political and administrative activity of the state organs. The leadership of the CPC in the state organs is not dependent on whether to adopt the legal system; It has always been there.

The principle governing the Party's leadership over the legislative work is: "The Party leads the people in formulating the Constitution and other laws."[28] The concrete procedure is as follows: the legislative work of the state is, in principle, presided over by the National People's Congress and its Standing Committee, but under the leadership of the CPC. When the National People's Congress and its Standing Committee examine laws, all important ones of principle shall be submitted to the Central Committee of the CPC in advance. As to the laws that are not so important, the Central Committee of the CPC gives the final word only on the guiding thought and major principles. The unimportant issues are left to the National People's Congress and its Standing Committee for decisions based on the opinions of the majority of deputies or members.

Second, the Party Commanding the Gun

The army is the pillar stone of the People's Republic of China, and is also one of the foundations for the leadership of the CPC over the state and society. After 1949, there has always been the Central Military Commission under the Central Committee of the CPC, except for a certain short period of time. In fact, the top leader of the CPC has served concurrently as the top leader of the Military Commission of the Central Committee of China.

The vital importance and influence of the army to the leadership of the CPC is inseparable from the history of the CPC and the important role of the army in the Chinese political and social life. The CPC won state power by armed struggle and the army was the main force and tool the Party relied on for seizing the political power. The army also has played a positive and important role in the peaceful years after 1949, and it sometimes even greatly influenced the political development in China. Because the army cannot separate itself from politics in China, the leadership of the Communist Party over the state and society naturally includes how to handle its relations with the army.

The Party commanding the gun is the tradition of CPC in handling its relations with the army and is the fundamental principle of its leadership over the army. Its basic meaning is that, on the one hand, the Party is above the army, politics above military affairs, and the political power above the power over military affairs in the relationship between the Party and the army; and on the other, the leadership of the CPC over the army is absolute. It is the CPC, not any other force that commands the army.

The principle of the Party commanding the gun embodies the CPC's absolute leadership over the army politically, ideologically and organizationally. The political leadership of the CPC over the army is manifested in the fact that the army must obey and implement the program, line, principles and policies of the CPC, and that the political aim of the CPC is the political aim of the army, and the army is not permitted to have any other political aim other than the political aim of the CPC.

The ideological leadership of the CPC over the army means that the army must follow the theory and ideology advocated by the CPC and arm itself with Marxism-Leninism, Mao Zedong Thought and Deng Xiaoping Theory. It is not allowed to propagate any anti-Marxist or non-Marxist theory and thoughts, and it must keep its own ideological purity, adhere to the Four Cardinal Principles and consciously obey the command of the CPC militarily.

By organizational leadership of the CPC over the army, it means that the CPC Central Committee and the Central Military Commission of the CPC hold the highest power to lead and command the army. Without the authorization of the Central Committee of the CPC and the Central Military Commission of the CPC, no organization or individual is allowed to intervene in or deal with affairs concerning the army, even the less to move or command troops without authorization.

Second, the organizational leadership of the CPC over the army is also manifested in the fact that the CPC establishes Party organizations at all levels of the army. Party branches are set up in the companies, Party committees are set up at the regimental level and above, and the Central Military Commission at the top level. The committees of the CPC at all levels in the army form a core of centralized leadership. All major issues concerning the army must be decided on by the Party committees, except in emergent cases in which commanders may handle them promptly as occasion requires. Once a decision concerning military affairs is made by the Party committee, the military commander is responsible for carrying it out. If it is a decision concerning political affairs, the political commissar will be responsible for its implementation.

The organizational leadership of the CPC over the army is exclusive. It forbids any other political party, political group or organization, except for the Communist Youth League, to establish organizations and recruit members in the army. Without the approval of the organizations of the CPC, the army does not permit the establishment of small groups or organizations of any nature and in any form.

Furthermore, the CPC guarantees its leadership over the army through its political work system with unique characteristic. The political work system in the army consists of the political commissar system. The political commissar system is an important system for the exercise of the leadership over the army by the CPC. The political commissar and the military commander are both the heads of an army unit. The political commissar usually presides over the Party work and political work of the unit, takes care of the day-to-day work of the Party committee at the same level. The basic duty of the political commissar is to ensure the implementation of the line, principles and policies of the CPC and do organizational work for the study of Marxism-Leninism, Mao Zedong Though and Deng Xiaoping Theory in his or her unit, etc.

Third, the Party Administering Cadres

The classical theory of the CPC holds that cadres are a decisive factor, once the political line is determined. To exercise leadership over the state power and the social life, the CPC is unable to achieve its goal if it does not have the final say of matters regarding cadres. This is the fundamental cause for the great attention it has paid to the cadre work. Being the sole ruling party for a long time, the CPC has pooled large numbers of outstanding talents, thus establishing its *de facto* monopoly over the finest talents of society.

The Party administering cadres is one of the fundamental principles of the CPC in exercising national leadership. The core of the implementation of the principle lies in CPC selecting, recommending and appointing the right people to important leading posts. Since the early 1950's, the following basic patterns have been established for the CPC to appoint and remove cadres.

(1) Direct appointments and removals by the CPC. This is applicable mainly to those cadres within the Party. The usual practice is to call Party meetings and decide on the appointments and removals .

(2) The CPC makes recommendations and the National People's Congress makes the appointments and removals. First, the Party committee prepares a list of candidates for leading posts that should be decided on by the people's congress at the corresponding level for appointments and removals. Then, it submits the list to the standing committee or presidium of the people's congress for inclusion in the election at the people's congress. Finally, the people's congress or its standing committee shall elect, appoint or decide to appoint the candidates through law-prescribed formalities. This applies mainly to the members of the standing committee of the people's congress, members of the government, president of the people's court, chief procurator of the people's procuratorate, as well as other state functionaries whose appointments and removals must go through the formalities of the people's congress or its standing committee in accordance with the stipulations of law.

(3) The CPC recommends and the government appoints. This applies mainly to the appointments and removals of the heads of government departments.

Fourth, the Party Exercising Leadership over Mass Organizations

In China, mass organizations are organized in certain forms to play different roles in different aspects of the social life and are composed of members of the society in different walks of life. The CPC provides leadership to all of them. Now, the major mass organizations include the All-China Federation of Trade Unions, All-China Women's Federation, the Communist Youth League of China, as well as various types of societies and associations.

In nature, the mass organizations in China are fundamentally different from similar organizations in other countries. First, they all carry out their activities under the leadership of the CPC. Second, they are all important social pillars supporting the CPC and the state power, and play an important supporting role in the leadership of the CPC over the state power and social life. Third, they are both the representatives of the interests of the masses and the representatives of the will of the state power, and serve as important links between the CPC and government on one hand and the general public on the other. Fourth, whether they are pure political or not, they play a distinct political role.

The All-China Federation of Trade Unions is a mass organization of physical laborers and mental laborers depending on wages as their major source of income under the leadership of the CPC. Featuring a high degree of organization, the federation has special setups and staff both at the central level and grassroots enterprises. It has hundreds of thousands of full-time staff members. With a certain financial capability, it has set up many undertakings and entities. It is a mass organization with considerable self-support.

The Communist Youth League of China is a mass organization of the youth under the leadership of the CPC. It also serves as a school where the CPC trains young people to learn communism, a mass organization for the CPC to unite and educate the young people. The Communist Youth League was the peripheral organization of the CPC for a long time in the past. Under the leadership of the CPC, it takes Marxism-Leninism and Mao Zedong Thought as its guide for action, practice democratic centralism, and features strict organizational discipline and organizational life.

The All-China Women's Federation is a women's mass organization under the leadership of the CPC. Specially set up for women in all walks of life, it also features a certain nature of a united front organization, in addition to the characteristics as a mass organization. Apart from the functions common to all mass organizations, it lays special emphasis on protecting the legitimate rights and interests of the women and children. One of its distinct organizational characteristics is that it practices the group membership system, with all women's organizations of the trade unions and other women's organizations being its group members.

Section 2 The Political Parties Participating in State Affairs in China

In China, there are eight democratic (non-communist) parties that participate in state affairs. They represent the interests of different groups of people in society under the leadership of the CPC since the CPC won state power. In accordance with the stipulations of the Constitution of the People's Republic of China, the system of multi-party cooperation and the political consultation under the leadership of the CPC shall exist and develop for a long time to come, and the democratic parties are all component parts of the patriotic united front under the leadership of the CPC. The Constitution of the CPC states that the CPC "adheres to the system of people's congresses and the system of multi-party cooperation and political cooperation under the leadership of the Communist Party of China."[29]

The eight democratic parties are the Revolutionary Committee of the Chinese Kuomintang, the China Democratic League, the China Democratic National Construction Association, the China Association for Promoting Democracy, the Chinese Peasants and Workers Democratic Party, the China Zhi Gong Dang, the Jiusan Society, and the Taiwan Democratic Self-Government League.

I. The Past and Present of the Democratic Parties

1. The Revolutionary Committee of the Chinese Kuomintang

The Revolutionary Committee of the Chinese Kuomintang was established on January 1, 1948. Chiefly, its members were the democrats in the Kuomintang and other patriotic democrats, and its representative figures were Soong Ching Ling and Li Jishen. At the initial stage after its founding, it took the political stand to overthrow the autocratic rule of the Kuomintang and strive for the independence of, democracy and peace in China.

The predecessors of the Revolutionary Committee of the Chinese Kuomintang were the Comrades' Association for the Three People's Principles established in October 1945 and the Democratic Promotion Association of the Chinese Kuomintang established in March 1946. The two organizations were both separated from within the Kuomintang for their discontent at the dictatorship and autocracy inside the Kuomintang. They stood for an end to the Kuomintang's one-Party dictatorship, the establishment of a coalition government and equality among all political parties.

At present, members of the Revolutionary Committee of the Chinese Kuomintang are mainly former Kuomintang officials, personages who have historical or social relations with the Kuomintang, personages who have relations with people of all circles in Taiwan, and other personages. It mainly recruits members chiefly from among the representative personages of the middle-level and senior intellectuals. Now, it has around 60,000 members.

According to its Constitution, revised in November 1988, the Revolutionary Committee of the Chinese Kuomintang practices democratic centralism, supports the system of multi-party cooperation and political consultation under the leadership of the CPC and endorses the leadership of the CPC. It adopts the congress and committee system. Its highest leading organ is its national congress or its central committee when the national congress is not in session. It does not adopts the system of limited tenure of office for its leading posts. Its local organizations are the congresses and committees at the provincial level, at the municipal level in cities directly under the provincial government, and at the county level. In some regions, it also has primary organizations. Its political program at the present stage is to lead all party members, unite patriots living in China and residing abroad in favor of the unification of the motherland to strive for the unification and rejuvenation of China, under the guidance of the basic line for the primary stage of socialism.

2. The China Democratic League

The predecessor of the China Democratic League was the "Association for Unification and Construction," established in November 1939. Its aim was to mediate the "disputes between the Kuomintang and the CPC" and urge the Kuomintang to adopt a democratic Constitution. When the Southern Anhui Incident happened in 1941, the "League of Chinese Democratic Political Groups" was founded in March that year. It was a merge of various small parties and political groups of the time, all of which favored the middle road and democracy. Included in the leader are some parties and organizations of considerable social and political influence at the time, such as the Young China Party, the National Socialist Party and the Action Committee for the Liberation of the Chinese Nation. Its main political goals were to persevere in the resistance to Japanese aggression, end the one-party rule by Kuomintang, exercise the rule by law, protect human rights, advocate equal political rights, nationalize the army, etc., with a distinct color of the middle road. It the current name in

September 1944. In May 1948, it endorsed the call of the CPC for convening the new Political Consultative Conference, supported the political views of the CPC, opposed the rule of the Kuomintang, and began political cooperation with the CPC. Now, the China Democratic League is mainly made up by middle-level and senior intellectuals in the fields of culture, education, science and technology. It has a total membership of 144,000.

In its Constitution adopted in 1997, the leader declares that it takes Marxism-Leninism, Mao Zedong Thought and Deng Xiaoping Theory as its guide, arms its members with Deng Xiaoping Theory, practices the principle of democratic centralism, adheres to the Four Cardinal Principles, and that its program is to hold high the banner of patriotism and socialism, implement the basic line for the primary stage of socialism, safeguard stability in the society, strengthen services to national unity and strive for the promotion of socialist modernization, establishment and improvement of a market economy, enhancement of political restructuring and socialist spiritual civilization, emancipation and development of productive forces, consolidation and expansion of the united patriotic front and realization of the grand goals of socialism with Chinese characteristics.

The leader practices the congress and committee system and does not limit the tenure of office for its leaders.

3. The China Democratic National Construction Association

The China Democratic National Construction Association was founded on December 16, 1945. Its principal initiators were Huang Yanpei, Hu Juewen, Zhang Naiqi and Shi Fuliang. The association's political stand at the time was to guarantee the basic political rights and human rights of citizens, protect and develop national industry and commerce and oppose the dictatorial rule of the Kuomintang.

The current Constitution of the China Democratic National Construction Association calls for the adherence of the Four Cardinal Principles, the implementation of the CPC's policy of focusing on economic construction under the guidance of Deng Xiaoping Theory, acceptance of the leadership of the CPC, persisting in the tradition of self-education, adhering to the principle of democratic centralism and carrying out the policy of multi-party cooperation and political consultation led by the CPC.

The central organization of the China Democratic National Construction Association is its National Congress and Central Committee. Now, it has a total membership of 78,000, most of whom are specialists and scholars in the economic field.

4. The China Association for Promoting Democracy

When it was founded on December 30, 1945, it was made up mostly by patriotic democrats working in cultural, educational and publishing institutions and patriotic figures in industry and commerce in Shanghai who stood for promotion of democracy and reform of the political power. It called on the Kuomintang to return the political power to the people, the establishment of a united and constitutional government.

The current Constitution of the China Association for Promoting Democracy declares that the association accepts the leadership of the CPC, persists in the system of multi-party cooperation and political consultation led by the CPC, upholds Deng Xiaoping Theory, adheres to the Four Cardinal Principles, and practices democratic centralism. It also stands for the promotion and improvement of socialist democracy, improvement of a socialist legal system, uplifting of the qualifications of the people, development of productive forces and turning China into a prosperous, culturally developed, democratic, strong and modern socialist country.

The organs of power of its organizations at all levels are the congresses and membership meetings. When the congresses are not in session, the committees elected are the leading organs of its organizations.

Now, the 73,000 members of the association are mostly from the educational institutions, and about 20% of them come from the cultural, arts, publishing, scientific, technical, medical, health and judicial fields. Of all members, 31% have obtained senior professional titles, and most of them live in large and medium-sized cities.

5. The China Peasants and Workers Democratic Party

Founded in March 1928, the predecessor of the China Peasants and Workers Democratic Party was the "Revolutionary Party of China" led by Tan Pingshan and Zhang Bojun. Its political stand of the time was to make a national democratic revolution and establish a common people's government. Its chief members were leftists of the Kuomintang with fairly high ranks and intellectuals. It was renamed the "Provisional Action Committee of the Chinese Kuomintang" in August 1930 on the initiative of Deng Yanda. It was again renamed the China Peasants and Workers Democratic Party in February 1947.

Before 1949, the China Peasants and Workers Democratic Party (including its predecessor) was a political Party which is distinctly different from the Kuomintang and the Communist Party. It strongly opposed the autocratic rule of the Kuomintang and stood for the establishment of a common people's government. Different from many political parties of the time, it engaged in a broad scope of political activities, waged armed struggles for a long time and devoted itself to mobilizing other social forces. Its chief aim was to oppose the Kuomintang regime and seize the political power. Due to cruel suppression from the Kuomintang, the Peasants and Workers Democratic Party gradually strengthened its relations with the CPC and finally decided to accept the leadership of the CPC.

The current Constitution of the Peasants and Workers Democratic Party declares that the party unswervingly endorses the leadership of the CPC, upholds the system of political consultation and multi-party cooperation, studies Marxism-Leninism, Mao Zedong Thought and Deng Xiaoping Theory, studies the line, principles and policies of the CPC, practices democratic centralism, and safeguards the rights and interests of its members and intellectuals who have ties with the Party. Organizationally, it adopts the congress and committee system. Its current Constitution does not stipulate for the limited tenure of office for its leaders.

Now, it boasts a membership of 73,000, with most of them being middle-level and senior intellectuals working in the medical and pharmaceutical circles of large and medium-sized cities.

6. The China Zhi Gong Dang

The China Zhi Gong Dang was mainly an overseas Chinese organization before 1950, In October 1925, the "Hong Men Zhi Gong Tang", an American overseas Chinese organization, founded the China Zhi Gong Dang. In October 1931, the China Zhi Gong Dang established its headquarters in Hong Kong, and declared its "opposition to Chiang Kai-shek" and resistance to Japanese aggression and took part in the domestic patriotic democratic movement. In May 1947, the Zhi Gong Dang convened a congress in Hong Kong, and decided to take an active part in the domestic revolutionary movement and join the people's democratic united front led by the CPC. In 1950, the Central Committee of the Zhi Gong Dang moved from Hong Kong to Guangzhou, and recruited members mainly from among returned overseas Chinese and their relatives. Now, It has a membership of nearly 18,000.

According to its current constitution, the China Zhi Gong Dang accepts the leadership of the CPC under the guidance of Deng Xiaoping Theory, assists the CPC and the Chinese government to consolidate and develop political stability, safeguards the rights and interests of party members and associated returned overseas Chinese and their relatives, reflects their opinions and demands and practices democratic centralism. It urges its members to study Marxism-Leninism, Mao Zedong Thought and Deng Xiaoping Theory and practices democratic centralism. Organizationally, it practices the congress and committee system.

7. The Jiu San Society

The predecessor of the Jiu San Society was the "Democracy and Science Forum" founded in 1944 by a group of well-known intellectuals who had close ties with the May Fourth Movement. At the initial stage after its founding, the Democracy and Science Forum took the political stand to inherit and carry forward the democratic and scientific spirit of the May Fourth Movement, promote democracy and science, and oppose one-Party dictatorship. Most of the members of the Forum were intellectuals in the cultural, educational, scientific and technical fields. The Jiu San Society was formally founded in May 1946. Now, it has a membership of 78,000.

The current program of the Jiusan Society stipulates that organizationally, it draws members from middle-level and senior intellectuals in the fields of science, technology, higher education and medicine, uses Deng Xiaoping Theory to guide its work, stands for the system of political consultation and multi-party cooperation led by the CPC, practices democratic centralism, and safeguards the rights and interest of its members.

8. The Taiwan Democratic Self-Government League

The Taiwan Democratic Self-Government League was founded in Hong Kong on November 12, 1947. The League of the time was a political organization founded and existed outside the Taiwan Province to seek

Taiwan's freedom from the Kuomintang's rule, and stand for democratic politics and regional autonomy in Taiwan. Its headquarters was moved from Hong Kong to Beijing in March 1949.

As compared with the other democratic parties, the Taiwan Democratic Self-Government League had close ties with the CPC right from the time of its founding. Among the founders and principal leaders of the League were members of the CPC.

Because of the changes in the relations between the mainland and Taiwan, the current Constitution of the League is also different from the time when it was founded. The current Constitution stipulates that the League safeguards the national sovereignty and territorial integrity, opposes split of the motherland and Taiwan's independence, opposes interference from foreign forces, establishes wide contacts with personages of all circles both in and outside Taiwan, promotes the "three links" — mail, transport and trade — and exchanges and cooperation across the Taiwan Straits, makes major efforts to facilitate the economic cooperation between the two sides of the Straits, promotes political talks across the Straits so as to achieve the reunification of the nation.

Politically and organizationally, it's the current Constitution of the League stipulates that it accepts the leadership of the CPC, supports the basic line of the CPC, unites its members and the compatriots in Taiwan with whom it has contacts to fight for the reform, opening-up and economic construction, to maintain stability and unity of China, promote socialist democracy and improve the legal system; it practices democratic centralism, and safeguards the rights and interests of the league members and personages in Taiwan with whom it has contacts.

Most of its more than 1,800 members are representative and upper-level Taiwan compatriots born in Taiwan and living in large and medium-size cities on the mainland.

II. The Nature and Position of the Chinese Democratic Parties

1. Evolution of the Nature of the Chinese Democratic Parties

(1) The Democratic Parties Were Independent Parties before 1949

Before the founding of the People's Republic of China in 1949, the basic dominating forces in the Chinese society were the Communist Party, the Kuomintang and their mutual struggles. The situation of the Chinese society and its future prospect were linked with the win or loss of the two parties. The Communist Party and the Kuomintang were the two powerful parties that represented the demands of the principal interests and the course of development of the society. Because there was no democratic political system in China and the competition between the different parties was apt to go to extremes, there was no possibility of adopting peaceful and competitive party politics and the struggle between the two parties grew fiercer and fiercer with each passing day. The cruel struggle between them worsened the social, economic and political environments, and inflicted severe and irrecoverable wounds on the cultural notions and psychological health of the members of the society. The two parties themselves kept going to extremes in the course of repeated struggles. The struggles between the two major parties objectively provided resources and space to the political parties and political factions that represented the demands of other social strata and interests, and the democratic parties found their own political resources and value of existence between the extremes. Therefore, during this historical period, the democratic parties represented and reflected the positions and demands of the middle-of-the-road forces and kept themselves away from the political ideas, political rules and political aspirations represented by the Communist Party and the Kuomintang. It can be said that the democratic parties were political parties that were different from the Communist Party and the Kuomintang, had their own goals to pursue and maintained independence politically and organizationally.

The existence of the democratic parties had also something to do with the social and political environments of the time. The Kuomintang exercised autocratic rule, suppressed the any alien forces and refused to carry out democratic politics for a long time. The rule of the Kuomintang and the political structure of the Chinese society it had created could not submit to the interests and demands of the members of society outside the ruling clique and their political ideas; it could only meet the interests and demands of the minority of the ruling classes. Yet, the rule of the Kuomintang had, after all, not penetrated into every corner of society, nor could it liquidate all non-governmental and anti-governmental activities and organizations. The efficiency of its autocratic rule was fairly low, making it impossible for its government to exercise comprehensive rule over the entire society and all members of the society. The low efficiency of the Kuomintang rule left certain room for the activities of social and democratic politics. During the entire period of the rule of the Kuomintang, political movements for the democracy and freedom erupted one after another, and all kinds of non-governmental political organizations and associations were established throughout the country. It was in these social and political environments that the democratic parties emerged and existed.

(2) The Democratic Parties — Component Parts of the United Front after the Founding of the People's Republic of China

The change in the nature of the democratic parties from being independent parties to being component parts of the united front began as early as on April 30, 1948 when the Central Committee of the CPC issued the "Slogans Commemorating May Day" and the subsequent responses made by leaders of the democratic parties to the call of the Central Committee of the CPC. In this document, the CPC proposed that the democratic parties and the patriotic democrats of all circles join the CPC in convening the political consultative conference to establish the democratic coalition government. It received positive support from the democratic parties. The leaders of the democratic parties and nonparty patriots issued open telegrams to the nation on May 5, 1948, expressing their endorsement of the proposal of the CPC. Beginning in August of the same year, representatives of the democratic parties and non-party patriots went to the liberated areas led by the CPC from various parts of the country and abroad to join the CPC in making preparations for the convention of the political consultative conference. On January 22, 1949, fifty-five representatives of the democratic parties and non-party patriots in the liberated areas issued "Our Opinions on the Current Situation," stating that "when the people's liberation war is going on, we will, under the leadership of the CPC, do all what we can to bring about the quick success of the Chinese people's democratic revolution and the early birth of an independent, free, peaceful and happy New China."[30] This indicated that the democratic parties had formed new political ties with the CPC. Before this, the relations between the CPC and the democratic parties were only political partnerships and their party-to-party relations were equal. Later, because the democratic parties accepted the leadership of the CPC, the relations between the CPC and the democratic parties were no longer equal partnerships, but the relations between the leader and the led politically. Therefore, after this statement was issued, Mao Zedong said: "All democratic parties, people's organizations and democrats without party affiliation are on our side."[31] Soon afterwards, the preparatory meeting for the New Political Consultative Conference was held from June 15 through 19, 1949. It was attended by 134 participants, representing the CPC, democratic parties, people's organizations, democrats of all circles, national minorities and overseas Chinese. On September 21, the First Chinese People's Political Consultative Conference was held and adopted the Common Program. The Common Program did not deal with the question of party politics and inter-party relations, but it was definitely stipulated in the preamble that the democratic parties and the CPC, just like the other political organizations and groups, were component parts of the people's democratic united front. The stipulations regarding the united front brought about a substantive change in the status of the democratic parties in the political system of the People's Republic of China. The united front nature of the democratic parties did not change after the founding of the People's Republic of China until the beginning of the reform and opening-up drive.

The united front nature of the democratic parties has changed the state of affairs of the democratic parties fundamentally. First of all, the nature of the democratic parties has changed. The democratic parties no longer take it as the highest goal of their existence and activities to compete and win political power, no longer use their unique political views and ideas to distinguish themselves from other social and political forces. Rather, they appeared more like parties of a political alliance. Second, their relations with the CPC have changed fundamentally. They are no longer political partners, but have formed a kind of relationship between the leader and the led, and the work of the democratic parties is often carried out under the leadership of the united front work department of the CPC. Third, because the united front carries out its work under the leadership of the CPC, the different component parts of the united front, that is, the various democratic parties, assume specific tasks respectively. There are also specific stipulations on the areas and goals for the activities carried out by the democratic parties. This determines their sizes and relations with the society, and the degree of their political influence and role as well.

(3) The Democratic Parties — Parties Participating in State Affairs under the Leadership of the CPC after 1990

After the reform and opening-up drive was launched, with the intensification of the restructuring of the economy and the changes in the social life, demands for political restructuring have emerged. As to the party system, in view of the lessons drawn from the ultra-"Left" politics rampant during the "cultural revolution" and the heightening of people's sense on the question of supervision over the power, a loud outcry was once heard on improving the leadership of the CPC. On the question of how to transform the leadership of the CPC, some people made repeated comparisons between the one-party system and multi-party system. As China practices the socialist system and adheres to the Four Cardinal Principles, there are inevitably inherent limits for the restructuring of the political system, and it is even so for changes of the party system. Deng Xiaoping said definitely that the multi-party system and the system of check-and-balance based on the division of power are not suited to the conditions in China. The way out for the solution of the question of the leadership of the CPC does not lie in the departure from the leadership of the CPC, but in how to strengthen and improve the leadership. Therefore, the fundamental way out is to continue to strengthen the centralized and unified leadership of the CPC and, at the same time, to give due play to the enthusiasm of the members of society.

The search for the new political structure began with the Thirteenth National Congress of the CPC convened in October 1987. This congress proposed the system of multi-party cooperation and political consultation under the leadership of the CPC for the first time, and listed it as an important component part of the Chinese political system. Later, in early 1989, Deng Xiaoping instructed to establish a special group "to draw up a plan on the participation of the democratic parties in state affairs and on their performance of the duty to exercise supervision, and to complete the work in one year, and begin to implement it the next year." At the end of 1989, the Central Committee of the CPC invited the leaders of the various democratic parties and the All-China Federation of Industry and Commerce and personages without party affiliation to discuss the "Opinions on Upholding and Improving the Multi-Party Cooperation and Political Consultation System Under the Leadership of the Communist Party of China" drafted by the United Front Department of the Central Committee of the CPC. The document was circulated to all Party committees for implementation in the form of Document No. 14 of the Central Committee of the CPC (1989), and it was published in the *People's Daily* on February 8 in the following year. In this document, the Central Committee of the CPC affirmed for the first time the political status of the democratic parties in the multi-party cooperation: the democratic parties are neither ruling parties nor opposition parties, but parties participating in state affairs with unique Chinese characteristics. It stated that the CPC is the leading core of the nation and the democratic parties are close friendly parties that accept the leadership of the CPC and they cooperate fully with the CPC and are dedicated together to the socialist cause. The main duties of the parties participating in state affairs are to participate in the political consultation and information briefing on major state affairs presided over by the CPC, play a role in the people's congresses and committees of the Chinese People's Political Consultative Conference at various levels, hold posts in the government and judicial organs, and exercise supervision.

III. Principal Forms of Participation in State Affairs by Democratic Parties

The "Opinions of the Central Committee of the CPC on Upholding and Improving the Multi-Party Cooperation and Political Consultation System under the Leadership of the Communist Party of China," formulated on December 30, 1989, included in it seven stipulations on upholding and perfecting the multi-party cooperation and political consultation system, namely, strengthening cooperation and consultation between the Communist Party of the China and the democratic parties, giving better play to the role of members of the democratic parties and personages without party affiliation in the people's congresses, recommending members of the democratic parties and personages without party affiliation to leading posts in the governments and judicial organs at various levels, giving further play to the role of members of the democratic parties and personages without party affiliation in the political consultative conference, and supporting the democratic parties in strengthening their own organizations. In accordance with these stipulations, the specific forms of participation in state affairs by democratic parties developed in recent years include:

1. Participating in and Discussing State Affairs

Under the leadership of the CPC, members of the democratic parties participate in the political activities on the state level, participate in the formulation and implementation of the major principles, policies, laws and regulations of the state, participate in the consultation on major political questions of the state and candidates for the leading posts of state organs, and participate in running state affairs. The usual form of participation in and discussion of state affairs is the consultation between the CPC and the democratic parties.

The CPC and the democratic parties hold consultations on specific matters mainly in the following ways:

(1) Democratic consultation meetings. The chief leader of the Central Committee of the CPC invites the chief leaders of the democratic parties and personages without party affiliation to attend meetings, consults with them on major policies and principles to be put forward, and listens to their comments and remarks. Such meeting is usually held once a year.

(2) Top-level heart-to-heart talks. The chief leader of the Central Committee of the Communist Party holds heart-to-heart talks with the chief leaders of the democratic parties and personages without party affiliation from time to time to exchange opinions on questions of common interest.

(3) Bimonthly discussions. Such discussions are presided over by the Central Committee of the CPC and attended by representatives of the democratic parties and personages without party affiliation to exchange information, read important documents and listen to suggestions of the democratic parties and personages without party affiliation on certain policies, or have discussions on special topics. Except for important matters, such discussions are usually held every two months. The leading Party members' group in the National Committee of the Chinese People's Political Consultative Conference is entrusted sometimes to convene the discussions.

(4) Leaders of the democratic parties and personages without party affiliation may submit written proposals to the Central Committee of the CPC on guiding principles of fundamental importance and specific major issues at any time they wish, or make appointments with responsible persons of the Central Committee of the CPC for dialogues.

2. Democratic Supervision

By democratic supervision, it means supervision exercised by the democratic parties over the work of the CPC and the state organs under the leadership of the CPC in the framework of multi-party cooperation and political consultation.

At present, supervision by the democratic parties is regarded as a component part of the entire system of supervision in China. Now, the democratic parties take democratic supervision as a means to participate in and discuss state affairs. They can make remarks, suggestions and criticisms, in their capacity as parties participating in and discuss state affairs, on the implementation of the Constitution, and laws and regulations, the formulation and implementation of the important principles of the CPC and the government, and the performance of the duties and observance of discipline by members of the CPC, leading cadres of the Party, the state organs and their staff.

The main forms of supervision are as follows: (1) The democratic parties make remarks, suggestions and criticisms to the Central Committee of the CPC at meetings of the Chinese People's Political Consultative Conference. (2) They put forward proposals and make criticisms on major political, economic and social problems of the state on the basis of their investigations and studies. (3) Members of the democratic parties who are elected deputies to the people's congresses or committee members of the Chinese People's Political Consultative Conference exercise supervision over the running of state affairs through their proposals, motions and check-ups. (4) Members of the democratic parties play the supervisory role in the capacity of special supervisors, procurators, auditors, and educational inspectors employed by the government.

The principle for the democratic parties to exercise supervision over the running of state affairs is: Making remarks, suggestions and criticisms on the principles and policies, and various aspects of work of the CPC and the government on the basis of adhering to the Four Cardinal Principles and persisting in the reform and opening. They are encouraged to speak out all they know and voice what they wish to say without reserve.

3. The Democratic Parties Participating in and Discussing State Affairs at the People's Congresses and the Committees of the Chinese People's Political Consultative Conference

In China, the people's congresses are not composed of only representatives of the various parties. The deputies are elected on the principle of regional division. Yet, the representatives of the various democratic parties can hold a given number of seats in the people's congress at all levels. The usual practice is that the list of candidates for the deputies to the people's congresses at various levels is prepared though consultation between the CPC and the democratic parties and personages without party affiliation. This is to ensure that a given number of members of the democratic parties can become deputies to the people's congresses. In the leading body of the people's congress — the presidium, the principal leaders of the democratic parties are usually members. In the special commissions and standing committees of the people's congresses, representatives of the democratic parties usually hold an appropriate percentage. The leading Party members' group established in the standing committee of the people's congress often exchanges information and views with the people's deputies who hold leading posts in the democratic parties.

The political consultative conference is composed on the group principle. Therefore, the democratic parties naturally hold a proper percentage of the seats. The leaders of the democratic parties are usually members of the presidium of the sessions.

4. Members of the Democratic Parties Are Recommended for Leading Posts in the Governments and Judicial Organs at All Levels

All the democratic parties have a certain number of members recommended by the CPC for leading posts in the governments and judicial organs. For example, from the beginning of the reform and opening-up drive to September 1997, about 8,300 members of the democratic parties and personages without party affiliation held leading posts at and above the county level in the local governments and judicial organs throughout China. Among them, 23 had served as vice or assistant governors or mayors at the provincial level, 13 members as vice mayors or assistant mayors of the cities at the deputy provincial level, 171 members as deputy or assistant leaders at the prefecture level, 181 members as departmental chiefs or deputy departmental chiefs in the provincial governments, and 6,274 as section chiefs or deputy section chiefs in the local government departments. All these people were members of the democratic parties, except for a few people without party affiliation.

As the democratic parties are not ruling parties after all, their members have relatively fewer opportunities to take leading posts in the governments. In view of this situation, the CPC usually relaxes the demands and age limits for the members of the democratic parties who are chosen to take leading posts in the government.

Notes:

[1] *Selected Works of Liu Shaoqi*, Vol. I. Beijing: People's Publishing House, 1981, p. 358.

[2] *Liu Shaoqi on Party Building*. Beijing: Central Document and Literature Press, 1999, p. 326.

[3] *Selected Readings from the Works of Mao Zedong*, Vol. II. Beijing: People's Publishing House, 1986, p. 819.

[4] *Selected Works of Liu Shaoqi*, Vol. I. Beijing: People's Publishing House, 1981, p. 359.

[5] *Liu Shaoqi on Party Building*. Beijing: Central Document and Literature Press, 1999, p. 340.

[6] "Speech Delivered at an Enlarged Working Conference of the Party Central Committee," *Selected Works of Deng Xiaoping, Vol. I (1938-1965)*. Beijing: Foreign Languages Press, 1995, second edition, p. 299.

[7] *Selected Works of Mao Tsetung, Vol. V* . Beijing: Foreign Languages Press, 1977, p. 467.

[8] *Selected Works of Deng Xiaoping (1975-1982)*. Beijing: People's Publishing House, 1983, p. 363.

[9] "Speech at the Rally to Celebrate the 40th Anniversary of the Founding of the People's Republic of China, September 29, 1989," *Xinhua Monthly*, Issue No. 10, 1989, pp. 5-12.

[10] *Selected Works of Mao Tsetung, Volume I* (English edition). Beijing: Foreign Languages Press, third printing, 1975, p. 192.

[11] *Selected Works of Deng Xiaoping (1975-1982)*. Beijing: People's Publishing House, 1983, p. 300.

[12] In January 1935, the Political Bureau of the CPC Central Committee convened an enlarged meeting in Zunyi, Guizhou Province. At the meeting, a new Central Committee leadership headed by Mao Zedong was established in place of the former "Left" opportunist leadership.

[13] *Selected Works of Deng Xiaoping, Volume III (1982-1992)*. Beijing: Foreign Languages Press, 1994, p. 301.

[14] Ibid.

[15] *Documents of the 16th National Congress of the Communist Party of China*. Beijing: Foreign Languages Press, 2002, p. 102.

[16] *Documents of the 16th National Congress of the Communist Party of China*. Beijing: Foreign Languages Press, 2002, p. 110-111.

[17] *Documents of the 16th National Congress of the Communist Party of China*. Beijing: Foreign Languages Press, 2002, p. 111.

[18] Ibid.

[19] *Documents of the 16th National Congress of the Communist Party of China*. Beijing: Foreign Languages Press, 2002, p. 112.

[20] *Documents of the 16th National Congress of the Communist Party of China*. Beijing: Foreign Languages Press, 2002, p. 102.

[21] *Documents of the 16th National Congress of the Communist Party of China*. Beijing: Foreign Languages Press, 2002, p. 101.

[22] "Preamble" of *Constitution of the People's Republic of China*. Beijing: Foreign Languages Press, Fourth Edition (with Chinese text), 1999.

[23] *Documents of the 16th National Congress of the Communist Party of China*. Beijing: Foreign Languages Press, 2002, p. 76.

[24] *Documents of the 16th National Congress of the Communist Party of China*. Beijing: Foreign Languages Press, 2002, p. 86.

[25] Ibid.

[26] Ibid.

[27] "Preamble" of *Constitution of the People's Republic of China*. Beijing: Foreign Languages Press, Fourth Edition (with Chinese text), 1999.

[28] Jiang Zemin: "Hold High the Great Banner of Deng Xiaoping Theory and Push the Cause of Building Socialism with Chinese Characteristics into the 21st Century – Report to the 15th National Congress of the Communist Party of China," included in *Collection of Important Documents of CPC National Party Congresses and Central Committee Plenary Sessions Since the Third Plenary Session of the 11th Party Central Committee*. Beijing: Central Document and Literature Press, 1997, p. 436.

[29] *Documents of the 16th National Congress of the Communist Party of China*. Beijing: Foreign Languages Press, 2002, p. 80.

[30] *Collection of Documents of the Central Committee of the Communist Party of China on the United Front during the War of Liberation*. Beijing: Archives Press, 1988, p. 319.

[31] *Selected Works of Mao Tsetung*, Vol. IV. Beijing: Foreign Languages Press, 1975, p. 371.

Chapter Three

THE PEOPLE'S CONGRESS

In China, the National People's Congress and local people's congresses represent a category of state organs. As prescribed by the Constitution of the People's Republic of China, they are organs of state power that exercise the supreme power, national or local, in accordance with this Constitution and law.

From the angle of comparative political science, China's people's congresses are distinctively different from the parliamentary systems in other countries. They are based on leadership by the CPC and on the principle of democratic centralism, thus showing many important differences from the parliamentary system in the Western democracies, especially those countries that practice the system of separation of legislative, executive and judicial powers. These differences are the key to studying and understanding Chinese politics, as well as the key to understanding China's system of people's congresses.

Section 1 The Nature and Status of the People's Congresses

I. The System of the People's Congresses Is China's Fundamental Political System

According to the Constitution of the PRC and official statements, the system of people's congresses is considered China's fundamental political system:

First, the system of the people's congresses directly reflects the nature of the Chinese state. The Constitution of the PRC stipulates that "The People's Republic of China is a socialist state under the people's democratic dictatorship led by the working class and based on the alliance of workers and peasants."[1] This means that the true masters and rulers of the People's Republic of China are the working class and other constituents of the masses of the people, and that all power in China belongs to the people, including the power to apply and exercise state power. For the ordinary "people" to exercise state power, it is imperative to establish proper channels and forms of political power. The people's congresses are the ideal organizational form for the ordinary people to exercise state power. In this sense, the people's congresses have a certain degree of "fundamentality" and are a "fundamental" political system.

Second, the system of people's congresses enjoys the status of the source of power of "a fundamental nature" in the entire setup of the political systems of the state, with the powers and legality of the other state systems and organs all deriving from the system of people's congresses. In terms of the Constitution and law, the people's congresses, in comparison with the other systems and organs, have the nature of the ultimate source and foundation.

Third, the people's congresses are organs of relatively low cost and fairly high accessibility through which the "people" exercise their power to rule and manage the state. In other words, as a state belonging to the people, the People's Republic of China is bound to have state organs and political facilities that are relatively easy for the people to access and exercise influence over. In comparison, among the existing state political systems, only the people's congresses are the closest to the people, the most accessible to the people and the easiest means for them to exercise their influence, and have the greatest ability to directly represent and reflect the will, aspirations and demands of the people. In this sense, the desire of the people to become the masters of their own country, and their mastery and use of the state's power can be truly realized only through the people's congresses. From this it can be seen that in a country where the people are its own masters, a political institution of such a political status naturally possesses a kind of "fundamentality."

Fourth, according to Marxism-Leninism, Mao Zedong Thought and Deng Xiaoping Theory, the state machine in a socialist state and its officials are servants of the people, and must enact and implement policies in accordance with the will and aspirations of the people. Then, where should the state machine and officials go in order to gather the will and aspirations of the people and how should they judge them? This is a difficult task. Therefore, to establish a political organ fully capable of representing and reflecting the will and aspirations of the people is a fundamental measure for realizing the political objectives of a socialist state. The availability of an organ of such a nature provides a fundamental guarantee for the *raison d'etre* of the politics of a socialist state. The people's congress system is such a political organ. Hence, the people's congresses have an indispensable role in ensuring and realizing the fundamental objectives and nature of the politics of a socialist state.

Fifth, the rich content of the system of the people's congresses determines that it has a kind of "fundamentality." As Li Peng said, "The very fact that our country's fundamental political system bears the name 'the people's congresses' obviously underlines the exceptionally important status and role of the people's congresses in this system. The system of the people's congresses is a system of state political power with the people's congresses as its cornerstone, defining the relationship between the people's congresses and the people who institute them; between the people's congresses on the one hand and the governments and people's courts and people's procuratorates and other state organs which the people's congresses create on the other; and between the CPC on the one hand and the people's congresses and other state organs on the other. The electoral system is the basis of this system. The system of democratic centralism is its organizational principle. These three relationships, one basis and one principle give a succinct, overall picture of the political life of our country, and embody the nature of our country in a concentrated form. In a word, the system of the people's congresses is an effective organizational form of political power for realizing leadership by the CPC and the exercise of their rights by the people as the masters of their own country."[2]

Sixth, the "fundamentality" of the people's congresses also lies in the fact that they are fundamentally different from the parliamentary democracies of the West. The People's Republic of China is the foremost country in the world that practices a political system fundamentally different from the Western ones. The fundamental difference between China's political system and the system in the West lies in the fact that China practices a system of multi-party cooperation and political consultation led by the CPC, while the Western countries practice a system of multi-party competition. The system of multi-party cooperation under one-party leadership and the system of multi-party competition with these parties enjoying equal status require a fundamentally different institutional dimension for the existence and competition of the political parties.

The institutional dimension for the activities of the political parties commensurate with the system of multi-party cooperation under the leadership of the CPC is the people's congress system, while the institutional dimension commensurate with the multi-party competition of the West is parliamentary democracy. At the same time, the different systems of political parties extend into and determine the modes of relationships among different state organs: The mode of relationship among the state organs commensurate with the system of multi-party cooperation under one-party leadership is democratic centralism, while the mode of relationship commensurate with parliamentary democracy is the separation of powers with checks and balances. Since it is of fundamental, political importance to practice in China a socialist political system with Chinese characteristics at the present stage, the dimension for the activities of the political parties as a natural outcome of the political system with Chinese characteristics — the people's congresses — likewise has status and significance of a fundamental nature. Top Chinese leaders have repeatedly emphasized this point at different times. At a meeting of the Political Bureau of the Central Committee of the CPC held in September 1948, prior to the founding of the People's Republic of China, Mao Zedong said, "The class nature of our political power is this: The people's dictatorship led by the proletariat and based on the alliance of workers and peasants, with the participation not only of workers and peasants, but also of bourgeois democrats." He added, "We adopt democratic centralism, not the bourgeois parliamentary system. The parliamentary system, which Yuan Shikai and Cao Kun both adopted, has been discredited. Democratic centralism is very suitable for China. We have proposed the convocation of the People's Congress....There is no need to introduce a bourgeois parliament, separation of powers, etc."[3] He thus explicitly expounded the nature and structure of the People's Republic of China, and laid down China's state system and form of government. Later, Deng Xiaoping emphasized, "In the reform of the political structure, one thing is certain: We must adhere to the system of the people's congresses instead of practicing the separation of the judicial, executive and legislative powers on the American pattern."[4] He also said, "As long as it keeps to the right policies and direction, such a legislative body helps greatly to make the country prosper and to avoid much wrangling."[5] Jiang Zemin pointed out, "In building socialist democratic politics, the most important thing is to persist in and perfect the system of the people's congresses."[6] Li Peng held the view that "the system of the people's congresses is one of our great political advantages and special features. It is essentially different from the bourgeois system of multi-party competition and of separation of powers and checks and balances.... To persist in and perfect the system of the people's congresses will become a powerful weapon for countering the preaching of Western countries for parliamentary democracy in an attempt to Westernize and divide China, ensure the stability of the country, national unity, economic development and social progress, and enable the country to stand various risks and tests. The practice over the past 45 years has proved that the system of the people's congresses is a system of people's democracy under the leadership of the CPC which conforms to China's conditions and the will of the people."[7]

II. The People's Congresses Must Accept Leadership by the CPC

The leadership role of the CPC over the people's congresses is determined by its status as the ruling party. Its role as China's sole ruling party is an outcome of Chinese history and a reflection of the actual political pattern of the country. As far as the origin of the political system of the People's Republic of China is concerned, the CPC was the founder of the People's Republic of China and maker of China's political system; and over a long period of political practice, the Chinese society has never produced a political force strong enough to compete with the CPC.

One of the points underlying the basic spirit of the current Constitution of the People's Republic of China is to emphasize adherence to the leadership by the CPC over the state. In terms of political theory and principles, this leadership is all-inclusive: Within the territory of the People's Republic of China, there exists no social organization that is in a position to ignore or break away from the CPC's leadership or its political influence, no matter what the nature of this social organization is or what its status. The people's congresses are the most important institution in China's fundamental political system. Nevertheless, they are, in essence, not different from any other social organization in accepting and following the CPC's leadership.

The leadership of the CPC over the people's congresses is mainly reflected on two levels: On the level of the Constitution, while the CPC exists and operates within the framework of the Constitution, it is in fact the principal maker and guardian of the Constitution, for the Constitution was formulated and amended under the CPC's leadership. Since the formulating and amending of the Constitution and the legislative power are the principal and most substantial powers of the people's congresses, which in fact are exercised under the leadership of the CPC, it can be said that the exercise of the principal powers of the people's congresses is carried out under the direct leadership and its influence of the CPC. In addition, none of the actual operations of the people's congresses can be carried out without the leadership or help of the CPC. A formal list of candidates for people's deputies is usually proposed by the organizational department of a Communist Party committee in consultation with other social organizations, and the actual elections of people's deputies are held under the leadership of the relevant department of a CPC committee. Since the deputies are grouped into regional delegations, and within each delegation a provisional CPC organization is established, deputies to the people's congresses, therefore, are usually placed within the limits of power of the local CPC committees. When the people's congresses are in session, the congress presidiums charged with the important functions of directing and controlling the sessions are mainly composed of principal leaders of the CPC at different levels. When the people's congresses are not in session, the CPC has leading Party groups within the standing committees of the people's congresses to carry out the CPC leadership on a daily basis over the standing committees, and each people's congress is headed concurrently by one of the principal leaders of the CPC committee at the corresponding level. With regard to the work procedures, important matters falling within the functions and powers of the people's congresses and their standing committees, such as plans for national economic and social development, draft budgets and final accounts, proposals on appointments and removals, and proposals for addressing questions and bills on recalls, shall, in view of their weight, usually receive consent from the CPC committee at the corresponding level or are proposed by such committees themselves before being placed on the agenda of the people's congress or its standing committee.

III. The NPC Is the Highest Organ of State Power Practicing Democratic Centralism

The People's Republic of China practices democratic centralism. The

NPC (NPC) is the highest organ of state power practicing democratic centralism. The nature of democratic centralism as practiced by the NPC is manifested in the following:

With regard to the relationship between the NPC and the other state organs, the NPC is the organ that has instituted the other state organs and supervises them and, constitutionally, the other state organs are all responsible to the NPC, and the exercise of their powers is subject to supervision and control by the NPC. This relationship is realized in two ways. First, since the NPC is the highest organ of state power as pre- scribed in the current Constitution, that is, under the prerequisite of the leadership of the CPC, it is the organ that has instituted and supervises the head of state, the state administration organs, the judicial organs and, in legal terms, the military organs, and therefore it has the power to in- stitute, supervise and remove from office the leaders of these organs. Hence, the relationship is not one of checks and balances, but of the former transcending and supervising the latter. Meanwhile, since these state organs are derived directly from and are responsible to the NPC, and correspondingly are subject only to the supervision by the people's congress, there does not exist a relationship of checks and balances among them. Second, the NPC is a people's representative body, which includes officials and functionaries from different state organs, who, apart from being people's representatives in the general sense, also ex- press and represent the interests and demands of the organs they work in. Therefore, the NPC is an institution where the views and demands of different state organs are pooled and find representation, and where the special interests and demands of different organs are integrated into a unified will, synthesizing the wills of the different state organs in a con- centrated way. Seen from the angle of the great capacity of the NPC to address the interests and demands of all the state organs, these organs are some of the sources of the will of the NPC, and at the same time bases for the NPC to practice democratic centralism.

With regard to the relationship of the NPC to the "people," the latter are the source and basis of democracy, while the NPC is the institution guaranteeing centralism. Most political systems recognize the "people" as the source and basis of democracy, but to the question of who consti- tute the "people," different political systems provide different answers, thus resulting in different inner relationships within the bodies of people's representatives and different modes of relationships among the state organs. In China, since there exist no clashes of fundamental interests among different sections of the "people," the differences in the interests and demands of the different sections of the "people" that the individual deputies to the NPC represent can be harmonized and unified. That is to say, any decision made by the NPC can contain and reflect the demands of the whole of the "people" rather than only one section of the "people." Since the "people" means the whole "people" and not simply one part or the simple addition of all parts, neither the "people" whom any particular deputy represents and their interests, nor the "people" whom all the particular deputies represent and the sum total of their interests are the "people" and the interests of the "people" as such. In other words, although the "people" are the basis of democracy under the people's congress system, they and their requirements and demands need to be identified and expressed through centralism. It is precisely in this sense that a deputy can fully exercise his or her democratic rights. However, whether he or she will be able to realize his or her specific objectives depends principally on the process of "centralism," that is, on the judgment that the people's congress, as an institution for "centralism," makes on whether the demands of that section of the "people" whom that particular deputy represents conform to the interests of the whole of the "people." Since "centralism" is a highly political and skillful activity, not merely a matter of the number of votes, although the "people" are the basis of the people's congress and the source of its powers, the determination of such questions as to who constitute the "people" and what the genuine interests of the "people" are cannot depend merely on the number of deputies. They must be settled on a higher level and through more complex procedures. The current Constitution and laws have relatively explicit and specific stipulations concerning the rights of the deputies, but the specific, operational stipulations on how the people's congresses shall carry out "centralism" in order to identify and express the interests of the "people" are not as yet adequate while at the same time being highly political. This results in the role of the deputies being manifested more in the "democratic" aspect, while their role is relatively weak in exercising their legislative power and administering their other functions prescribed by the Constitution and law. To a great extent, the main functions of the people's congresses are manifested in providing the deputies, who share identical fundamental interests, with a mechanism to express, pool and integrate the demands of different sections of the "people" and ultimately find and express the interests and demands of the whole of the "people." In this way, the various sections of the "people," through the procedure of "democratic centralism," are integrated into the "people" in a general sense. As opposed to the whole of the people, the demands of any part of the "people" need to be weighed within the framework of "democratic centralism" of the people's congresses in order to determine their share and degree of importance in the system of the fundamental interests and demands of the whole of the people. In this way, the people's congresses, as institutions for "centralism," can give play to and realize the "people's" democracy, and at the same time prevent, in the manner of "centralism," ultra-democratic tendencies from interfering and adversely affecting the interests of the "people," thereby more efficiently exercising the legislative power and the other powers as prescribed by the Constitution and laws.

Within a people's congress, democratic centralism is manifested in the relationship of the deputies to the congress as well as the deputies to all organizations and institutions within the congress, and in the relationship among the various organizations and institutions. The deputies are the basic components and the foundation of the congress, enjoying the most basic and broadest functions and powers. In addition, the people's congress is the main body that creates the other organizations and institutions within the congress. With regard to the relationship between the deputies and the congress, on the surface, the congress appears to be constituted by the individual deputies. But, in fact, the group as a result of a simple addition of the individual deputies is not the congress as such; a group composed of deputies becomes the congress as such only when it contains the element of "democratic centralism." Although the congress is an institution where deputies express their personal views and positions, their views and positions must go through the process of "democratic centralism" before they can become part of the position and will of the congress. Therefore, the relationship between the deputies and the congress is not one of numbers only, but of "democracy" and "centralism" too: The function of the deputies embodies democracy while that of the congress embodies centralism.

Within the people's congress, there are mainly two types of organizations and institutions. One covers the organizations and leading bodies when the congress is in session, including groups of deputies, delegations and the congress presidium; the other refers to the permanent institutions that exercise the functions of the congress on its behalf when it is not in session. On the one hand, these organizations and institutions are charged with the specific functions of organizing the deputies, and on the other, they, being established among the deputies and forming tiers, are conducive to the operations of "democratic centralism." To illustrate the point, "democratic centralism" during a session of the congress roughly goes through two tiers of operation. The first tier is the process of "democratic centralism" at the level of groups of deputies and delegations. When the congress is in session a deputy exercises his or her functions and powers usually at the meetings of his or her group or delegation. The groups and delegations are formed on a geographical basis (the People's Liberation Army delegation being an exception), and within these, *ad hoc* leading bodies and chains of leadership are established. Owing to the fact that currently officials from the local governments make up a high proportion of the deputies, the chain of leadership within the groups and delegations is in fact a replica of the original local chain of leadership. In this way, the various groups and delegations are able to exercise effective leadership over the deputies at a relatively small cost, in order to meet the objective of "centralism." The second tier involves the process of "democratic centralism" performed by the congress presidium vs. the various delegations. Charged with the function of conducting the congress, the presidium is composed of the heads of the various delegations, the principal leaders of the CPC organizations and the various state organs at the corresponding level of the congress, as well as some other deputies. After the various delegations complete their process of "democratic centralism," the presidium will have to conduct "democratic centralism" among the various delegations at the level of the congress, in order to form the unified will of the congress. In time sequence, the "democratic centralism" processes at the two levels are usually mixed and intercrossed. When the congress is not in session, this process is realized through the institution of its standing committee. The standing committee of a people's congress (at the county level and above) is a permanent body composed of not many people, which performs the functions and powers of the congress on its behalf to a large extent. Because a session of the congress is very short, the broad range of functions and powers granted to the congress by the Constitution and law cannot be performed in a comprehensive and timely manner by the congress. So, a considerable part of its functions and powers must be left to be performed by its standing committee, hence the transfer of functions and powers from the congress to its standing committee. Moreover, because the members of the standing committee have been elected mutually from among the deputies at the same level, the transfer, to a certain extent and in a certain sense, is of some portions of functions and powers from those deputies who do not sit on the standing committee to those deputies who sit on the committee. Through these two forms of transfer, the degree of "democratic centralism" in the people's congress is enhanced.

Section 2 Deputies to the NPC

I. Qualifications of the Deputies and Their Composition

1. Qualifications of the Deputies

The Constitution of the People's Republic of China, the Electoral Law of the National People's Congress and the Local People's Congresses of the People's Republic of China, the Law of the People's Republic of China on the Deputies to the National People's Congress and the Local People's Congresses at Various Levels and the Methods of the People's Liberation Army on Electing Deputies to the National People's Congress and the Local People's Congresses at Different Levels provide the necessary legal conditions for the deputies to the NPC: (1) NPC deputies must hold Chinese citizenship, but there are no stipulations on the acquisition of the citizenship and minimum number of years. (2) They must have reached the age of 18. (3) They must be entitled to political rights as prescribed by law. The Chinese law stipulates that some anti-social persons and those who oppose the current social system may be removed of the political rights that they are otherwise entitled to, as one of the forms of legal punishment. Therefore, all those who have been removed of their political rights are no longer qualified to serve as deputies to the NPC. (4) They must be mentally sound, so that they have the capability of judgment and action. The Electoral Law has a special provision that mentally ill persons are not to be listed on the roll of voters, and it follows that such persons are disqualified as candidates for deputies to the NPC. (5) Those who have been punished by law, but not yet removed of their political rights still enjoy the right to vote and stand for election, and thus are eligible for candidacy as NPC deputies. Under the current law, there are explicit provisions that those removed of their political rights do not have the right to vote or stand for election. Therefore, in a legal sense, those persons who have not been removed of their political rights although they have been punished by law still have the right to vote and stand for election. However, the history of the election of NPC deputies shows not a single case of a convict who still enjoys political rights ever having been elected as an NPC deputy. On the contrary, an NPC deputy convicted of a crime during his or her term of office is more often than not recalled, no matter whether he or she has been removed of political rights or not.

Viewed from the legal stipulations, Chinese law is fairly generous about the qualifications of NPC deputies, having no legal restrictions as to property, sex, occupation or educational status; it can even be said that basically there are no restrictions. On the one hand, this shows that Chinese law embodies the nature of the law of a modern state. But, on the other hand, at the present stage, invariably and completely ignoring the qualifications of the NPC deputies is not necessarily beneficial to raising the quality of the deputies and perfecting the system of the people's congresses. The current system of electing deputies has shown the unintended result of making the voters (electoral units) overlook the need for an all-round appraisal of the abilities of the candidates to discharge their functions as deputies, so some incompetent persons have unjustifiably filled valuable seats at the NPC. Meanwhile, the NPC will play a specific role in the future changes and development of Chinese politics, and, correspondingly, the political status of NPC deputies will become more important and of substantial significance. Therefore, to appropriately stipulate the qualifications of NPC deputies, for instance, the minimum qualifications showing their educational level and capability of participation in the exercise of state power, minimum length of residence and work of a candidate in a specific place under regional representation, exclusion of persons in certain professions or fields from serving as deputies or restrictions imposed on such persons, and approval ratings from the constituencies (electoral units) for those deputies seeking re-election will considerably promote the improvement of the qualities of the deputies and the substantive exercise of their functions.

On the other hand, although the current Constitution and law have fairly generous stipulations on the qualifications of the NPC deputies, the actual process of electing them is subject to considerably strict control. Therefore, the generosity of the legal stipulations on the qualifications of the deputies and the control to which the process of electing the deputies is subject show that there is room for improvement in the extent of the authority and institutionalization of the people's congresses in China's political system.

2. The Composition of the Deputies

The NPC is China's highest organ of state power, and the deputies who make up the NPC are its basic units. Therefore, it is by no means pointless to inquire as to the composition of the deputies. From the perspective of comparative political science, the representative institutions of countries in general are composed of members who serve on a full-time basis, with the deputies (parliamentarians) being career politicians, showing no direct connection between their original status and their functions as deputies. At the same time, since the deputies are closely connected with political parties and organizations representing particular social strata, there exists a marked difference in political positions between the deputies. In China, owing to the fact that the deputies serve on a part-time basis, their original status will affect to a certain extent the exercise of their functions. They take part in the elections and discharge their functions basically in their personal capacities, showing no direct connection with political parties or organizations, so their representativeness has to be expressed through other channels. There is no close connection between the elections and personal electoral inputs by the candidates, while elections are carried out in such a way that the organizations charged with holding elections of NPC deputies will allocate numbers of candidates for deputies, according to certain rules, and to various social strata and groups, classified by different special status features. Thus, the statuses of the deputies in China will affect the exercise of the functions of the NPC to a certain extent.

The composition of the deputies refers to their occupations, party affiliations, ethnic origins, sex, etc. As shown by data on the successive NPCs, the composition of the NPC deputies has remained basically stable.

Table 1 Proportion of NPC Deputies of Different Statuses in the Total Number of Deputies (%)

	1st NPC	2nd NPC	3rd NPC	4th NPC	5th NPC	6th NPC	7th NPC	8th NPC	9th NPC
Workers & Peasants	5.1	11.1	12.6	51.61	47.3	16.6	23	20.6	18.89
Intellectuals				12	15	23.5	23.4	21.8	21.07
Cadres				11.2	13.4	21.4	24.7	28.3	33.16
Armed Forces	4.9	4.9	3.9	16.8	14.4	8.97	9	9	8.90
Returned Overseas Chinese	2.5	2.5	2.5	1	1	1.3	1.6	1.2	2.45*
Total	12.5	18.5	19	92.6	91.1	71.77	81.7	80.9	84.47

*Including the deputies from Hong Kong, who account for 1.21 percent.

Table 2 Party Affiliations of NPC Deputies (%)

	1st NPC	2nd NPC	3rd NPC	4th NPC	5th NPC	6th NPC	7th NPC	8th NPC	9th NPC
CPC	55.5	57.8	54.8	76.3	72.8	62.5	66.8	68.4	71.48
Democratic Parties & Personages Without Party Affiliation	25.5	42.2	45.1	8.3	14.2	18.2	18.2	19.1	15.44
Non-Party Masses				15.4	13	19.3	15	12.5	
Total	81.0	100	99.9	100	100	100	100	100	86.92

Table 3 Proportion of Women and Ethnic Minority Deputies in the Total Number of Deputies (%)

	1st NPC	2nd NPC	3rd NPC	4th NPC	5th NPC	6th NPC	7th NPC	8th NPC	9th NPC
Women	12	12.2	17.8	22.6	21.2	21.2	21.3	21	21.81
Ethnic Minorities	14.4	14.7	12.3	9.4	10.9	13.6	15	14.8	14.36

The above data gives a rough picture of the special features with regard to the status of the NPC deputies and the composition of the NPC. However, when releasing this data, the relevant office did not provide detailed explanations about the criteria for the collection and classification of the data, thereby limiting the value for analysis.

The data can still tell us something, though. First, in Table 1, the sum total of the figures representing the deputies of different occupations is not equal to the overall total. This means that some additional deputies must have been allocated to other occupations, or that there are gross errors, so that the figures representing the deputies of some particular occupations are not accurate. Second, because most deputies have more than one capacity at the same time, it is entirely up to the will of the proper offices to fit a particular deputy into a certain category. To illustrate the point, most deputies are officials, but they may at the same time have other capacities, for instance, they may hold leading posts in universities or work in factories, or may be from families of minority ethnic groups, or may be women. Such deputies may be classified into different professional groups at different times. Therefore, it is a reasonable assumption that in the circumstances where the criteria for classifying the professions of the deputies are not clear, the number of officials among the deputies will by far exceed the officially released figures. Third, relative to other professional groups, the workers' and peasants' deputies (even if these are not representatives of the workers and peasants in a genuine sense), women and non-Communist people are seriously underrepresented, the proportion of deputies representing them being grossly lower than their proportions of the population, while the percentages of the deputies representing cadres, intellectuals, democratic parties and returned overseas Chinese are relatively high. Fourth, the percentage of the deputies from the armed forces is high relative to the proportion of the armed forces to the population as a whole. Fifth, owing to the fact that the NPC is a unicameral legislature at present, the deputies have the dual capacity of representing localities and voters at the same time. This has created a certain dilemma in the distribution of seats: It is necessary to take into consideration the rights of the ethnic minorities to national representation and at the same time the universality of the voters, resulting in an inherent tension between the seats occupied by deputies from the minority ethnic groups (which vary in size, but some are tiny) and the need for representation of the whole population.

II. Election of Deputies

Article 3 of the Electoral Law of the National People's Congress and the Local People's Congresses of the People's Republic of China stipulates that all citizens of the People's Republic of China who have reached the age of 18 have the right to vote and stand for election, regardless of ethnic status, race, sex, occupation, family background, religious belief, education, property status or length of residence, except for persons removed of political rights according to law.

In China, deputies to the people's congresses below the county level are elected directly by their constituencies. Deputies to the people's congresses above the county level are elected by the people's congresses at the next-lower level. The deputies to the NPC are elected by the people's congresses of the provinces, autonomous regions and the municipalities directly under the central government, and by the armed forces.

The number of NPC deputies shall not exceed 3,000.[8] The Standing Committee of the current NPC decides the allocation of the seats. Specifically, prior to the convocation of the next NPC, the Standing Committee of the current NPC puts forward a draft "Resolution on the Issues Concerning the Number and Election of NPC Deputies," covering the total number, specific numbers for each electoral unit and timetable of elections, to be examined and adopted at the last session of the current NPC. Apart from this resolution, the NPC Standing Committee may also make specific decisions on the allocation of seats and election matters concerning such special areas as the armed forces, minority ethnic groups, returned overseas Chinese, Hong Kong and Macao, and Taiwan. The resolution of the NPC on the number of deputies and their allocation is valid only for one time. In a legal sense, the NPC, during its term, has no right to change the number and allocation plans beyond the next NPC.

The number of NPC deputies is distributed roughly as follows: (1) The number of deputies to be elected by a province, autonomous region or municipality directly under the central government shall be allocated by the NPC Standing Committee in accordance with the principle that the number of people represented by each rural deputy should be four times the number of people represented by each urban deputy, that is, in rural areas, one deputy for every 830,000 people, with the total coming to 1,091, while in urban areas, one deputy for every 210,000 people, with the total coming to 1,263.[9] (2) The numbers of NPC deputies whom the minority ethnic groups are eligible to elect are allocated in the light of the populations of the minority nationalities and their geographical distribution by the NPC Standing Committee to the people's congresses of the provinces, autonomous regions and municipalities directly under the central government, which shall elect them accordingly. When a minority ethnic group is exceptionally small, it must have one deputy to the NPC. The minority ethnic groups account for about 6.7 percent of the national total population, but their deputies account for no less than 12 percent of the total number of the NPC deputies. (3) The deputies from the armed forces are elected, in accordance with the Electoral Law and the Methods of the People's Liberation Army on Electing Deputies to the National People's Congress and the Local People's Congresses at Different Levels, by the congresses of military personnel of the various headquarters of the PLA, the military area commands, the services and arms, the Science and Technology Commission for National Defense, the Office for the National Defense Industry, the Academy of Military Science, the Military Academy, the Political Academy and the Logistics Academy, in line with the seats allocated by the PLA Electoral Committee. Since the Sixth NPC, the deputies from the PLA have accounted for about 9 percent of the total. (4) Since the Electoral Law was revised in 1979, the number of deputies from among returned overseas Chinese has remained at around 50. (5) Beginning with the Fifth NPC, the Hong Kong-Macao region has been allocated around 20 deputies. (6) Around 13 deputies represent Taiwan Province. They are elected through consultations among the representatives sent by the people of Taiwan origin in various provinces, autonomous regions and municipalities directly under the central government and the PLA, in accordance with the methods adopted by the Standing Committee of the NPC.

There is a relatively big difference in the number of NPC deputies of a locality or unit in relation to the total population of that locality or unit, and the number of people each deputy represents.

Table 4 Relationship between the Numbers of Deputies to the 6th, 7th and 8th NPCs and Populations Represented

Serial Number	By order of total population (Progressive decrease)		By order of total number of deputies (Progressive decrease)		By order of number of people each deputy represents (Progressive decrease)	
	Ranking	Population (in thousands)	Ranking	Number of deputies	Ranking	Population (in thousands)
1	Sichuan	101,880	Armed forces	267	Guangxi	610

2	Henan	77,130	Sichuan	192	Shandong	590
3	Shandong	76,950	Shandong	167	Yunnan	580
4	Guangdong	62,530	Henan	142	Hebei	550
5	Jiangsu	62,130	Liaoning	136	Henan	540
6	Hunan	56,230	Guangdong	131	Hunan	540
7	Hebei	55,480	Jiangsu	123	Anhui	540
8	Anhui	51,560	Heilongjiang	121	Sichuan	530
9	Hubei	49,310	Zhejiang	105	Gansu	520
10	Zhejiang	40,300	Hunan	104	Jiangsu	510
11	Guangxi	38,730	Hubei	102	Guangdong	480
12	Liaoning	36,860	Hebei	100	Hubei	480
13	Jiangxi	34,600	Anhui	95	Jiangxi	460
14	Yunnan	34,060	Jilin	82	Shaanxi	460
15	Heilongjiang	33,110	Jiangxi	76	Guizhou	460
16	Shaanxi	30,020	Shaanxi	65	Fujian	440
17	Guizhou	29,680	Guizhou	65	Shanxi	440
18	Fujian	27,130	Guangxi	64	Zhejiang	380
19	Shanxi	26,270	Fujian	62	Inner Mongolia	360
20	Jilin	22,980	Shanxi	60	Xinjiang	360
21	Gansu	20,410	Yunnan	59	Jilin	280
22	Inner Mongolia	20,070	Shanghai	59	Liaoning	270
23	Xinjiang	13,610	Inner Mongolia	56	Heilongjiang	270
24	Shanghai	12,170	Beijing	56	Ningxia	260
25	Beijing	9,600	Tianjin	43	Qinghai	250
26	Tianjin	8,080	Gansu	39	Shanghai	200
27	Ningxia	4,150	Xinjiang	38	Tianjin	190
28	Qinghai	4,070	HK-Macao	20	Beijing	170
29	Armed forces	3,200*	Ningxia	16	Tibet	120
30	Tibet	1,990	Qinghai	16	Armed forces	15
31	HK-Macao		Tibet	16	HK-Macao	
32	Taiwan		Taiwan	13	Taiwan	
33	Chongqing		Chongqing		Chongqing	
34	Hainan		Hainan		Hainan	
35	HK		HK		HK	

* During this period, the population of the armed forces changed drastically. The official released figure in 1992 was 3.2 million. See *Statistics Yearbook of Population of China, 2001*, p. 197, by China Statistics Publishing House, 2001.

Table 5 Relationship between the Number of Deputies to the 9th NPC and Populations Represented

Serial number	By order of total population (Progressive decrease)		By order of total number of deputies (Progressive decrease)		By order of number of people each deputy represents (Progressive decrease)	
	Ranking	Population (in thousands)	Ranking	Number of deputies	Ranking	Population (in thousands)
1	Henan	92,430	Armed forces	268	Henan	567
2	Shandong	87,850	Shandong	185	Sichuan	558
3	Sichuan	84,300	Guangdong	166	Anhui	547
4	Jiangsu	71,480	Henan	163	Guizhou	546
5	Guangdong	70,510	Sichuan	151	Hebei	544
6	Hebei	65,250	Jiangsu	151	Hunan	543
7	Hunan	64,650	Hubei	126	Gansu	542
8	Anhui	61,270	Hebei	120	Shaanxi	533
9	Hubei	58,730	Hunan	119	Jiangxi	525
10	Guangxi	46,330	Liaoning	116	Chongqing	524
11	Zhejiang	44,350	Anhui	112	Guangxi	515
12	Jiangxi	41,500	Heilongjiang	105	Fijian	513
13	Liaoning	41,380	Guangxi	90	Zhejiang	498
14	Yunnan	40,940	Zhejiang	89	Shandong	475
15	Heilongjiang	37,510	Yunnan	88	Jiangsu	473
16	Guizhou	36,060	Jiangxi	79	Hubei	466
17	Shaanxi	35,700	Jilin	72	Yunnan	465
18	Fujian	32,800	Shanxi	68	Shanxi	462
19	Shanxi	31,410	Shaanxi	67	Guangdong	425
20	Chongqing	30,420	Shanghai	67	Hainan	413
21	Jilin	26,280	Guizhou	66	Inner Mongolia	408
22	Gansu	24,940	Fujian	64	Jilin	365
23	Inner Mongolia	23,260	Beijing	59	Liaoning	357
24	Taiwan	21,740	Xinjiang	59	Heilongjiang	357
25	Xinjiang	17,180	Chongqing	58	Ningxia	294
26	Shanghai	14,570	Inner Mongolia	57	Xinjiang	291
27	Beijing	12,400	Gansu	46	Qinghai	261
28	Tianjin	9,530	Tianjin	45	Shanghai	217

29	Hainan	7,430	HK	36	Tianjin	212
30	HK	6,500	Tibet	20	Beijing	210
31	Ningxia	5,300	Qinghai	19	HK	186
32	Qinghai	4,960	Ningxia	18	Tibet	124
33	Armed forces	3,200	Hainan	18	Macao	37
34	Tibet	2,480	Taiwan	13	Armed forces	12
35	Macao	440	Macao	12	Taiwan	--

Table 6 Increase or Decrease in the Number of Deputies to the 9th NPC Compared with the 6th, 7th and 8th Congresses

Serial number	Ranking	Increase or decrease in number of deputies
1	Guangdong	35
2	Yunnan	29
3	Jiangsu	28
4	Guangxi	26
5	Hubei	24
6	Henan	21
7	Xinjiang	21
8	Hebei	20
9	Shandong	18
10	Anhui	17
11	Hunan	15
12	Shanxi	8
13	Shanghai	8
14	Gansu	7
15	Tibet	4
16	Jiangxi	3
17	Beijing	3
18	Qinghai	3
19	Shaanxi	2
20	Fujian	2
21	Tianjin	2
22	Ningxia	2
23	Guizhou	1
24	Inner Mongolia	1
25	Jilin	-10
26	Heilongjiang	-16

27	Zhejiang	-16
28	Liaoning	-20
29	Sichuan	-41
30	Armed forces	
31	Chongqing	
32	HK	
33	Hainan	
34	Taiwan	
35	Macao	

From the above tables it can be seen that, first, the allocation of the numbers of seats is directly related to the size of the population of the various localities (units), yet it is, at the same time, subject to influence from other important factors. The reason that the number of deputies from a particular area is not closely related to the size of its population is that the current Electoral Law confirms the long-standing system of separate administration for urban and rural areas. This system has retained and expanded the already existing demographic features of different areas, and the Electoral Law, by differentiating the urban and rural representation, has, in terms of representation, recognized and legalized this system to a considerable extent. Since the system of the people's congresses is the fundamental political system of China and it touches upon the basic nature of the state and the citizens' rights. Therefore, the issue of the relationship between the number of deputies and the population may, therefore, become a problem to be solved in the system of the people's congresses. Second, the number of deputies is closely related to the level of urbanization of an area. This relationship is manifested in two ways: (1) The average base figure of people represented by each deputy in a municipality directly under the central government is far smaller than that in other areas. (2) Among the deputies from other areas, the relative numbers of the deputies representing urban residents are by far bigger than those representing rural residents. Moreover, since there is a large proportion of Party and government officials among the NPC deputies at present, even in rural areas, most of those elected live and work in towns and cities. Therefore, the NPC bears a fairly heavy urban and industrial coloring. Since the NPC is a representative and legislative institution, its obvious demographic, industrial and professional features will affect its rationality and legitimacy to a certain extent. Third, The number of deputies from the areas inhabited by ethnic minorities is not only guaranteed but show a considerably large ratio of deputies to population. But, when it comes to a particular minority ethnic group, since the deputies of ethnic minorities only have the same rights and status as deputies in general, attempts to solve the rights and status of a particular minority ethnic group in the political life of the state by ensuring seats for that particular group can only be less than satisfactory. Fourth, There is a certain relationship between the allocation of numbers of deputies and the political importance of the localities and units in national politics, as well as the policy direction of the central government in a given period. The number of deputies from the armed forces, whether in terms of the ratio between the number of deputies and the population or the absolute number, has remained stable, indicating the strong influence of the armed forces on national politics. During the periods from the Sixth, Seventh to Eighth NPCs, Liaoning, Jilin and Heilongjiang provinces had an edge in the allocation of number of deputies, but during the Ninth NPC, the shares of Shandong and Guangdong grew remarkably. Apart from changes in population size, the increase or decrease in the number of deputies is obviously also related to other factors, for instance, how important a given locality in the politics of the central government, whether the development of a given locality conforms to the immediate policy objectives of the central government, or whether a given locality fits into an exemplary role that the central government hopes to promote. In other words, although the allocation of the NPC deputies is basically tied to the population, there exist also political considerations, which in turn have a certain impact on the direction of the legislation and exercise of the powers of the NPC. In fact, the extent of the importance of a given locality to the overall national politics can also be examined and proved through other channels, for instance, whether officials of that locality hold posts in the central government concurrently. A look at the increase or decrease in the number of deputies during the last few congresses reveals that those localities that are in a favorable position in the allocation of numbers of deputies often see their top leaders holding posts concurrently in the top echelons of the central authorities.

In addition, it needs to be explained that a portion of the total number of deputies (roughly 7 percent of the total, or around 230, during the Seventh and Eighth NPCs) is reserved by the NPC Standing Committee for direct allocation to the provinces, autonomous regions and municipalities directly under the central government in accordance with certain conditions, outside the general allocation of number of deputies. Fitting into this category are those persons whom the Central Committee of the CPC deems suitable for acting as NPC deputies and who do not live or work in that area, or even have no connections whatever with that area, but are influential and highly placed on the national political scene. Specifically, the CPC Central Committee first proposes a list of candidates for deputies, then the General Office of the NPC Standing Committee recommends them to various localities as candidates, and the localities make practical electoral arrangements. Customarily, such persons are often assigned to their native places, units in which they once worked, or other places.

In accordance with the stipulations of the Electoral Law, the election of the NPC deputies is presided over by the NPC Standing Committee. The elections of the NPC deputies fall into two categories: general elections at the provincial level, and elections within the armed forces.[10] The elections are indirect and secret balloting is adopted, with the number of candidates larger than the actual number of deputies to be elected.

With regard to the local general elections at the provincial level, the Election Law stipulates that deputies to the NPC are to be elected indirectly, "by the people's congresses at the next-lower level."[11] Thus it follows that, generally speaking, a deputy to the NPC is chosen through two to three levels of elections. The deputies at the county level, who are elected directly by their constituencies, elect deputies to the people's congress at the provincial level, and then the people's congress at the provincial level elect deputies to the NPC. Where counties are administered by a city and there are autonomous prefectures, the directly elected deputies at the county level must first elect deputies to the people's congresses at the level of the city or prefecture, and then the people's congresses at the city or prefectural level elect deputies to the people's congress at the provincial level, before the latter elects deputies to the NPC.

In the elections conducted within the armed forces, the deputies to the NPC are elected by the congresses of military personnel, which are set up in indirect elections. The Methods of the People's Liberation Army on Electing Deputies to the National People's Congress and the Local People's Congresses at Different Levels, formulated in accordance with the Electoral Law, stipulates that the "congresses of military personnel of the various general headquarters, the various military area commands, the various services and arms, the Science and Technology Commission for National Defense, the Office of the National Defense Industry, the Academy of Military Sciences, the Military Academy, the Political Academy and the Logistics Academy elect deputies to the NPC." What is slightly different as compared with the local general elections at the provincial level is that the electoral organs for the NPC deputies from the armed forces are the congresses of military personnel, while the electoral organs of the localities are the people's congresses at the provincial level.

The specific operational procedures of the elections are: First, nomination of candidates. Under the stipulations of the current law, the subjects that have the right to propose candidates are: the various political parties and the various public organizations, which may either jointly or separately recommend candidates. A joint group of ten deputies or more may also recommend candidates. Second, deciding on the formal list of candidates. The Electoral Law stipulates that in electing deputies to the NPC, the presidium of a people's congress at the provincial level shall preside, submit the list of candidates recommended by the various subjects to all the deputies for deliberation and consultation, and then decide on a formal list of candidates. In finalizing the candidates, the Electoral Law stipulates that the number of candidates shall be 20 percent to fifty percent greater than the number of deputies to be elected; and candidates shall not be limited to the current deputies to the people's congress at the lower level. Third, briefing on the candidates and balloting. The Electoral Law explicitly says that the presidium of a people's congress at the provincial level may brief all the deputies on the candidates and that the political parties, public organizations and deputies to the people's congresses at the provincial level that have recommended candidates may brief deputies on those candidates at group meetings of deputies. It can be seen that the procedure for proposing candidates for deputies to the NPC is rather democratic and open, but in the absence of a system of candidates running for office and that of introducing candidates on a large scale, the openness of the nomination procedure has been greatly weakened. Within provinces and autonomous regions, the degree of familiarity of a candidate's name and his exposure to the public has become an important restraint on a truthful, effective election process. Except for local Party and Government officials and prominent figures whose names may be very familiar in their areas, other candidates lack the necessary means and media to present and promote themselves. Even if they are nominated as candidates, very often they can hardly win enough votes to get elected, for lack of name familiarity.

This has resulted in a lack of potential candidates and low competitiveness. In the circumstances in which the voters do not have a full range of candidates to choose from, the briefings on the candidates prepared by the congress presidium and the presidium's inclinations may become an important factor on whether a candidate will be elected, and the voters, more often than not, will tend to rely on or follow the guidance or hints of the presidium. Therefore, it can be said that a candidate's chance to get elected as a deputy to the NPC will partly rely on the backing of the congress presidium. Those candidates who may receive support from the presidium will have a better chance of winning the elections because of their ability to get wider publicity. As the election results show, the fact that there are a large number of local officials and prominent figures among the NPC deputies is the result of such institutional arrangements.

During the elections, voters may vote for or against a candidate, or abstain, or vote instead for any other voter. Candidates shall be elected only if they have obtained more than half of the votes of all the deputies. If the number of the candidates who have obtained more than half of the votes exceeds that of the deputies to be elected, the ones who have got more votes shall be elected. Where the number of votes for some candidates is tied, making it impossible to determine the ones to be elected, another round of balloting shall be conducted for these candidates to resolve the tie, and the ones who have obtained the most votes shall be elected. The presidium of the people's congress shall determine whether or not the election result is valid, and shall make an announcement accordingly.

The Standing Committee of the NPC presides over the elections, with the funds for elections to be disbursed by the state treasury. A deputy to the NPC may submit his or her resignation to the standing committee of the people's congress that elected him or her. When a deputy leaves a vacancy for any reason before serving out the law-prescribed term, the original electoral unit may hold a by-election in accordance with the law to fill the vacancy.

Taken as a whole, the relevant stipulations of the current law concerning the election of deputies, compared with the days when there were no legal stipulations to abide by, represent historical progress. But, there are still areas of ambiguity. For instance, the current law provides that the list of candidates for NPC deputies shall be published 20 days prior to the election. But how should the timing of the people's congress at the provincial level, the indirect electoral unit, be fixed? Should it be correspondingly advanced and extended to 20 days, so that the deputies to the provincial people's congress will have the necessary time and opportunity to get full information and make proper choices? Moreover, the current law only provides that a candidate shall be elected only if he or she has obtained more than half of the votes, without further specifying whether a new candidate shall be put forward if the original candidate has failed to secure that majority vote even after several rounds of balloting. Furthermore, as a candidate for the NPC may not be a deputy to the people's congress at the corresponding level or of the electoral unit and, such being the case, he or she is not entitled to attend the meetings to elect NPC deputies, how then can he or she become known to and accepted by the voters? In the absence of campaigning, how can the program of the nominated person be ascertained? Is it the case that once someone is nominated, he or she will have to accept the nomination? When the people's congress at the level of a province or autonomous region elects someone as an NPC deputy, should the person in question be notified and should his or her opinion be canvassed? Suppose after the conclusion of the election, an elected deputy indicates his or her inclination to turn down the offer to serve as an NPC deputy, should a by-election by called to elect a new deputy? These questions are not merely legal details, but contain considerable political import.

III. Recall and Disqualification of Deputies

The current law has corresponding stipulations on the procedure concerning the recall and disqualification of deputies.

On the recall of deputies, Article 40 of the Electoral Law says: "All deputies to the national and local people's congresses shall be subject to supervision of the voters and the electoral units which elect them. Both the voters and the electoral units shall have the right to recall the deputies they elect." The relevant laws have no provisions on the conditions for recalling deputies, but do have stipulations on the procedure for the original electoral units to recall deputies.

1. Proposals for Recall

The electoral units of the NPC deputies are the people's congresses at the provincial level and organizations of the armed forces. Therefore, a decision to recall must be made by a people's congress at the provincial level or an armed forces organization. When a people's congress at the provincial level or the congress of an armed forces organization is in session, the congress presidium or more than one tenth of the deputies may jointly submit a demand for recalling deputies. When the congress is not in session, the council of chairmen of its standing committee or more than one fifth of its members may jointly submit a proposal for recall.

2. The Procedure for Examining a Proposal for Recall

After being examined by the presidium of a people's congress or the council of chairmen of its standing committee, a proposal for recall must be submitted to the plenary meeting of the congress or its standing committee for voting by secret ballot. The adoption of a proposal for recall requires approval votes of more than half of the members (the deputies or the members of the standing committee). Upon its adoption, the person in question shall be notified, and a report shall be sent to the Standing Committee of the NPC for the record.

3. Disqualification of Deputies and Suspension of Performance of Functions of Deputies

With regard to the disqualification of deputies, the Electoral Law and the Law on Deputies provide the conditions for the disqualification of deputies: (1) Expiration of term; (2) Death; (3) Forfeit of Chinese nationality; (4) Resignation; (5) Absence without leave from two sessions of the people's congress at the corresponding level; and (6) Loss of political rights in accordance with the law.

In addition, the law also stipulates the circumstances in which the functions of a deputy shall be suspended: Being held in custody and subjected to investigation and trial in a criminal case; or being sentenced to public surveillance, criminal detention or fixed-term imprisonment but without the supplementary punishment of deprivation of political rights and serving a sentence. In either of the above circumstances, the performance of the person's functions as a deputy shall be temporarily suspended. As soon as the above circumstances no longer exist during the term of the deputy in question, the performance of his or her functions as a deputy shall be restored.

The disqualification of a deputy, and suspension and restoration of his or her functions as a deputy shall be reported by the Credentials Committee of the NPC to the Standing Committee of the NPC or the presidium of the NPC for confirmation and public announcement.

IV. The Functions and Powers of Deputies

In accordance with the Constitution and the Organic Law of the National People's Congress of the People's Republic of China (hereafter referred to as the NPC Organic Law), the term of office of the NPC deputies is five years, that is, beginning with the convocation of the first session of an NPC and ending with the convocation of the first session of the succeeding NPC. The term of office for those deputies who have been elected to fill vacancies lasts from the day of their by-election to the expiration of the current NPC.

The NPC is composed of deputies who, as the component members of the NPC, collectively exercise the highest power of the state. The deputies have corresponding functions and powers, which fall into two categories, functions and powers exercised during a session of the NPC and those exercised when the NPC is not in session.

1. The Functions and Powers during a Congress Session

(1) The Right to Submit Bills and Proposals

NPC deputies have the right, in accordance with the law, to put forward bills and proposals to the congress. Amendments to the Constitution are to be proposed by more than one fifth of the deputies; bills on legislative matters of a general nature and other bills shall be submitted by a delegation or joint action of at least 30 deputies.

(2) The Right to Advance Suggestions, Criticism and Opinions

The deputies have the right to advance suggestions, criticism and opinions to relevant state organs. These are not bills, but a right of the deputies to expression, which is relatively flexible and with less legal binding force.

(3) The Right to Vote in Elections and Decisions on Appointments

The NPC deputies are legal electors of members of the NPC Standing

Committee, the president and vice-president of the state, the chairman of the Central Military Commission, the president of the Supreme People's Court and the procurator-general of the Supreme People's Procuratorate. They may also participate in the process of deciding on the choice of the premier and other members of the State Council, and on the choice of all those on the Central Military Commission other than the chairman. In addition, they may also vote on the composition of the various special committees. When voting in elections, they may cast ballots for or against, or abstain, or vote instead for another person. When voting to decide on choices, they can only vote for or against, or abstain.

(4) The Right to Deliberation

The NPC deputies, when attending an NPC session, have the right to discuss and deliberate on the topics already on the agenda. During the deliberations, they may express their opinions and have the right to propose revisions and submit bills.

(5) The Right to Propose Removals

Three or more provincial delegations or more than one-tenth of the deputies to the NPC may propose removals from office of whoever has been elected or decided by the deputies.

(6) The Right to Address Questions and Make Inquires

During a congress session, a delegation or a group of 30 deputies or more may make a proposal in writing for addressing questions to the State Council and/or the various ministries and commissions, which must answer the questions.

(7) The Right to Propose Investigations

A group of one-tenth of the NPC deputies or more may put forward a proposal to set up a committee for investigation of a specific question.

(8) The Right to Vote

The deputies have the legal right to vote, which is an important right of the deputies and at the same time the most important of the forms of expression of the deputies' rights. When the congress is in session, the deputies may vote freely.

(9) The Right to Exemption

The NPC deputies shall have no legal liability for their speeches or votes at its meetings.

The right to exemption is a protective right universally practiced by modern states for popular representatives. Owing to special conditions in China, the stipulations in this respect are somewhat different from similar laws in other countries. First, the scope of this right is too narrow, limiting itself mainly to the meetings. Since the deputies do not exercise their functions and powers at the meetings only, their exercise of functions and powers outside the meetings are not covered by this protection. Second, speeches and votes are only part of the forms in which the deputies exercise their functions and powers, which are protected by the right to exemption, but other forms the deputies may adopt to exercise their functions and powers are not exempt from exemption. Third, owing to the fact that the level of law coverage and enforcement in China is relatively low, there are numerous forms of extralegal punishments while legal punishments are only one of the various means of punishment. Therefore, merely limiting the right to exemption to exemption from legal liability is not enough to remove the misgivings of the deputies in the course of performing their functions. Fourth, should the statements and actions of deputies during the exercise of their functions clash with the Constitution or with the basic political principles, would this right to exemption still apply?

2. Functions and Powers When the Congress Is Not in Session

When the congress is not in session, the status of the deputies still remains. Therefore, they still enjoy corresponding functions and powers. Owing to the fact that when the NPC is not in session, the institutions that were established during the congress session to direct the congress no longer exist, the circumstances in which the deputies perform their functions and powers are different from those they enjoy during the congress session. Therefore, the Law on Deputies stipulates that when the congress is not in session, the performance of the deputies' functions and powers is, generally speaking, conducted by the deputies organized as the NPC Standing Committee. This further strengthens the institutional characteristic that the functions and powers of deputies do not depend solely on the individual deputies, but on the institutions of the congress. Therefore, when the congress is not in session, the exercise of the deputies' functions and powers is not their personal action, but the continuation of the collective action of the congress. The exercise of the deputies' functions and powers outside the congress is more indicative of the responsibility of the congress than of the responsibility and rights of the individual deputies, especially in the sense that the deputies represent and reflect the opinions and demands of the localities.

When the congress in not in session, the offices which organize the deputies to exercise their functions and powers are usually the standing committees of the people's congresses at the corresponding level and at the next lower level. The Law on Deputies provides that the standing committees of the people's congresses above the county level, when entrusted by the standing committees of the people's congresses at the next-higher level, shall organize the deputies they have elected to the congresses at the next-higher level to carry out activities. Therefore, when the NPC is not in session, the offices for organizing the NPC deputies to exercise their functions and powers are the standing committees of the NPC and the people's congresses at the provincial level. This shows to a certain extent that, when the NPC is not in session, the standing committees of the people's congresses at the provincial level have a certain right to organize and arrange for the exercise of the extra-congress functions and powers of the NPC deputies.

The current Law on Deputies has no stipulations on whether or not the deputies are obliged to perform their functions and powers outside the congress.

(1) The Right to Maintain Ties with the Original Electoral Units

When the congress is not in session, the deputies shall keep in touch with their original electoral units, and listen to and reflect the opinions and demands of their original electoral units. They shall adopt a variety of forms to collect people's opinions and answer inquires from their original electoral units about their work and activities as deputies. Deputies who are to be recalled by their original electoral units shall have the right to attend the meetings called for that purpose, and the right to speak at the meetings or hand in written statements to defend themselves.

At present, the Electoral Law only has stipulations on the relationship between the deputies and their original electoral units in general terms, without going further to cover the *de facto* trusteeship and relationship of agency between the two, and without defining their respective rights and obligations in cases in which acts of deputies in performing their functions clash with the interests and demands of their original electoral units.

The Law on Deputies does not have further stipulations on matters related to the ties between the deputies and their original electoral units. Nor does it touch on the respective rights and obligations of the original electoral units and the deputies in case deputies fail to perform their function of "listening to and reflecting opinions." For instance, is a deputy under obligation to reflect whatever he "listens to"? Does "listen to" necessarily mean "reflect"? How should the relationship between the original electoral units and deputies be harmonized if the deputies fail to perform that function? Is an opinion of the "people" equal to an opinion of an "original electoral unit" in value? Does "inquire" have sufficient binding power on the deputies? The Law on Deputies does not have stipulations on these matters.

Owing to the fact that in the process of electing NPC deputies, the qualification requirements for deputies are rather lax (such as a lack of requirements with regard to the length of residence and political experience) as well as the *de facto* existence of non-electoral factors to a certain extent (like the direct allocations by the central authorities of certain candidates who must be elected), the relationship of the deputies to their original electoral units is only of symbolic significance to a certain extent. Therefore, the seemingly loopholes of a structural nature in the Law on Deputies are perhaps deliberate institutional arrangements. So, to apply the general viewpoints of comparative political science to the examination of the system of the people's congresses sometimes does not lead to a real understanding of the essence of China's system of people's congresses.

(2) The Right of Inspection

The right of inspection is exercised by the deputies mainly when the NPC is not in session. The content of the inspections is related to the agenda of the congress and related matters. In practice, before each session of the congress, the NPC Standing Committee organizes the deputies to inspect relevant areas and units. Deputies may conduct inspections on their own.

There are usually two forms of inspection by NPC deputies: those arranged by the NPC Standing Committee of state organs or related units at the corresponding or a lower level; and near-by inspections arranged by the standing committees of the local people's congresses at the request of deputies. Except for the inspections arranged by the Standing Committee of the NPC, the main places inspected by NPC deputies are state organs and relevant units in their localities.

During inspections of the first type, NPC deputies may propose interviews with leaders of relevant state organs at the corresponding or a lower level, and the leaders or their representatives interviewed shall listen to the suggestions, criticisms and opinions of deputies. In the second form of inspections, deputies carry out inspections on the strength of their deputies' cards, and may give their suggestions, criticism and opinions to the inspected units, but shall not deal with problems directly.

(3) The Right to Propose an Interim Session

Deputies may propose the convocation of an interim session of the NPC in accordance with the stipulations of the relevant law.

(4) The Right to Attend Meetings of the NPC Standing Committee and Special Committees as Non-voting Participants

Deputies may, when invited, attend meetings of the Standing Committee of the NPC and the special committees as non-voting participants.

(5) The Right to Participate in Committees for the Investigation of Specific Issues

Deputies may join committees for the investigation of specific issues in accordance with decisions of the NPC Standing Committee.

(6) The Right to Attend Meetings of the People's Congresses of the Original Electoral Units and Their Standing Committees as Non-voting Participants

Deputies may attend meetings of the people's congresses of their original electoral units and, when invited, attend meetings of the standing committees of the people's congresses of their original electoral units, all as non-voting participants.

3. Special Habeas Corpus

No deputy to the NPC may be removed of his or her personal freedom unless a special procedure is completed. The law provides that no NPC deputy may be arrested or put on criminal trial without the consent of the presidium of the current NPC or, when the NPC is not in session, the consent of its Standing Committee. If a deputy is caught in a criminal act and detained, the organ that has executed the detention shall report to the presidium of the NPC or its Standing Committee immediately. If any other restriction of personal freedom is imposed on a deputy, such as temporary custody for examination, administrative detention, legal detention, house surveillance or bail, approval from the presidium of the NPC or its Standing Committee must be obtained as soon as possible.

4. Special Privileges of Deputies

When deputies are performing their functions, the state and various relevant areas and units shall give them proper subsidies and conveniences in terms of time and materials. No unit or individual is permitted to find any excuse for obstructing or hindering deputies from exercising their functions or their personal freedoms.

V. Non-Voting Participants of NPC Meetings

In accordance with the stipulations of the Rules of Procedure of the National People's Congress, the following personnel can attend meetings of the NPC as non-voting participants: members of the State Council, members of the Central Military Commission, the president of the Supreme People's Court, and the procurator-general of the Supreme People's Procuratorate. Leaders of other organs and organizations may, with permission from the NPC Standing Committee, attend NPC meetings as non-voting participants.

In normal circumstances, members of the National Committee of the Chinese People's Political Consultative Conference may also attend meetings of the NPC as non-voting participants.

Usually, the number of non-voting participants at the meetings of the NPC is larger than the scope allowed in the Rules of Procedure of the National People's Congress. Take, for example, the list of non-voting participants adopted at the 20th meeting of the Standing Committee of the Ninth NPC allowed to attend the Fourth Session of the Ninth NPC: (1) 27 members of the State Council (those members of the State Council who were not on the list were all deputies to the NPC); (2) 2,261 members of the National Committee of the Chinese People's Political Consultative Conference (CPPCC); there are altogether 2,266 on the National Committee of the CPPCC, with the exception of five members who are concurrently deputies to the NPC — all the other 2,261 members were invited as non-voting participants; (3) one deputy secretary-general of the NPC; (4) 12 persons acting as deputy secretaries-general of the Standing Committee of the NPC, vice-chairman of the Working Committee on Legal Affairs under the NPC Standing Committee, vice-chairman of the Working Committee on Budget, and the chairman of the committee on the Basic Law of the Hong Kong Special Administrative Region under the NPC Standing Committee; (5) two deputy secretaries-general of the State Council; (6) one vice-president of the Supreme People's Court and one Procurator-General; (7) 10 principal leaders of Communist Party committees, standing committees of people's congresses and governments of provinces, autonomous regions and municipalities directly under the central government; (8) the chief executive of the Hong Kong Special Administrative Region; and (9) 15 persons from the People's Liberation Army and the Chinese People's Armed Police Force (3 of them were members of the Central Military Commission).

Owing to the fact that there are no stipulations under the current law on the rights and duties of the non-voting participants at the meetings, and that the scope of such participants, prescribed and actual, is so extensive, their roles, legal and political, are ambiguous. As the NPC is the country's highest organ of state power, as well as its highest representative organ, an excessively large attendance of non-deputies will have the unintended result of weakening the solemnity of the NPC and, to a certain extent, its representativeness. Moreover, owing to the fact that the NPC is already bulky enough and the duration of a session is limited, and the time and forms available to the deputies are limited by the scale of the congress, an addition of a large number of non-voting participants to the formal deputies would further increase the difficulties of the congress and affect the exercise of the deputies' functions and powers.

Section 3 The Organizations of the NPC

Every state organ has its corresponding organizational structure. The NPC, being China's highest organ of state power, has the following main organizations: the Session, the Standing Committee, and the special committees, as well as the working organs.

I. The Session of the NPC

The session of the NPC is both a form of assembly of the NPC and at the same time an organization of the NPC. Unlike the organizations of the general type, an NPC session, as an organization, lasts for the duration of the meeting, that is, that organization exists only during the meeting; once the meeting adjourns or closes, the meeting as an organization ceases to exist with it.

The Constitution and other relevant laws include fairly complete stipulations on matters related to the sessions of the NPC, which fall into two categories — regular and interim. The regular sessions take place once a year, with the right to convene them vested in the NPC Standing Committee. An interim session may be called when the Standing Committee deems it necessary or more than one fifth of the NPC deputies so propose.

Whether as a form or as an organization, a session of the NPC has within itself component parts that play their respective roles in the congress session and have the nature of organizations. Among them are preparatory meetings, the presidium and secretary-general, the plenary meetings and delegation meetings.

II. The Standing Committee of the NPC

1. The Nature and Status of the Standing Committee of the NPC

The Standing Committee of the NPC is the permanent body of the NPC. When the NPC is not in session, it exercises the supreme state power. It is subject to supervision by and responsible to the NPC, and reports on its work to the NPC.

When the NPC is not in session, the State Council is responsible to the Standing Committee of the NPC, and reports on its work to it, as do the chairman of the State Central Military Commission, the Supreme People's Court and the Supreme People's Procuratorate. The NPC Standing Committee has the right to supervise the work of the State Council, the State Central Military Commission, the Supreme People's Court and the Supreme People's Procuratorate.

The NPC Standing Committee is composed of the chairman, several vice-chairmen, the secretary-general, and members.

The members of the Standing Committee are elected at a plenary meeting by the NPC deputies by balloting during the first session of the current NPC. The steps before the elections are: first, the presidium of the first session of a new NPC proposes a list of candidates from among the deputies, and then submits it to the various delegations for discussion and consultation before the presidium decides on the formal list of candidates based on the opinions expressed by the majority of deputies. Generally speaking, the members of the Standing Committee include: (1) deputies from the CPC; (2) deputies from the various democratic parties and personages without party affiliation; (3) deputies from social organizations, such as the trade unions, the Communist Youth League and women's federations; (4) deputies from the armed forces; and (5) deputies from minority ethnic groups each with a population exceeding one million people.

The Constitution of the People's Republic of China provides that no one on the NPC Standing Committee shall concurrently hold any post in any of the administrative, judicial or procuratorial organs of the state. Otherwise, he or she must resign from the NPC Standing Committee.

Beginning with the Seventh NPC in 1988, elections of the standing committee members include a greater number of candidates than the number of posts to be filled, while the number of candidates for chairman and vice-chairmen has remained the same as the number of the posts to be filled.

The NPC Standing Committee shall be elected for the same five-year term as the NPC. The term of the NPC Standing Committee is calculated from the time when the Standing Committee is elected by the current NPC at its first session until a new Standing Committee is elected by the succeeding NPC at its first session.

2. The Chairman of the NPC Standing Committee and the Council of Chairmen

The Constitution of the People's Republic of China provides that the chairman of the NPC Standing Committee presides over the work of the Standing Committee and convenes its meetings; the vice-chairmen and the secretary-general assist in the work of the chairman; the vice-chairmen of the Standing Committee may exercise such of the functions and powers of the chairman as may be deputed by the chairman; when the chairman cannot carry on his or her work because of bad health or leaves the post vacant, the Standing Committee shall select one of the vice-chairmen to be the acting chairman until the health of the chairman is back to normal or a new chairman is elected by the NPC.

The chairmen and vice-chairmen of the Standing Committee shall be elected for a term of five years and shall serve no more than two consecutive terms.

The council of chairmen of the NPC Standing Committee, with the participation of the chairman, vice-chairmen and secretary-general of the

NPC Standing Committee, is the main form of handling day-to-day work of the Standing Committee. Deputy secretaries-general attend the council meetings as non-voting participants, as may responsible members of relevant state organs, with the approval of the chairman or the executive vice-chairman. The main functions of the council include: (1) fixing the date for convening the meeting of the Standing Committee and its duration, and drawing up a draft agenda; (2) submitting to the Standing Committee bills within the scope of its functions and powers; (3) deciding, during the meeting of the Standing Committee, to refer to a relevant special committee or a Standing Committee meeting for examining proposals submitted by a group of ten or more of the Standing Committee members for addressing questions; (4) deciding whether the leader of the organ addressed should make an oral or written reply to the questions at the Standing Committee meeting or at the relevant special committee meeting; (5) deciding whether to submit bills and proposals to the Standing Committee for examination or to first refer them to a relevant special committee for examination and report before the council decides to send them to the Standing Committee for examination; (6) deciding to send reports on the work of state organs it has received to relevant special committees for examination and comment; (7) directing and coordinating the day-to-day work of the various special committees; (8) proposing, when the NPC is not in session, choices of individual vice-chairmen of special committees and some members, as additional appointments by the NPC Standing Committee; and (9) handling other important work of the Standing Committee.

The chairman convenes and presides over the meetings of the council of chairmen. He may also entrust a vice-chairman to preside over the meetings. The agenda of the council of chairmen is prepared by the secretary-general and approved by the chairman. The documents adopted by the council of chairmen are to be signed by the secretary-general or a deputy secretary-general whom the secretary-general has entrusted for this task. The issues decided at the council of chairmen may be made public, with the consent of the secretary-general.

3. Meetings of the Standing Committee

The meetings of the NPC Standing Committee usually are held once every two months, with the duration of each meeting varying from 7 to

15 days. The meetings of the Standing Committee may be held only when more than half of its members attend.

The meetings of the NPC Standing Committee may have the following personnel as non-voting participants: (1) leaders of the State Council, the State Central Military Commission, the Supreme People's Court and the Supreme People's Procuratorate; (2) those vice-chairmen and members of the special committees of the Standing Committee who are not on the Standing Committee or advisers to the special committees; (3) the chairman or one vice-chairman each of the standing committees of the people's congresses of the provinces, autonomous regions and municipalities directly under the central government; (4) NPC deputies who are relevant to the agenda of the meetings; and (5) leaders of relevant departments.

At present, meetings of the NPC Standing Committee have three forms: plenary meetings, group meetings and joint group meetings.

III. The Special Committees

Before 1982, the NPC basically had no special committees of a permanent nature, with only some committees for the duration of the congress when the congress was in session. But, beginning in that year, some special committees were established, in accordance with the Constitution, as permanent working bodies of the NPC. Some special committees are explicitly listed in the Constitution and law, but the Constitution also says that some other special committees, though not explicitly listed, may be established. On a technical level, the establishment of the special committees is aimed at strengthening the building of the system of the NPC and improving its working efficiency, but the move has also helped China's NPC to move closer to the parliaments in other countries in terms of set-ups.

The Ninth NPC, for instance, had nine special committees: Nationalities; Law; Financial and Economic; Education, Science, Culture and Health; Foreign Affairs; Overseas Chinese; Civil and Legal Affairs; Environment and Resources Protection; and Agriculture and Rural Areas.

Different in nature from the session of the NPC or the NPC Standing Committee, the special committees do not have the nature of organs of power, but are bodies charged with certain special tasks under the direction of the organs of power.

IV. The Credentials Committee of the NPC Standing Committee

The credentials committee was established in accordance with the Organic Law of the National People's Congress by the NPC Standing Committee as a permanent body for examining the credentials of the NPC deputies. Its main functions are to examine those deputies who have been added to the current NPC, and to examine the credentials of the newly elected deputies to the succeeding NPC.

The credentials committee is composed of the chairman, vice-chairmen and members, all of whom are nominated by the council of chairmen of the NPC Standing Committee from among the members of the Standing Committee, and are to be endorsed by the plenary meeting of the Standing Committee.

V. Committee for the Investigation of a Specific Question

A committee for the investigation of a specific question is established by the NPC to inquire into a certain matter. The Organic Law of the National People's Congress and the Rules of Procedure of the National People's Congress provide that a proposal for setting up a committee for the investigation of a specific question may be put forward by the presidium, or a joint action of three or more provincial delegations, or of more than one tenth of all the deputies, to be submitted by the presidium to a plenary meeting of the congress for adoption.

A committee of investigation is composed of the chairman, several vice-chairmen and several members, all of whom are to be nominated by the presidium from among the deputies and the nominations must be submitted to a plenary meeting of the congress for approval. The committee may invite experts to take part in the work of inquiry.

When the NPC is not in session, the NPC Standing Committee may be authorized by the NPC to hear the committee's reports, make resolutions and report to the NPC for the record.

A committee of investigation is not a permanent body, and must be abolished immediately upon the completion of the investigation.

So far, neither the NPC nor its Standing Committee has established any such committee.

Section 4 The Main Functions and Powers of the NPC and Its Standing Committee

I. Main Functions and Powers of the NPC

Under the Constitution of the People's Republic of China and the law, the NPC is the highest organ of state power, and enjoys important, wide-range and comprehensive legal powers.

1. The Power to Formulate and Amend the Constitution

In accordance with the stipulations in Articles 62 and 64 of the Constitution, the NPC enjoys the power to amend the Constitution. That is, the amendments to the Constitution are to be proposed by the NPC Standing Committee, or by more than one-fifth of the deputies to the NPC and adopted by a majority vote of more than two-thirds of all the deputies. At the same time, the NPC also has the power to supervise the enforcement of the Constitution.

Owing to the fact that the Constitution has no stipulations on the special procedure for amending it, and that in fact since 1949, most Constitutions of the People's Republic of China (except the Common Program) have been formulated by the NPC, the NPC, therefore, in legal terms, enjoys the *de facto* power to formulate the Constitution.

Since the Constitution not only provides for the power of the NPC to amend the Constitution, but also implies its *de facto* power to formulate the Constitution, the NPC has the powers to formulate the Constitution and amend it. As all the Constitutions since the Constitution of 1954 were promulgated in the name of amendments to the previous texts of the Constitution (altogether three overall amendments and five partial amendments), the power of the NPC to formulate the Constitution, therefore, has never been used in practice, or it can be said that the power to amend the Constitution, as exercised by the NPC a number of times, is tantamount to the power to formulate the Constitution.

The NPC's exercise of the power to amend the Constitution has shown marked features. Some scholars have noticed that China's basic mode of amending the Constitution is to make timely amendments to the Constitution in accordance with the policies of the CPC and incorporate the main spirit of its policies into the Constitution to become the guidelines for state activities. They have also summed up the following special features: First, each amending of the Constitution (whether overall or partial) took place after a national congress of the CPC. For instance, the amended Constitution of 1975 was promulgated after the Tenth CPC National Congress; the amended Constitution of 1978 was adopted after the 11th National Congress of the CPC; the amended Constitution of 1982 was formulated after the 12th National Congress of the CPC was held earlier that year; the amended Constitution of1988 was promulgated after the 13th National Congress of the CPC in 1987; the amending of the Constitution in 1993 took place after the 14th National Congress of the CPC in 1992; and the CPC's 15th National Congress was held in 1997, followed by the amending of the Constitution in 1999. Second, it has become a "constitutional practice" that each time it is the CPC that proposes the amending of the Constitution or drafted such amendments. Third, each amending has been tied to the revision of the CPC Constitution. For instance, the CPC Constitution was revised at its 12th National Congress in 1982, and the Fifth NPC, convened soon afterwards, promulgated the new amended Constitution; in 1992, the 14th National Congress of the CPC promulgated revisions to the CPC Constitution, and in March 1993, the Constitution of the People's Republic of China was amended a second time; and in September 1997 the CPC Constitution was revised at its 15th National Congress, resulting in the third amending of the Constitution of China in March 1999. Fourth, the amendments to the Constitution of China each time were roughly similar in content to the keynote reports to the CPC National Congresses in question and the revisions of the CPC Constitution, or sometimes even directly copied from the relevant resolutions of the CPC congresses. For instance, the CPC made a breakthrough at its 14th National Congress with regard to the theory concerning the planned economy, and the amended Constitution of China in 1993 provided that "The state practices a socialist market economy." In the report to the CPC's 15th National Congress, the guiding role of Deng Xiaoping Theory and the principle of "governing the country accord to law" were established, and the amended Constitution in 1999 made corresponding amendments: "Under the guidance of Deng Xiaoping Theory" and "govern the country according to law and build a socialist country under the rule of law." Fifth, the successive amendments of the Constitution of China have been basically caused by policy changes, which have required corresponding changes in the content of the Constitution. For instance, in the 1980s, the CPC called for adhering to the Four Cardinal Principles, and the 1982 Constitution of China included in it the phrase "taking the Four Cardinal Principles as the guide." Another striking example is the attitude toward the non-public economic sector. As a result of the CPC policy changes, the Constitutions following the 1954 one showed a gradual process of wiping out private ownership, while beginning with the 1987 Constitution the non-public sector experienced a gradual return. Sixth, as far as the contents of successive amendments is concerned, most were related to the changes in principles and policies, and mostly economic policies at that. For instance, on April 12, 1988, at the First Session of the Seventh NPC, two bills on the amendments to the Constitution were adopted, their main thrust covering economic policies: provisions allowing the private sector to exist and grow within the scope prescribed by law, and allowing the transfer of the right to the use of land in accordance with the stipulations of the law. On March 29, 1993, nine bills on amendments to the Constitution were adopted at the First Session of the Eighth NPC, with their main points as follows: confirming that China is in the primary stage of socialism with special features of historical development and establishing the guiding role of the theory of building socialism with Chinese characteristics; providing that China practices a socialist market economy; and providing that the system of multi-party cooperation and political consultation led by the CPC is to exist and develop for a long time to come. The bills from the third to the ninth congresses were almost exclusively devoted to economic policies. For instance, "adherence to the reform and opening-up" was written into the Preamble, "state-operated economy" was rephrased as "state-owned economy," "rural people's communes" was deleted, and "practicing a socialist market economy" and "expanding the independent decision-making power of enterprises in business operations" were included. Half of the amendments to the Constitution in 1999 dealt with the economy, such as raising the status of the non-public sector, and re-establishing new forms of ownership and modes of distribution.

The amending of the Constitution must follow normal practices and legal procedures. In reality, normal practices perhaps have greater practical significance than legal procedures. The normal practices are: First, the CPC Central Committee puts forward a proposal for amending the Constitution, and then sends it to the Standing Committee of the NPC for discussion. The NPC Standing Committee arranges for a draft constitutional amendments plan to be advanced in accordance with legal procedures. Although the subjects enjoying the right to propose constitutional amendments are not limited to the CPC, only the CPC has actually proposed such amendments. This is because adherence to the leading role of the CPC is an unshakable principle of political life in China, and an important aspect of the leading role of the CPC is its right to formulate the Constitution and laws. Take the amending of the Constitution in 1999 for example. In the wake of the CPC's 15th National Congress, the Central Committee of the CPC, in November 1997, set up a Constitution Amendment Group, with Li Peng as its head. This group, in accordance with the Report to the CPC's 15th National Congress and the series of principles and policies that had come into being in the previous years and on the basis of collecting and studying opinions from various quarters on this topic, drafted preliminary opinions on partial amendments to the Constitution. The preliminary opinions, after being examined and finalized by the Standing Committee of the Political Bureau of the CPC Central Committee and adopted in principle by the Political Bureau at its meeting, were sent to various quarters for comment. The preliminary opinions were sent on December 5, 1998 to the Party committees of all provinces, autonomous regions and municipalities directly under the central government, the departments under the CPC Central Committee, the leading Party members' groups or Party committees in the ministries and commissions of the State Council, the General Political Department of the Central Military Commission and the leading Party members' groups in the various people's organizations, as well as members and alternate members of the CPC Central Committee, with a view to collecting their opinions. On December 21, the CPC Central Committee held a forum of non-Communist personages presided over by Jiang Zemin, to canvass opinions on the preliminary opinions on partial amendments to the Constitution from the leaders of the central committees of the various democratic parties and the All-China Federation of Industry and Commerce, as well as representatives of personages without party affiliation. On December 22 and 24, the Constitution Amendment Group of the CPC Central Committee held a forum, presided over by Li Peng, to canvass opinions from legal and economic experts. Finally, after being revised by the CPC Central Committee and discussed and adopted by the Standing Committee of the Political Bureau and the Political Bureau of the CPC Central Committee, the preliminary opinions became the Proposal of the

CPC Central Committee on Partial Amendments to the Constitution of the People's Republic of China, and this was sent to the Standing Committee of the NPC. In January 1999, the Standing Committee of the Ninth NPC discussed the proposal of the CPC Central Committee at its 7th meeting, and in accordance with Article 64 of the Constitution proposed amendments to the Constitution of the PRC. On March 9, the Second Session of the Ninth NPC heard an explanation presented by NPC Standing Committee Vice-Chairman Tian Jiyun about the proposed amendments to the Constitution. Afterwards, the various delegations examined the amendments. On March 15, the amendments were put to the vote by secret ballot, in accordance with the Rules of Procedure of the National People's Congress at the Second Session of the Ninth NPC, and adopted with an overwhelming majority. (Note: A total of 2,862 ballots were issued, and 2,858 were returned; 2,858 votes were valid, of which 2,811 were "for," 21 were "against," and 24 were "abstentions.")

2. The Power to Supervise the Enforcement of the Constitution

The power to supervise the enforcement of the Constitution is an important state power the NPC exercises. That the NPC enjoys that power is one of the results of China practicing the system of democratic centralism. Under this system, the NPC is the highest organ of state power, while the other state organs are, in legal terms and theory, secondary state organs created by the NPC through elections, and there is no horizontal relationship of checks and balances between them. Therefore, the function of safeguarding the constitutional security and dignity cannot be realized through the relationship of checks and balances between the various state organs, but can only be left to the NPC to guarantee and safeguard the enforcement of the Constitution.

As far as practice is concerned, the NPC has never really exercised its power to supervise the enforcement of the Constitution, as it lacks the requisite conditions for exercising such power. For instance, the relevant law lacks specific stipulations on the exercise of this power by the NPC, which transfers part of the power to supervise the enforcement of the Constitution to its Standing Committee. Take the Eighth NPC and its Standing Committee for example. During the five years of its term, they examined and adopted 118 laws and decisions concerning laws and legal affairs, averaging as many as 23 a year, but did nothing about constitutional supervision.

The power of the NPC to supervise the enforcement of the Constitution also faces the challenge of whether it is equal to the function of constitutional supervision, and whether the NPC and its Standing Committee should serve as the organs of constitutional lawsuits and reviews on unconstitutionality. In legal terms, the NPC is also a state organ regulated by the Constitution, and any legislation it makes, if found to contravene the Constitution, shall be null and void. Therefore, in this sense, the NPC is also subject to the supervision by the Constitution, although it is a kind of self-supervision. On the other hand, if the supreme power of constitutional enforcement is vested only in the supreme legislative organ, and if the legislation of the legislative organ contravenes the Constitution, the Constitution will be in lack a guarantee, especially in light of the fact that the NPC's permanent organ, its Standing Committee, has a monopoly of the power to interpret the Constitution and that the NPC itself has the power to amend the Constitution on the strength of a majority vote of more than two-thirds of its deputies. Obviously, in the light of the usual practice worldwide, having a legislative organ supervise the enforcement of the Constitution cannot solve the problem of legislative unconstitutionality. Therefore, the power of the NPC to supervise the enforcement of the Constitution can at the most only play the role of constitutional guarantee within certain limits and to a certain extent.

To be specific, constitutional supervision shall include review of the constitutionality of the laws and documents of a legal nature; review of the constitutionality of acts of state organs and their staff, as well as political parties, social organizations and citizens; and settlement of conflicts between state organs over limits of power. In practice, the emphasis of the unconstitutionality reviews in China is often on unconstitutional acts of an abstract nature, while seriously neglecting the reviews of concrete unconstitutional acts as well as conflicts between state organs over limits of power. The supervision over and review of abstract unconstitutional acts is often carried out by different organs of state power and administration, as prescribed by the Constitution and relevant organic laws and through the systems of report for the record, approval and cancellation to achieve the objective of reviewing and dealing with abstract unconstitutional acts. According to statistics, between 1988, when the NPC and its Standing Committee began the practice of reviewing and supervising the enforcement of laws and 1998, they had reviewed and supervised the enforcement of a total of 58 laws and decisions on legal issues. In addition, between 1993 and June 1997, 3,692 local rules and regulations were reported to the NPC for the record, and the various special committees of the NPC Standing Committee completed reviews on 2,045 of them, 93 of which were found contravening the Constitution and current laws, accounting for 4.54 percent of the total reviewed.[12] On the other hand, there was a serious lack of review of the constitutionality of the acts of state organs and their staff, political parties, social organizations, enterprises and undertakings, as well as the general public, while, in fact, concrete unconstitutional acts in China were particularly widespread, serious and blatant, and therefore more harmful.

3. Legislative Power

The NPC exercises the legislative power of the state, in accordance with the spirit and stipulations of the Constitution currently in force, to enact and amend basic statutes concerning criminal offenses, civil affairs, state organs and other matters.

At present, with regard to the legislative power the NPC enjoys, in addition to the legislative power explicitly prescribed by the Constitution, the "basic statutes...on other matters" referred to by the Constitution include:

(1) Legislation concerning the fundamental rights and duties of citizens

The Constitution already has provisions on the fundamental rights and duties of citizens, but these should be further developed into specific laws. The NPC has the power to enact laws on some aspects of the fundamental rights and duties of the citizens.

In the light of comparative study of constitutions, owing to the fact that legislation concerning the fundamental rights and duties of citizens involves the question of guaranteeing the citizens' fundamental rights as prescribed in the Constitution, it is therefore up to the state law to guarantee them, and no restriction or deprivation by any organ or individual in the form of legislation is permitted; nor shall an administrative organ or local government have any scope of legislative power in this respect. In practice, if this power is not exclusive to the highest legislative organ of the state, which has the nature of a representative organ, then the guarantee of citizens' fundamental rights will not be assured.

Because the legislative power of the NPC in this respect cannot cover all aspects of the citizens' fundamental rights and duties, the Law on Legislation of the People's Republic of China, which was adopted at the Third Session of the Ninth NPC and went into force on July 1, 2000, delegates some aspects of the legislative power concerning citizens' fundamental rights and duties to the administrative organs of the state and local legislative organs. The transfer of legislative power in this respect by the NPC has considerably restricted the scope of the exclusive legislative power of the NPC concerning the freedom of the person of citizens and their right to property, leaving considerable scope of legislation to the administrative organs and local legislative organs.

(2) Legislation concerning the fundamental political and administrative systems of the state

Included in this category is legislation concerning the establishment of organs of state power, administrative organs, judicial organs and procuratorial organs, and their functions and powers, and their mutual relationships, laws on civil servants and other matters.

(3) Legislation concerning the fundamental economic systems of the state

Included in this category is legislation concerning the state economic planning, system of finance and budget, taxation, banking, ownership, issuance of money, customs houses, foreign trade system and other matters.

4. Functions and Powers in Other Respects

(1) The power to organize other supreme organs of state power

In accordance with the Constitution, the NPC has the power to elect to or remove from office members of the NPC Standing Committee, the president and vice-president of the state, the president of the Supreme People's Court and procurator-general of the Supreme People's Procuratorate; to decide on the choice of the premier of the State Council upon nomination by the president of the state, and to decide on the choice of the vice-premiers, state councilors, ministers in charge of ministries or commissions, auditor-general and secretary-general upon nomination by the premier; to elect the president of the Central Military Commission and to decide on the choice of the other component members of the Central Military Commission upon nomination by the chairman of the Central Military Commission.

(2) The power to decide on major issues of state

As the highest organ of state power in China, the NPC has the supreme power to decide on major issues concerning China's social, political, economic and all other fields. According to the current Constitution, the power of decision of the NPC mainly includes examining and approving the plan for national economic and social development, and reporting on its implementation; examining and approving the state budget, and reporting on its implementation; approving the establishment of provinces, autonomous regions and municipalities directly under the central government; deciding on the establishment of special administrative regions and the systems to be instituted there; and deciding on questions of war and peace.

(3) The power of supervision

The NPC exercises the supreme power of supervision, which is manifested as follows: The NPC Standing Committee is responsible to the NPC and reports on its work to the congress; the NPC has the power to alter or annul inappropriate decisions by the NPC Standing Committee; the State Council is responsible to the NPC and reports on its work to the congress; the president of the State Central Military Commission is responsible to the NPC; and the Supreme People's Court and the Supreme People's Procuratorate are responsible to the NPC and report on their work to the congress.

The basic form of supervision by the NPC over other state organs is by hearing and examining reports on the work of the NPC Standing Committee, the State Council, the Supreme People's Court and the Supreme People's Procuratorate, as well as by addressing questions.

In recent years, especially since the Ninth NPC, the NPC has set steadily higher requirements on the exercise of supervision power, and attached increasingly greater attention to it. On the whole, since the beginning of the reform and opening-up program, the NPC and its Standing Committee have shaped a number of specific supervision systems, such as the system of constitutional supervision, the review and supervision system over the enforcement of laws, the system of hearing and deliberating on work reports, the system of examining and approving plans and budgets, etc.

The supervision power of the NPC and its Standing Committee consists of two aspects: "urging" and "disposing." By "urging," it means collection of information, reviewing and deliberating the work of those supervised and of their enforcement of the Constitution and laws; by "disposing," it means dispositions and corrections of and sanctions against, by the NPC and its Standing Committee, violations of the Constitution and law, and other inappropriate acts. Those to be supervised by the NPC and its Standing Committee, as prescribed by the Constitution and law, are the administrative, judicial and procuratorial organs of state that are created by, and are responsible to, the NPC and its Standing Committee, namely, the State Council, the Supreme People's Court and the Supreme People's Procuratorate, as well as their members, in addition to the president of the state, and the Central Military Commission. In terms of legal supervision, the NPC and its Standing Committee may also supervise the people's congresses of the provinces, autonomous regions and municipalities directly under the central government and their standing committees. But the NPC and its Standing Committee shall not supervise ordinary citizens or civil servants directly.

(4) Such other functions and powers as the highest organ of state power should exercise

The Constitution provides that the NPC has the power to exercise "such other functions and powers as the highest organ of state power should exercise,"[13] which are not listed in the Constitution. This has constitutionally vested the NPC with a widespread, open-ended stipulation on its functions and powers.

II. The Main Functions and Powers of the Standing Committee of the NPC

1. Legislative Power

According to the Constitution, the Standing Committee of the NPC exercises legislative power jointly with the NPC itself. The NPC Standing Committee has the power to enact all laws except the fundamental statutes that must be enacted by the NPC only. In other words, the NPC Standing Committee has the power to enact and amend all laws, except the fundamental statutes concerning criminal offenses, civil affairs, state organs and other matters that are to be enacted and amended by the NPC. It has the power also to add partial supplements and amendments to statutes enacted by the NPC provided that they do not contravene the basic principles of these statutes. In fact, this puts a large amount of legislative work on the NPC Standing Committee.

As the practice of the NPC and its Standing Committee in their legislative work shows, with the exception of the Constitution and a small number of fundamental statutes that have been enacted by the NPC, a large number of laws have been enacted by the NPC Standing Committee. On the technical level, the sharing of the legislative power of the NPC by its Standing Committee has greatly speeded up the process of China's legislative work, but as people pay increasingly greater attention to legislative work and become increasingly more conscious of the legal system, the need for legislative work has, although unintended, resulted in a gradual shift of the supreme legislative power of the NPC to its Standing Committee, which is not only in a position to enact laws other than the fundamental statutes but has also acquired increasingly greater legislative power in some areas related to the fundamental systems of the state and the fundamental rights of citizens. Because the NPC Standing Committee does not enjoy the status of the highest representative body, it has, while speeding up the process of legislative work, brought about a certain degree of confusion to the building of a society featuring rule of law, due to its lack of representativeness and inadequate legal basis. At the same time, an excessive transfer by the NPC of its legislative power has weakened its status and functions as the highest legislative organ of the state.

2. Power to Interpret the Constitution and Laws

The Standing Committee of the NPC is the only organ with the power to give legislative interpretation of the Constitution and other laws. The laws to be interpreted by the NPC Standing Committee are not limited to those enacted by the Standing Committee itself but also cover those formulated by the NPC.

3. The Power to Supervise Constitutional Enforcement

The NPC and its Standing Committee jointly exercise the power to supervise the enforcement of the Constitution.

Because the NPC Standing Committee has an edge over the congress in technical terms and in terms of the quality of personnel, the substantive part of the supervision over the enforcement of the Constitution has thus been placed more on the NPC Standing Committee, and with assistance from the special committees established under the NPC and its Standing Committee, the aim of supervising the enforcement of the Constitution has thus been realized. This amounts to a supplement to the functions of the NPC. In fact, it is very difficult for the NPC to exercise this function and power on a regular basis, so, to a greater extent, its Standing Committee has the actual power to supervise the enforcement of the Constitution.

4. The Power to Supervise Other Work of State Organs

The Standing Committee of the NPC supervises the work of the State Council, the Central Military Commission, the Supreme People's Court and the Supreme People's Procuratorate. It has the power to annul administrative rules and regulations, decisions or orders of the State Council that contravene the current Constitution or statutes. It also has the power to annul local rules and regulations, and resolutions of the state organs of the provinces, autonomous regions and municipalities directly under the central government that contravene the current Constitution, statutes, or administrative rules and regulations.

In addition to supervision in the above areas, an important aspect of the expanded power of supervision by the NPC Standing Committee in recent years is its supervision over economic work. On March 1, 2000, the 14th meeting of the Standing Committee of the Ninth NPC adopted the Resolution of the Standing Committee of the National People's Congress on Strengthening Supervision over Economic Work, which includes the following stipulations:

(1) The Standing Committee of the NPC exercises the power of supervision over the economic work of the State Council;

(2) The draft annual plan for national economic and social development, draft five-year plan and draft long-term plan drawn up by the State Council are to be reported to the NPC Standing Committee one month before the convening of a session of the NPC;

(3) When the Congress is in session, the Financial and Economic Committee examines the draft plans, and reports on them in the light of the opinions expressed on the results of examinations by the delegations and special committees, and prepares a report on the results of the examination, which, upon approval by the presidium, is to be printed for distribution at the congress;

(4) The focal points of the Financial and Economic Committee in examining the draft annual plan and the report on it are to ensure that the guiding principle for drawing up the plan shall conform to the five-year national economic and social development plan as well as the long-term plan, which the NPC has already approved; that the main objectives and

targets meet the demands for developing the national economy in a sustained and stable way; and that the main measures to be taken conform to the requirements for strengthening macro-regulation, optimizing the economic structure, making appropriate arrangements for national priority construction projects, improving the people's livelihood in a thoroughgoing way, vigorously promoting employment, and being conducive to bolstering social security and sustainable development;

(5) In the case of an exceptionally important national construction project which will have a long-term impact, affect a wide range of sectors and require a large amount of investment, the State Council may propose a bill to the NPC or its Standing Committee for deliberation and decision;

(6) When the annual plan, the five-year plan and long-term plan that the NPC has approved need partial adjustments in the course of economic operations, the State Council shall propose such adjustments to the Standing Committee for examination and approval. Except in special cases, the State Council shall report its plan for adjustments to the Standing Committee one month in advance of a Standing Committee meeting; the State Council shall in August report on its implementation for the period of the first six months; when major changes occur in the economic operations, the State Council shall report to the Standing Committee and give explanations; the Standing Committee may, when it deems this necessary, hear and deliberate on reports on special subjects related to the economic work by the State Council; the Standing Committee shall exercise supervision over the implementation of the national economic and social development plan, and may, when necessary, hear work reports from the State Council on national key construction projects listed in the plan;

(7) With regard to treaties and agreements that China has concluded with foreign countries or international organizations, or which it intends to annul, all those which are subject to ratification by the NPC Standing Committee in accordance with the Law of the People's Republic of China on the Procedure for the Conclusion of Treaties must be reported by the State Council to the NPC Standing Committee for deliberation and decision;

(8) Entrusted by the Council of Chairmen, relevant special committees may hold plenary meetings to hear reports on special subjects by relevant departments of the State Council. Such reports are to be arranged by the State Council in a unified way. The Financial and Economic Committee shall hold plenary meetings before the 15th day of April, July

and October, respectively, to hear reports by relevant departments of the State Council concerning economic operations in the first, second and third quarters of the year, and to carry out analyses and studies;

(9) When the NPC Standing Committee meets to deliberate and discuss matters listed in this "decision," the State Council shall provide requested information, data and explanations in a timely manner, and arrange for its responsible members or responsible members of relevant departments to appear at the meetings, listen to opinions and respond to inquiries; when a special committee holds plenary meetings to deliberate on and discuss matters listed in this "decision," the relevant departments of the State Council shall provide requested information, data and explanations in a timely manner, and arrange for relevant responsible members to appear at the meetings, listen to opinions and respond to inquiries;

(10) A special committee shall, after hearing a report by a relevant department of the State Council at its plenary meetings, report its opinions and suggestions to the council of chairmen. The latter shall decide whether or not to refer such opinions and suggestions to the State Council and relevant departments for study and disposal, followed by a report back to the NPC Standing Committee;

(11) The NPC Standing Committee shall release accounts of its supervision of economic work to the general public, with exceptions as prescribed by law.

5. The Power to Appoint and Remove Personnel of Other State Organs

Whether the NPC is in session or not, the NPC Standing Committee has the power to appoint or remove from office relevant personnel of the highest administrative, military, judicial and procuratorial organs of the state. That is to say, it can decide on the choice, upon nomination by the premier, of the ministers in charge of the various ministries and commissions, auditor-general and secretary-general; on the choice, upon nomination by the president of the Central Military Commission, of the other members of the commission; on the appointment and removal, at the suggestion of the president of the Supreme People's Court, vice-presidents of the court, judges and members of the judicial committee, as well as the president of the military court; on appointment and removal of deputy procurators-general of the Supreme People's Procuratorate, procurators, members of the procuratorial committee and president of the military procuratorate, at the suggestion of the procurator-general of the

Supreme People's Procuratorate, and approval of the appointments and removals of the chief procurators of the people's procuratorates of the various provinces, autonomous regions and municipalities directly under the central government; and on appointment and recall of plenipotentiary representatives abroad.

6. The Power to Decide on Important Issues of State

This power covers the following specific aspects: When the NPC is not in session, examining and approving the national economic and social development plans, and partial adjustments to the state budget in the course of its implementation; deciding on the ratification or abrogation of treaties and important agreements concluded with other countries; instituting systems of titles and ranks for military and diplomatic personnel, and others; instituting state medals and honors, and deciding on their conferment; deciding on the granting of special pardons; deciding, when the National People's Congress is not in session, on the proclamation of a state of war in the event of an armed attack on the country or in fulfillment of international treaty obligations concerning common defense against aggression; deciding on general mobilization or partial mobilization; and deciding on the enforcement of martial law throughout the country or in particular provinces, autonomous regions or municipalities directly under the central government.

7. Such Other Functions and Powers as the NPC May Assign to It

Apart from the above functions and powers, the NPC Standing Committee has also the power to exercise such other functions and powers as the NPC may assign to it: to preside over the election of deputies to the NPC; to convene sessions of the NPC; and to direct the work of the various special committees when the NPC is not in session, etc.

Section 5 Local People's Congresses at Different Levels

The local people's congresses at different levels refer to the people's congresses and their standing committees at the levels of provinces (including autonomous regions and municipalities directly under the central government), cities divided into districts (including autonomous prefectures), and counties (including autonomous counties, districts of cities, cities not divided into districts); and people's congresses of townships (including ethnic minority townships and towns).

I. Deputies to the Local People's Congresses and Their Election

1. The Legal Status and Political Relationships of Deputies to Local People's Congresses

The local people's congresses made up by deputies elected to them are local organs of state power at different levels.

According to Article 2 of the Electoral Law, the election of deputies to the local people's congresses at different levels falls into two categories: direct election and indirect election. Deputies to a people's congress of a city that is not divided into districts, municipal district, county, autonomous county, township, ethnic minority township or town are directly elected by their electoral districts; deputies to a people's congress of a province, autonomous region or a municipality directly under the central government, of a city divided into districts or an autonomous prefecture are elected indirectly, that is, by people's congresses at the next-lower level.

The directly elected deputies to a local people's congress are connected with particular electoral districts, while the indirectly elected deputies to a local people's congress are not connected with particular voters or electoral districts, but with people's congresses at the next-lower level. Therefore, the local people's deputies differ in their representativeness and power of representation because of the different forms of election, that is, those local people's deputies who are directly connected with particular constituencies and voters are legally elected directly by voters of particular electoral districts. Therefore, there exists a certain specific political representative relationship between the deputies on the one hand and the people and groups which voted for them on the other. As a legal principle, the deputies elected in this manner do not represent all residents in that locality in a general, abstract sense, but represent, to a greater extent, the voters of their electoral districts. Local people's deputies elected by a local people's congress at the next-lower level, not being directly connected with any specific voters or groups of voters, do not have a direct representative relationship with the residents in that locality, but represent only in a general sense all the "people" in the locality at that level, as representatives of the residents in that area as a whole. Therefore, the two categories of deputies are very different in their representativeness and scope of representation, with different legal status and political standing.

2. Election of Deputies

(1) Dividing of Electoral Districts

According to Article 22 of the Electoral Law, the number of deputies to the people's congresses in cities not divided into districts, municipal districts, counties, autonomous counties, townships, ethnic minority townships, and towns shall be allocated to the electoral districts, and elections shall be held in the electoral districts. Zoning of electoral districts may be decided according to the voters' residence or on the basis of production units, institutions or work units. [14] In actual elections, urban residents who belong to work units usually vote in the electoral district to which their work units belong, while those who do not belong to work units vote in the electoral districts of their residences. Electoral districts in cities and towns generally fall into the categories of independent electoral districts, that is, a work unit or a residential area constituting an electoral district; joint electoral districts, that is, several work units combining to form an electoral district; and mixed electoral districts, that is, electoral districts formed by a residential area mixed with several work units. Rural electoral districts are formed according to administrative divisions, as well as villages and villagers' groups. When rural areas elect deputies to a county people's congress, usually several villages combine to form an electoral district, while a village with an exceptionally large population or a township with an exceptionally small population may form a separate electoral district. In elections of deputies to the people's congress of a township, usually several villagers' groups combine to form an electoral district, while a villagers' group with a relatively large population or a village with a relatively small population may form a separate electoral district. According to Provisions of the Standing Committee of the National People's Congress for the Direct Election of Deputies to People's Congresses at or below the County Level, adopted in 1983, the zoning of electoral districts shall be decided on the basis of one to three deputies to be elected from each electoral district.

An electoral district is further divided into several voters' groups. A voters' group is a basic unit for organizing the voters and carrying out electoral activities. Voters elect one of themselves to be the head of the group and carry out certain electoral activities, such as nominating candidates for deputies and introducing them.

(2) Registration of Voters

Article 23 of the Electoral Law provides that the registration of voters shall involve ascertaining that the voter has reached the age of 18, and that he or she is not subject to restrictions on the freedom of the person in accordance with the law. In this latter case, registration shall be based on the decisions of the judicial organs (Current law provides that those who are under investigation, prosecution or trial on charges of endangering state security or any other serious criminal offence may, upon the decision of a people's procuratorate or people's court, be suspended from exercising their voting rights during detention). A voter shall be registered for one election only.

The roll of voters shall be made public 20 days prior to the date of the election by the election committee.

(3) Organization and Leadership of Elections

The leading organs and working organs for elections are different for direct and indirect elections. Election committees shall be established for direct elections, the members of which shall be appointed by the standing committees of the people's congresses at the corresponding or next-higher level, and which shall work under the direction of the standing committees of the people's congresses at the next-higher level. In the case of indirect elections, the standing committee of the people's congress at the corresponding level is the leading organ for the elections. The main reason for not establishing an election committee to direct indirect elections but making the standing committee of the people's congress act in its capacity instead is that such indirect elections are held within the congress at the corresponding level, and only the deputies to the people's congress at the corresponding level have the right to vote, and therefore the number of persons and scale involved are much smaller. Moreover, the electoral activities throughout the indirect elections are not directly related to the voters, nor is it necessary to zone electoral districts. Therefore, the workload of the leading organ for elections is not heavy. Moreover, the manner of indirect elections of deputies is not significantly different from those of other elections taking place in the congress at the corresponding level. Therefore, it is not hard for the standing committee of the people's congress to lead and organize the indirect elections.

The main functions of the standing committees of the local people's committees at different levels during elections are as follows: (1) The standing committee of the people's congress of a province, autonomous region or municipality directly under the central government decides on the number of deputies to the local people's congresses at different levels within its administrative area, draws up detailed regulations for implementation in accordance with the Electoral Law and presides over the election of deputies to the congress at the corresponding level. (2) The standing committee of the people's congress of a city divided into districts, municipal district, county or autonomous county appoints the members of the election committee at the corresponding level, and directs its work, and appoints members of election committees of townships, ethnic minority townships and towns, and directs their work.

The main functions of the election committees of a county (city or urban district at the county level) and a township (a town or autonomous township or autonomous town) are to preside over the election of deputies at the corresponding level; to set the election date; to carry out registration of voters, review voters' qualifications and make public the roll of voters; to handle any objection to the roll of voters and make relevant decisions; to divide the electoral districts for the election of deputies to the people's congress at the corresponding level, and allocate the number of deputies to be elected by each electoral district; to collect and make public lists of nominees for deputies; to decide, in accordance with the opinions of the majority of voters, upon a formal list of candidates for deputies and publish it; to send out personnel to preside over the elections at the polling stations or election meetings; and to decide whether or not election results are valid, and make public the list of elected deputies.

An election committee may establish working organs or agencies for handling specific matters related to elections.

(4) Nomination of Candidates for Deputies

The Electoral Law provides that candidates for deputies to local people's congresses at different levels shall be nominated on the basis of electoral districts or electoral units; and that political parties and people's organizations may either jointly or separately recommend candidates for deputies. A joint group of at least ten voters may also recommend candidates.

Those who submit recommendations shall inform the election committee or the presidium of the local people's congress meeting of their candidates' backgrounds. Where direct elections are held, the candidates for deputies nominated or recommended by political parties, people's organizations and voters shall, after being collected by the election committee, all be put on the list of nominees for candidates, without any replacement, addition or deletion by the election committee permitted.

The candidates on a formal list of candidates for deputies that has been determined after a preliminary election shall be listed in the order of the number of votes they have obtained in the preliminary election.

The number of candidates for deputies to be directly elected by the voters shall be from one third to 100 percent greater than the number of deputies to be elected. The number of candidates for deputies to be elected by local people's congresses at different levels to the next-higher level shall be 20 to 50 percent greater than the number of deputies to be elected. Candidates for deputies to the people's congresses to be directly elected by the voters shall be nominated by the voters in the various electoral districts, and by the various political parties and people's organizations. The election committee shall collect and publish, 15 days prior to the date of the election, the list of nominees for deputies for repeated deliberation, discussion and consultation by voter groups in the respective electoral districts, and shall decide, in accordance with the opinion of the majority of the voters, a formal list of candidates to be made public five days prior to the date of the election. When a local people's congress at or above the county level is to elect deputies to a people's congress at the next-higher level, the presidium of the people's congress meeting at the said level shall distribute the list of the candidates nominated by the various political parties, people's organizations and deputies to all the deputies for deliberation and discussion, and decide, in accordance with the opinion of the majority of the deputies, upon the formal list of candidates.

The election committee or the presidium of the local people's congress meeting shall brief the voters or deputies on the backgrounds of the candidates for deputies. The political parties, people's organizations and voters that have nominated candidates may brief voters on those candidates at group meetings of voters or deputies. However, such briefings may not be held on the day of the election.

(5) Voting and Announcement of Voting Results

Where voters directly elect deputies to people's congresses at the county and townships (town) levels, polling stations shall be set up and mobile polling boxes provided in each electoral district, or election meetings shall be held. Polling stations shall be generally set up or election meetings held according to electoral districts and presided over by the election committee.

Elections shall be by secret ballot. A voter may entrust another voter to write his or her ballot or entrust him or her with a proxy vote. A voter shall not stand proxy for more than three persons.

When balloting has been concluded, scrutineers and vote-counters, and those sent by the election committee to preside over the balloting shall check the number of people who voted against the number of votes cast, and make a record of this. The record shall be signed by the scrutineers. An election shall be valid if the number of votes cast is equal to or less than the number of people who voted; it shall be null and void if the number of votes cast is greater than the number of people who voted. Whether or not an election is valid must be announced immediately; when an election is not valid, another one must be held. After the validity of an election has been determined, the votes shall be counted. A ballot shall be valid if an equal number of candidates or fewer candidates are voted for than the number of deputies to be elected.

In a direct election of deputies to the people's congresses, candidates for deputies shall be elected only if they have obtained more than half of the votes cast, provided that more than half of all the voters in an electoral district cast their votes. In an indirect election of deputies to the people's congresses, candidates for deputies shall be elected only if they have obtained more than half of the votes of all the deputies. Where the number of candidates who have obtained more than half of the votes exceeds the number of deputies to be elected, the ones who have obtained more votes shall be elected. Where the number of votes for some candidates is tied, making it impossible to determine the ones to be elected, another round of balloting shall be conducted for these candidates to resolve the tie, and the ones who have obtained more votes shall be elected. If the number of elected deputies who have obtained more than half of the votes is less than the number of deputies to be elected, another round of balloting shall be held among the remaining candidates, and the ones who have obtained more votes than others shall be elected. However, the number of votes they have obtained shall not be less than one third of the votes cast.

The election committee, upon the completion of the vote counting, shall determine whether or not the result of an election is valid, and shall make an announcement to that effect accordingly.

3. The Main Functions and Powers of Local People's Congresses at Different Levels

(1) Functions and Powers When the Congress Is in Session

a) The power to put forward bills, proposals, suggestions, criticism and opinions

A group of ten or more deputies to a people's congress at or above the county level has the right to put forward bills and proposals to the congress at the corresponding level within the scope of the functions and powers of the congress at the said level. A group of five or more deputies to a congress at the level of a township or town has the right to put forward bills and proposals to the congress at the corresponding level within the scope of the functions and powers of the congress at the said level.

Deputies to a people's congress at or above the county level have the right to advance suggestions, criticism and opinions to the congress at the corresponding level and its standing committee concerning various aspects of work in its administrative area. Deputies to a people's congress at the level of a township or town have the right to advance suggestions, criticism and opinions to the congress at the corresponding level concerning various aspects of work within its administrative area. The standing committee (or the presidium in the case of a township or town) shall refer such suggestions, criticisms and opinions to the relevant departments for study and disposal, which shall be responsible for replies.

b) The power to nominate

A joint group of ten or more deputies to a people's congress at or above the county level may nominate candidates for members of the standing committee of the congress at the corresponding level, and the choice of the leaders of the people's government at the corresponding level, and the president of the people's court and chief procurator of the people's procuratorate at the corresponding level.

A candidate recommended by a joint group of ten or more deputies must be referred to all deputies for deliberation and discussion. Then the presidium shall decide, in accordance with the opinion of the majority of the deputies, whether or not to place the said candidate on the formal list of candidates. During the balloting, deputies may vote for any other deputy or voter.

c) The power to propose removals

When a local people's congress at or above the county level meets, one tenth or more deputies may jointly make a proposal for the removal from office of any member of the standing committee of the congress at the said level, leader of the government, president of the people's court and chief procurator of the people's procuratorate at the said level. The proposal shall be submitted to the congress for deliberation and discussion. When the people's congress of a township or town is in session, the presidium or a joint group of one fifth or more deputies may make a proposal for the removal from office of the head or deputy head of a township or a town. The proposal shall be submitted by the presidium to the congress for deliberation and discussion.

d) The power to address questions and make inquiries

When a local people's congress meets, a joint group of ten or more deputies may table a bill addressing questions in writing to the people's government at the corresponding level and its departments, the people's court or the people's procuratorate at the corresponding level, which shall be referred by the presidium to the organs addressed. The organs addressed shall be responsible for answering the questions during the session.

When a local people's congress is deliberating a bill, deputies have the right to make inquiries to the relevant department and acquire relevant information in order to facilitate their deliberation. The departments concerned must dispatch people to the congress to give explanations.

e) Special habeas corpus

No deputy to a local people's congress at or above the county level may be arrested or placed on criminal trial without the consent of the presidium of the congress at the corresponding level when it is in session, or without the consent of its standing committee when the congress is not in session. If a deputy is caught in an illegal act and detained, the public security organ executing the detention shall report the matter to the people's congress at the corresponding level or its standing committee immediately. If any other restriction on personal freedom prescribed by law is imposed on a deputy to a people' congress at or above the county level, it shall be subject to the approval of the presidium of the congress at the corresponding level or of its standing committee.

If a deputy to a people's congress of a township is arrested or placed under criminal trial, or subjected to any other restriction on personal freedom prescribed by law, the executing organ shall report the matter to the congress at the township level immediately.

f) The right of exemption from liability

Deputies to local people's congresses at and above the county level and the members of their standing committees shall hold no legal liability for their speeches or votes at meetings of the people's congresses and their standing committees. This right of exemption for liability shall cover speeches and votes at congress sessions, joint group meetings, group meetings and meetings of special committees (or working committees). Deputies shall hold no legal liability for any statement in their speeches or votes.

g) The right to ask for necessary material conveniences

When a deputy attends meetings of people's congresses or performs functions as a deputy, he has the right to receive necessary material help, such as traveling expenses. The unit to which the deputy belongs must ensure him the needed time, salary and other benefits of the unit on a normal basis. Deputies with no fixed income in wages or salaries shall, for the performance of their functions as deputies, be appropriately subsidized by the government financial office at the corresponding level. And the funds for a deputy's activities shall be included in the budget of the governments at the corresponding levels.

The standing committees of local people's congresses at different levels shall, in various ways, maintain contact with the deputies to the people's congresses at the corresponding levels.

(2) Functions and Powers When the Congress Is Not in Session

a) Right of Inspection

When a people's congress is not in session, deputies have the right to participate in study tours on special topics and inspection tours organized by the standing committee of the congress at the corresponding level, with a view to acquiring information on the work of the government, court and procuratorate at the corresponding level, and collecting voters' opinions, suggestions and demands.

b) Ties with voters and the electoral units that elected them

Deputies shall maintain contact, regular or otherwise, with voters and the electoral units that elected them in various ways, such as holding meetings or paying visits, to listen to voters' opinions and demands; and to convey voters' opinions and demands to the standing committees of the people's congresses and governments at the corresponding levels.

c) Right to attend other meetings as non-voting participants

Deputies to people's congresses at and above the county level have the right to attend, upon invitation, meetings of the standing committees of the people's congresses at their respective corresponding levels as non-voting participants.

Deputies to the people's congresses at the level of a province or a city divided into districts may attend, as non-voting participants, meetings of the people's congresses of the electoral units that elected them, and may also attend in such capacity meetings of the standing committees of the people's congresses of the electoral units that elected them. They may also attend, upon invitation, meetings of special committees of the people's congresses at their respective corresponding levels.

d) Right to propose the convening of an interim congress

Deputies to local people's congresses at all levels have the right to propose, in accordance with the stipulations of the law, the convening of interim sessions of the people's congresses at their respective corresponding levels.

4. Non-voting Participants

Members of local governments, presidents of people's courts and chief procurators of people's procuratorates at different levels may attend, as non-voting participants, meetings of the people's congresses at their respective corresponding levels, and responsible members of other relevant organs and organizations may, with the approval of the presidiums of the congresses, attend meetings of the people's congresses at their respective corresponding levels as non-voting participants. There are no further legal stipulations in this respect.

II. Number of Deputies to Local People's Congresses at Different Levels and Sizes of Local People's Congresses at Different Levels

According to articles 9 and 10 of the Electoral Law, the methods of determining the number of deputies to local people's congresses are as follows:

(1) The number of deputies to local people's congresses at different levels are to be determined by the standing committees of the people's

congresses of provinces, autonomous regions and municipalities directly under the Central Government independently;

(2) The number of deputies shall be appropriate;

(3) The various ethnic groups, areas and walks of life must have an appropriate number of deputies to the people's congresses at various levels. In areas where minority ethnic groups live in compact communities, every minority ethnic group must be represented at the local people's congresses. The number of their deputies shall be determined and allocated in accordance with the ratios prescribed in the Electoral Law. However, a minority nationality with an exceptionally small population must have at least one deputy.

The Electoral Law as revised in 1995 at the 18th meeting of the Standing Committee of the Eighth NPC has stipulations on the specific numbers of deputies to the local people's congresses at different levels. They are as follows: The base number of deputies to the people's congress of a province or an autonomous region is 350, and one more deputy may be added for every 150,000 people, with the total number of deputies for a province or autonomous region ranging generally from 350 to 1,000. The base number of deputies to the people's congress of a municipality directly under the central government is 350, and one more deputy may be added for every 25,000 people, with the total number of deputies of a municipality directly under the central government generally ranging from 625 to 790. The base number of deputies to the people's congress of a city divided into districts, or an autonomous prefecture is 240, and one more deputy may be added for every 25,000 people, with the total number of deputies to the people's congress of a city divided into districts, or an autonomous prefecture ranging generally from 240 to 650. The base number of deputies to the people's congress of a county, an autonomous county, a city not divided into districts, or a municipal district is 120, and one more deputy may be added for every 5,000 people, with the total number of deputies to the people's congress of a county, an autonomous county, a city not divided into districts, or a municipal district ranging generally from 120 to 450. The base number of deputies to the people's congress of a township, an ethnic minority township or a town is 40, and one more deputy may be added for every 5,000 people, with the total number of deputies to the people's congress of a township, an autonomous township or a town ranging generally from 40 to 130.

III. Organizations of the Local People's Congresses at Different Levels

1. The Sessions of the Local People's Congresses at Different Levels

(1) Term of office of local people's congresses at different levels

The term of office of the people's congresses of provinces, autonomous regions, municipalities directly under the central government, autonomous prefectures, and cities divided into districts, which are all elected indirectly, shall be five years. The term of office of the people's congresses of counties, autonomous counties, cities not divided into districts, municipal districts, townships, autonomous townships and towns, which are all elected directly, shall be three years.

(2) The sessions of the local people's congresses at different levels and their main agenda

The sessions of the local people's congresses at different levels are the main form of activities of the local people's congresses at different levels, as well as the main form for them to exercise their functions and powers.

Local people's congresses at or above the county level shall meet in session at least once a year; in special circumstances, a session of a local people's congress may be conveyed at any time upon the proposal of more than one fifth of its deputies.

A local people's congress generally lasts for four to five days, during which at least six reports must be examined, and the time for hearing reports and voting generally takes four half-days.

A preliminary meeting shall be held for each session of a local people's congress at or above the county level. The preliminary meeting for the first session of a local people's congress shall be presided over by the standing committee of the preceding people's congress at the corresponding level. A preliminary meeting must be held prior to the convening of the formal session, and the main items on its agenda are to elect the presidium and secretary-general of the session, examine and adopt the agenda for the session, and elect working organs to be set up in accordance with the needs of the session.

When a local people's congress at or above the county level meets, its session shall be presided over by the executive chairmen of the presidium. The choice of the executive chairmen of the presidium is decided on at the first meeting of the presidium in accordance with the proposal of the standing committee of the preceding people's congress.

When a local people's congress of a township, a ethnic minority township or a town meets, its session shall be presided over by the presidium elected by the congress.

The main functions and powers of local people's congresses at different levels are: to examine and approve the work reports of the people's governments at the corresponding levels; to examine and approve the reports by the planning commissions of the people's governments at the corresponding level on the implementation of the local national economic and social development plan for the previous year and the draft plan for the following year; to examine and approve the reports by the finance departments of the people's governments at corresponding levels on the implementation of the budgets for the previous year and the draft budget for following year; to examine and approve the reports on the work of the standing committees of the people's congresses at corresponding levels; to examine and approve the reports on the work of the people's courts and people's procuratorates at corresponding levels; to examine and adopt local rules and regulations within their administrative areas; and to elect and remove from office members of the standing committees of the people's congresses at corresponding levels, and responsible members of the people's governments, people's courts and people's procuratorates at corresponding levels.

2. Standing Committees of the Local People's Congresses at or above the County Level

(1) The standing committees of the local people's congresses at or above county level

The standing committee of a local people's congress at or above the county level is the permanent organ of that people's congress, and exercises most of the functions and powers of the congress when the latter is not in session.

The standing committee of a local people's congress is elected by that people's congress, is responsible to it, reports on its work to it and is subject to supervision by it. The standing committee of the people's congress of a province, autonomous region or municipality directly under the central government is composed of the chairman, vice-chairmen, secretary-general and members, all of whom are elected from among the deputies to the people's congress at the corresponding level. The standing committee of the people's congress of a county, autonomous county, or a city not divided into districts is also elected by the people's congress at the corresponding level, but the post of secretary-general is not instituted.

The number of members on the standing committees of local people's congresses of the provinces, autonomous regions and municipalities directly under the central governments ranges from 35 to 65, and up to 85 for a province with an exceptionally large population; 13 to 35 for standing committees of people's congresses of autonomous prefectures and cities divided into districts, and up to 45 for autonomous prefectures and cities divided into districts, which have exceptionally large populations; and 11 to 19 for counties, autonomous counties and cities not divided into districts, and up to 29 for counties, autonomous counties and cities not divided into districts, which have exceptionally large populations.

The chairman, vice-chairmen, secretary-general and members of the standing committee of a local people's congress at or above the county level may not hold any office in an administrative, judicial or procuratorial organ of the state.

The standing committee of a local people's congress shall have the same term of office as that of the congress.

(2) Meetings of the standing committees of local people's congresses at or above the county level

Meetings of the standing committee of a local people's congress at or above the county level shall be convened by its chairman, and held at least once every other month. Resolutions of a standing committee shall be adopted by a majority vote of more than half of its members. The way of voting shall be decided by the standing committee independently, either by a show of hands or a secret ballot. The general practice is, when it comes to voting on personnel appointments and removals, vote is usually by secret ballot, while a show of hands is used in adopting resolutions on other matters.

(3) The council of chairmen of the standing committee of a people's congress at or above the county level

The council of chairmen of the standing committee of a people's congress of a province, autonomous region, or municipality directly under the central government, or a city divided into districts is composed of the chairman, vice-chairmen and secretary-general of that standing committee; while the standing committee chairman and vice-chairmen of people's congress of a county, autonomous county, or a city not divided into districts form a council of chairmen. Charged with the day-to-day work of the standing committee, the council of chairmen's main functions and powers are:

a) To propose partial nominations for members of special committees. When the people's congress is not in session, its standing committee may appoint individual additional vice-chairmen and members of special committees, upon the nomination by the council of chairmen to be adopted at the meeting of the standing committee.

b) To nominate the candidates for presidents of the intermediate people's courts. The standing committee of a people's congress at the provincial level has the power to appoint or remove from office the presidents of the intermediate people's courts, which are established in areas within a province or autonomous region.

c) To decide, when the standing committee is in session, whether or not to refer inquiries put forward by members of the standing committee to the relevant government, judicial or procuratorial organs. A group of five or more standing committee members of the people's congress of a province, autonomous region, municipality directly under the central government, autonomous prefecture, or a city divided into districts or a group of three or more standing committee members of a people's congress at the county level may submit to the standing committee written proposals for addressing questions to the people's government, people's court or people's procuratorate at the corresponding level. The council of chairmen shall decide whether to refer the proposals to the organs addressed for a decision.

3. Agencies of Local People's Congresses at the Provincial Level

Such agencies are working organs of a people's congress at the provincial level, which its standing committee has established in the seats of the prefectural offices — prefectural liaison offices (or section or group) of the people's congress.

A prefectural liaison office of the people's congress at the provincial level shall not constitute an organ of state power, but is mainly charged with communication between the standing committee of the people's congress at the provincial level and those of the people's congresses of the counties under the jurisdiction of the prefectures. Its main functions are to gather information about the implementation in that area of the Constitution, laws, rules and regulations of the state, as well as the resolutions and decisions by the NPC and the provincial people's congress, and report to the standing committee of the provincial people's congress; to relay relevant guidelines of the standing committee of the provincial people's congress to the standing committees of the people's congresses of the counties in that area for implementation, and carry out various assignments of the standing committee of the provincial people's congress; to follow the work of the standing committees of the people's congresses of the counties in that area and help with the resolution of difficulties and problems they may encounter in their work; to get relevant departments of the administrative office to handle in a responsible manner bills, proposals, criticisms, suggestions and opinions put forward by deputies to the provincial people's congress at its meetings, and make timely reports on the progress of this work to the standing committee of the people's congress at the provincial (autonomous regional) level.

IV. Main Functions and Powers of Local People's Congresses at Different Levels and Their Standing Committees

The basic functions and powers of the local people's congresses at and above the county level and their standing committees are to discuss and decide on major issues; and exercise the power of election, appointment and removal, local legislative power and the power of supervision. The local people's congresses at and above the county level shall exercise these functions and powers, and when they are not in session, their standing committees shall exercise these functions and powers.

1. The Power to Discuss and Decide on Major Issues

From the perspective of legal stipulations, the local people's congresses at and above the county level and their standing committees have the power to discuss and decide on major issues in political, economic, educational, scientific, cultural, public health, and civil and ethnic affairs in their administrative areas, and the resolutions and decisions they make on such issues shall have the highest authority and the legal binding power.

2. Power of Election, Appointment and Removal

(1) The power of election, appointment and removal of the people's

congresses at and above the county level

The people's congresses at and above the county level shall elect and remove from office component members of the standing committees at the corresponding levels, the chairmen, vice-chairmen and members of various special committees, and deputies to the people's congresses at the next-higher level; elect and remove from office governors, deputy governors, chairmen and vice-chairmen of autonomous regions, mayors and deputy mayors, prefects and deputy prefects, and heads and deputy heads of counties and districts; and elect and remove from office presidents of people's courts and chief procurators of people's procuratorates at the corresponding levels. However, the election or removal of the chief procurator of a people's procuratorate shall be reported to the chief procurator of the people's procuratorate at the next-higher level, who shall submit it to the standing committee of the people's congress at the same level for approval.

A member of the standing committee of a local people's congress at or above the county level, a leading person of a local people's government, the president of a people's court or the chief procurator of a people's procuratorate at or above the county level may submit resignation to the people's congress at the corresponding level, which shall decide whether or not to accept the resignation. A resignation of the chief procurator of a people's procuratorate must be reported to the chief procurator of the people's procuratorate at the next-higher level, who shall refer it to the standing committee of the people's congress at the corresponding level for approval.

(2) The power of election, appointment and removal of the standing committees of the local people's congresses at and above the county level

The standing committees of the local people's congresses at and above the county level shall exercise the power to decide, upon the nomination by the governor, chairman of the autonomous region, mayor, prefect, or head of the county or district, on the appointment or removal of the secretary-general, and the department and bureau directors, commission chairmen and section chiefs of the people's governments at the corresponding levels and to report such decisions to the people's government at the next-higher level for the record.

The standing committees of the local people's congresses at and above the county level shall exercise the power to decide, when their congresses are not in session, on the appointment or removal of individual deputy governors, vice-chairmen of an autonomous region, deputy mayors, deputy prefects and deputy heads of the counties or districts; and when the head of a local government, president of a court or the chief procurator of a procuratorate is unable to perform his or her duties, to choose a person from among the deputy heads of the government, court and procuratorate at the corresponding level to act on his or her behalf. The choice of an acting chief procurator must be reported to the people's procuratorate and the standing committee of the people's congress at the next-higher level for the record.

They shall appoint or remove vice-presidents, chief judges and associate chief judges of divisions, members of the judicial committees and judges of the people's courts, appoint or remove deputy chief procurators, members of the procuratorial committees and procurators of the people's procuratorates, and approve the appointment or removal of the chief procurators of the people's procuratorates at the next lower level.

The standing committee of a people's congress of a province, autonomous region, or municipality directly under the central government shall, upon nomination by its council of chairmen, decide on the appointment or removal of presidents of intermediate people's courts established within a province, autonomous region or municipality directly under the central government and, upon nomination by the chief procurator of the people's procuratorate of a province, autonomous region or municipality directly under the central government, decide on the appointment or removal of chief procurators of branch people's procuratorates.

The standing committees of the people's congresses at and above the county level shall decide, when the people's congresses are not in session, on the removal from office of individual deputy leading members of governments (deputy governors, vice-chairmen of the autonomous region, deputy mayors, deputy prefects and deputy heads of the county or district); and decide on the removal from office of personnel it has appointed among other members of the governments, vice-presidents, chief judges and associate chief judges of divisions, members of the judicial committees and judges of the people's courts, deputy chief procurators, members of the procuratorial committees and procurators of the people's procuratorates, presidents of intermediate people's courts and chief procurators of branch people's procuratorates, all at the corresponding level.

They shall conduct by-elections, when the people's congresses are not in session, in the event that a post of deputy to the people's congress at the next-higher level becomes vacant, and remove from office individual deputies.

They shall accept, when the people's congresses are not in session, the resignation of component members of the people's congress standing committees, leading persons of the governments, presidents of the people's courts and chief procurators of the people's procuratorates at the corresponding levels that the people's congresses at the corresponding levels have elected, and decide whether or not to accept the resignation. Once a decision to accept the resignation is made, the standing committee shall report it to the people's congress at the corresponding level for the record. However, the resignation of the chief procurator must be reported to the chief procurator of the people's procuratorate at the next-higher level, who shall submit it to the standing committee at that same level for approval.

3. Local Legislative Power

In accordance with relevant stipulations in the Organic Law of the Local People's Congresses and Local People's Governments of the People's Republic of China, local rules and regulations may be formulated by the people's congresses of the provinces, autonomous regions, and municipalities directly under the central government, and the people's congresses of cities where provincial and autonomous regional people's governments are located and the people's congresses of relatively larger cities with the approval of the State Council, and by their standing committees when the congresses are not in session, in the light of the political, economic and cultural features of their respective administrative areas.

(1) Scope of local rules and regulations

a) Detailed rules and regulations and methods formulated for the implementation of state laws;

b) Local rules and regulations enacted upon authorization by the NPC and the law;

c) Rules and regulations enacted in the absence of state laws, local rules and regulations which the administrative areas in question need badly; and

d) Local rules and regulations enacted on issues peculiar to the localities which do not deserve the enactment of national laws.

(2) Procedure for enacting local rules and regulations

a) Submission of bills and proposals on local rules and regulations

According to the Organic Law of the Local People's Congresses and Local People's Governments, the standing committees of local people's congresses at and above the county level, special committees, governments at the corresponding level and a joint group of ten or more deputies to the people's congresses of a province, autonomous region or municipality directly under the central government, or a city divided into districts may submit bills and proposals for formulating local rules and regulations to the people's congresses at the corresponding level; special committees and a group of five or more members of the standing committee may submit bills and proposals for formulating local rules and regulations to the standing committee. A draft of local rules and regulations drawn up by working departments of the government must be first adopted at an executive meeting of the government and signed by the governor before it is sent as a bill to the provincial people's congress and its standing committee.

b) Deliberations on bills on local rules and regulations

The presidium of a people's congress shall decide whether to refer a bill on local rules and regulations directly to the congress for deliberation or to first refer it to a relevant special committee for deliberation and a report before deciding whether to submit it to the congress for deliberation. Those who have submitted such bills and proposals shall make explanations on the bills and proposals, which shall then be sent to the delegations for discussion, deliberation and comment. The organs that have sponsored such bills and proposals shall send representatives to hear opinions from the delegations and answer their inquiries. The bills and proposals are to be revised by relevant special committees on the basis of the discussions.

c) Adoption of bills

The revised bills on local rules and regulations shall be read out at the congress meetings accompanied by explanations on the revisions, and are to be adopted by a majority vote of more than half of the deputies to the people's congress or members of the standing committee. The Organic Law of the Local People's Congresses and Local People's Governments has no specific stipulations on the manner of voting, although the usual practice is by a show of hands. There are two forms of adoption: formal adoption, which means that a bill so adopted shall immediately be promulgated for implementation; and adoption in principle, which means that a bill so adopted needs individual revisions or textual changes before it is promulgated for implementation.

d) Reporting of local rules and regulations for the record

Local rules and regulations formulated by the people's congresses of the provinces, autonomous regions and municipalities directly under the central government shall be reported to the Standing Committee of the NPC and the State Council for the record. Local rules and regulations formulated by the cities where provincial and autonomous regional governments are located and relatively larger cities with the approval of the State Council shall be reported to the standing committees of the people's congresses of the provinces and autonomous regions for approval before implementation, and be submitted to the Standing Committee of the NPC and the State Council for the record.

e) Promulgation of local rules and regulations

Local rules and regulations are generally published in the gazettes of the standing committees of the local people's congresses, as well as in local newspapers and gazettes of the local governments at the corresponding level. Local rules and regulations the implementation of which does not require a period of preparation shall go into force on the date of promulgation; and local rules and regulations the implementation of which requires a period of preparation shall have a clause on the date of their going into force.

4. Power of Supervision

(1) Scope of supervision

a) To annul the decisions and orders of the local people's governments at the corresponding level that contravene the Constitution, law, and administrative rules and regulations of the state, and to correct major violations of the law by the governments at the corresponding level or to get them to correct such violations;

b) To raise opinions with the court or procuratorate at the corresponding level over decisions, judgments and rulings that do not conform to the stipulations of law and to get the court or procuratorate to correct them;

c) To correct acts of appointing and removing personnel in violation of legal provisions by the government, court or procuratorate at the corresponding level or to get them to correct such acts; and

d) To remove or to dismiss state functionaries from office for serious violations of the law or neglect of duty.

(2) Forms of supervision

a) Hearing work reports of local government, judicial and procuratorial organs and holding deliberations on them. This is the principal and basic form of supervision. Generally speaking, there are two forms of reports: annual hearing of and deliberation on regular work reports; and work reports concerning special issues. Relevant resolutions and decisions are made after hearing such reports;

b) Addressing questions and making inquiries. When a local people's congress meets in session, a group of ten or more deputies may make a written proposal for addressing questions to the government, court or procuratorate at the corresponding level; a group of five or more members of the standing committee of the people's congress of a province, autonomous region, municipality directly under the central government, autonomous prefecture or a city divided into districts, and a group of three or more members of the standing committee of a people's congress at the county level may make a proposal to the standing committee for addressing questions to the government, court and procuratorate at the corresponding level.

When a people's congress or its standing committee is deliberating bills and proposals, deputies or members of the standing committee may make inquiries to the relevant state organs, which must answer their inquiries.

c) Setting up committees for investigation on specific questions

The standing committees of the local people's congresses at and above the county level have the power to establish specific committees for investigation on certain questions and conduct special investigations into major cases of legal violations and neglect of duty, or other major issues, and make corresponding resolutions on the basis of the investigation results.

d) Investigations and inspections

Deputies to a local people's congress or members of its standing committees are organized to conduct investigations and inspections on some aspects of work of the local government, court and procuratorate and advance opinions on it. They may submit proposals concerning important issues to the people's congresses or their standing committees for deliberation.

e) Handling appeals and opinions from citizens concerning state organs and state functionaries. The standing committee may pick what it deems important from among the appeals and opinions from the citizens, organize special investigations, send its opinions to relevant departments, and see to it that they act upon them.

V. The Functions and Powers of the People's Congresses in Autonomous Areas and Their Standing Committees

The people's congress of an autonomous region corresponds to a local organ of state power at a provincial level. The people's congress of an autonomous prefecture corresponds to a local organ of state power at the level of a city divided into districts. The people's congress of an autonomous county (banner) corresponds to a local organ of state power at the county level.

The people's congresses and their standing committees in autonomous areas, in addition to exercising the functions and powers of the local people's congresses and standing committees at the corresponding level, may also exercise the right of autonomy as prescribed by the Constitution of the People's Republic of China and the Law on Regional National Autonomy. The people's congresses in ethnic minority autonomous areas and their standing committees exercise the right of autonomy mainly as follows: by formulating, in the light of the political, economic and cultural characteristics of their ethnic autonomous areas, provisions that contain adaptations or additions to the state laws; and by formulating autonomy regulations and separate regulations.

Regulations on autonomy are regulations the people's congress in an ethnic minority autonomous area formulates in accordance with the Constitution and the Law of the People's Republic of China on Regional Ethnic Autonomy, and in the light of the special local political, economic and culturalconditions, and the rules for its organ of self-government in managing local affairs. Separate regulations are formulated by the people's congress in an autonomous area to solve special problems in order to protect the local characteristics.

The regulations on autonomy and separate regulations of an autonomous region shall be reported to the Standing Committee of the NPC for approval before going into force. Those of an autonomous prefecture or an autonomous county (banner) shall be reported to the standing committee of the people's congress of a province or an autonomous region for approval before going into force, and to the Standing Committee of the NPC for the record.

VI. The Functions and Powers of the People's Congresses of Townships, Autonomous Townships and Towns

The people's congresses of townships, autonomous townships and towns shall be elected for a term of three years, with a presidium, a chairman and vice-chairmen. The presidium shall be responsible for convening the congress.

The functions and powers of the people's congresses of townships and towns include:

a) The power to deliberate and decide on major issues

The people's congresses of townships, autonomous townships and towns decide, in accordance with state plans, on plans for the development of the economy, cultural affairs and public services in their respective administrative areas; examine and approve the budgets of their respective administrative areas as well as the reports on the implementation of the budgets; and decide on plans for civil affairs in their respective administrative areas.

b) The power of election, appointment and removal

The people's congresses of townships, autonomous townships and towns have the power to elect or remove from office heads and deputy heads of townships and towns.

The procedure for elections is: the candidates for the choice of heads and deputy heads of townships and towns shall be nominated by the presidiums of the people's congresses of townships and towns, or a joint group of ten or more deputies.

When a people's congress of a township, autonomous township or town is in session, the presidium and more than one fifth of the deputies to the congress may jointly put forward a proposal for removing from office any of the above personnel. A proposal for removal shall be submitted by the presidium to the congress for deliberation.

c) Power of supervision

The people's congresses of townships, autonomous townships and towns examine reports on the work of the governments of townships, autonomous townships and towns, annul all inappropriate decisions and orders, and have the power to remove and dismiss from office component members of such governments.

Notes:

[1] "General Principles," *Constitution of the People's Republic of China.* Beijing: Foreign Languages Press, 1999, Fourth Edition (with Chinese text), p. 8.

[2] See "NPC Chairman Li Peng on Some Important Issues Concerning the System of the People's Congresses and the Work of the People's Congresses," *Studies of the People's Congresses*, Lanzhou, Issue No. 1, 2000, pp. 4-6.

[3] Quoted from *Recollections of Some Major Policy Decisions and Events*, Book One, by Bo Yibo. Beijing: Central Party School Press, 1991, p. 29.

[4] *Selected Works of Deng Xiaoping, Vol. 3.* Beijing: Foreign Languages Press, 1994, p. 299.

[5] Quoted from "NPC Chairman Li Peng on Some Important Issues Concerning the System of the People's Congresses and the Work of the People's Congresses," *Studies of the People's Congresses*, Lanzhou, Issue No. 1, 2000, pp. 4-6.

[6] Research Office of the General Office of the Standing Committee of the NPC: *Documents and Data of the People's Congresses of the People's Republic of China, 1949—1990.* Beijing: China Democracy and Legal System Publishing House, March 1991, p. 623.

[7] See "NPC Chairman Li Peng on Some Important Issues Concerning the System of the People's Congresses and the Work of the People's Congresses," *Studies of the People's Congresses*, Lanzhou, Issue No. 1, 2000, pp. 4-6.

[8] The number of deputies to the successive NPCs varies. The number stood at 1,226 at the first and second Congresses, 3,040 at the third, 2,885 at the fourth and 3,497 at the fifth. The Electoral Law of the National People's Congress and the Local People's Congresses at Different Levels of the People's Republic of China adopted in 1979 stipulated for the first time that the number of NPC deputies should be 3,500. A decision made at the Fifth Session of the Fifth NPC in 1982 set the number at around 3,000. At its 18th meeting, the Standing Committee of the Sixth NPC made amendments to the Electoral Law, stating that the number shall not exceed 3,000. It is believed that before there were any legal stipulations, there had been no sound basis for setting the number of NPC deputies. Please see relevant speeches by Peng Zhen, carried in the *Collection of Documents and Data of the National People's Congress of the People's Republic of China, 1949-1990*, compiled by the Research Office of the General Office of the Standing Committee of the NPC. Beijing: China Democracy and Legal System Press, March 1991, pp. 152-154.

[9] This figure is the result of tabulation based on the population censuses, the number of NPC deputies and the respective percentages.

[10] Article 59 of the *Constitution of the People's Republic of China.* Beijing: Foreign Languages Press, fourth edition (with Chinese text), 1999, p. 27.

[11] Article 2 of "The Electoral Law of the NPC and the Local People's Congresses at Different Levels of the People's Republic of China."

[12] Liu Han and Li Lin: "Twenty Years of Achievements in the Building of China's Legal System and Its Prospects," *Qiu Shi* (Seeking Truth), Issue No. 23, 1998, pp. 12-15.

[13] Article 62 of the *Constitution of the People's Republic of China.* Beijing: Foreign Languages Press, fourth edition (with Chinese text), 1999, p. 30.

[14] *The Laws of the People's Republic of China (1983-1986).* Beijing: Foreign Languages Press, 1987, p. 322.

Chapter Four

THE STATE COUNCIL

The State Council of the People's Republic of China, namely the central people's government, is the executive body of the highest organ of state power and the highest state administrative body.

The State Council of the People's Republic of China was established in 1954. Before that, the highest organ of state administration was the Government Administrative Council of the Central People's Government. The first session of the National People's Congress (NPC) held in 1954 established the State Council to function as the Central People's Government in accordance with the stipulations of the Constitution. From then on, the State Council has existed as the highest state administrative body in both form and functions.

The nature and functions of the State Council in the system of state organs are stipulated in a number of laws and regulations. At present, the main relevant laws are the Constitution of the People's Republic of China and the Organic Law of the State Council.

Section 1 The Nature, Position and Power of the State Council

I. The Nature and Position of the State Council

1. The State Council Is the Executive Body of the Highest Organ of State Power

Article 85 of the Constitution stipulates, "The State Council, that is, the Central People's Government, of the People's Republic of China is the executive body of the highest organ of state power; it is the highest body of state administration."[1]

The National People's Congress is the highest organ of state power under the people's congress system. Only the NPC has the overall, unified and supreme state power, and the other state organs are legally partial and specific executive bodies of the highest organ of state power. Strictly speaking, there is no fundamental division of work or relations of check and balance between the highest organ of state power and the other state organs. Therefore, the State Council does not enjoy a position or authority equal to the highest organ of state power, and legally it is subordinate to the highest organ of state power, ranking as a second-grade state organ.

On the other hand, although the Constitution stipulates that the State Council is the executive body of the highest organ of state power, neither the Constitution nor other relevant laws stipulate specifically the exact ways or channels for the State Council to act as the executive body; and the State Council has no specific directives on how to exercise or how to differentiate between its executive powers and its responsibilities. That means that the present stipulations do not make clear the relationship between the decision-making powers of the highest organ of state power and the executive powers of the State Council. In a word, the nature of the State Council as an executive body of the highest organ of state power needs to be further clarified or the stipulations shall be cancelled.

2. The State Council Is a State Organ Produced without Electoral Procedure

Of the main state organs, the State Council is the only one the members of which are decided without electoral procedure. The premier of the State Council is decided by the NPC based on nomination by the state president. It is similar to the cabinet system in some other countries, where the leader of the majority party becomes the premier of the state. So, it is unnecessary for the state to elect the premier through some other method; it only needs a formal and symbolic procedure to confirm the leader of the majority party as premier by the head of state. The NPC system is similar to parliamentarianism in form, and the State Council is responsible to the NPC. So the method of naming the premier under the NPC system is almost the same as that of the countries exercising parliamentarianism. The difference is that in the process of producing the premier of the State Council there is no competition between candidates. Yet, theoretically, nominating the premier has to embody the state's will and purpose. So he or she has to be nominated by a person who represents the state — the president.

Viewed from the practical angle, there is not much difference essentially between the "determining" of the premier and the election of the other leaders of the state organs. In fact, the only difference is that the premier is nominated by the president, while the power of nominating the candidates for leaders of the other state organizations is widely dispersed. Though the premier of the State Council is also decided by the NPC, the premier is directly linked with the president of the state as compared with other state organizations because the premier is nominated by him. The direct link between the premier and the president, on the one hand, relatively weakens the premier's political position, while on the other it also weakens the link between the State Council and the NPC. This puts the premier of the State Council in a strong and relatively unconventional political position. Since there is no substantial competition in the election of the premier, and the president does not hold real political power, the candidate for the premier must be a person with great political capability and influence.

3. The State Council Is the Highest Organ of State Administration

According to the stipulations of the Constitution, the State Council exercises unified leadership over the work of local organs of state administration at various levels throughout the country, and formulates the detailed division of functions and powers between the central government and the organs of state administration of provinces, autonomous regions, and municipalities directly under the central government.[2]

The Constitution places the State Council in the highest position among all the organs of state administration, giving the central government absolute and centralized power and authority. There is no distinct and legal division of power between the central government and local governments, which, fundamentally speaking, are established and exist as agencies of the central government. Therefore, the central government can exercise direct or indirect leadership over local governments at any place and level. In addition, the highest administrative position of the State Council also means that there are no administrative organs undertaking special tasks independent of the State Council. The State Council exercises all the administrative functions of the central government in a unified way. So the state administrative power is unified and centralized, and supreme.

It should be noted that all the administrative acts of the State Council are of the highest legal and political force, overriding all administrative acts of local governments. Therefore, the local governments have to follow the leadership of the central government — in the form of the State Council — all the time and in all circumstances.

II. The Functions and Powers of the State Council

According to the Constitution, the State Council has overall and unified direct powers to lead the political activities of the state, and indirect powers ensuring the exercise of the direct powers.

1. Direct Powers

(1) Enacting Administrative Rules and Issuing Orders

The State Council adopts administrative measures, enacts administrative rules and regulations, and issues decisions and orders in accordance with the Constitution and the law.

(2) Exercising Administrative Leadership over Subordinate Agencies and Local Governments

The State Council has the power of absolute leadership over the work of the various ministries and commissions under it, and the work of local governments at all levels.

The State Council adopts the premier responsibility system. It lays down the tasks and responsibilities for the various ministries and commissions and exercises unified leadership over their work. It establishes special departments to exercise jurisdiction over the administrative work of a national character that does not fall within the jurisdiction of any of the ministries and commissions.

The State Council exercises unified leadership over the work of local organs of state administration at all levels throughout the country, and lays down the detailed division of functions and powers between the central government and the organs of state administration of the provinces, autonomous regions and municipalities directly under the central government. It does not need to negotiate with any departments, including the local governments.

(3) Administrative Power

The State Council, the highest organ of the state administration, manages all administrative affairs of the country, including directing and administering economic affairs as well as urban and rural development; education, science, culture, public health, physical culture and family planning; civil affairs, public security, judicial administration and supervision and other related matters; buildup of national defense; affairs concerning national minorities, and safeguarding the equal rights of ethnic groups and the right of autonomy of the autonomous areas; approving the geographical divisions of provinces, autonomous regions, and municipalities directly under the central government, and the establishment and geographical divisions of autonomous prefectures, counties, autonomous counties and cities; examining and deciding on the size of administrative organs and, in accordance with the law, appointing, removing and training administrative officials, appraising their work, and rewarding or punishing them.

(4) Drawing up and Implementing the Plan for National Economic and Social Development, and the State Budget

The State Council draws up and implements the plan for national economic and social development, and the state budget.

(5) Foreign Affairs

The State Council conducts foreign affairs and concludes treaties and agreements with foreign countries; protects the legitimate rights and interests of Chinese nationals residing abroad, and protects the lawful rights and interests of returned overseas Chinese and of the family members of Chinese nationals residing abroad.

The Constitution and law stipulate that the State Council is the main body responsible for foreign affairs of the state and the legal body of the state for signing diplomatic documents with foreign governments.

2. Indirect Power

(1) Submitting Bills

The State Council may submit bills to the National People's Congress or its Standing Committee concerning affairs beyond its authority, so as to gain the power to handle such affairs following legislation or authorization by the NPC or its Standing Committee.

(2) Veto Power

The State Council does not make a direct decision or order on a cer-

certain matter. But when a department under it or a local government makes a decision or order on a matter the State Council may alter the decision or order. Moreover, the State Council can also alter or annul the orders, directives, regulations and decisions made by the ministries and commissions, and local organs of administration at various levels.

(3) Imposing Martial Law

The State Council can decide on the imposition of martial law in any parts of the provinces, autonomous regions and municipalities directly under the central government.

The State Council may impose martial law if it deems that normal administrative measures are inadequate. The imposition of martial law is only a remedial measure available to the State Council.

(4) Other powers

The State Council directs and administers affairs with the power conferred upon it by the NPC and the NPC's Standing Committee. This means that the NPC and its Standing Committee, through legislation, can confer upon the State Council more powers than are prescribed in the Constitution and the laws.

Section 2   The System of Leadership of the State Council

I. Premier Responsibility System

The concrete manifestations of the premier responsibility system are as follows:

1. The Premier Takes the Overall Responsibility for the Work of the State Council and Is Answerable to the NPC and Its Standing Committee

Among all the major state organs, the State Council is the only one practicing the system under which its head assumes full responsibility. This is a manifestation of democratic centralism. Generally speaking, compared with the committee responsibility system, the premier responsibility system is more effective for administration. Since the State Council is the top administrative organ of the state, it is extremely important to guarantee its administrative efficiency. The purpose of practicing the premier responsibility system is to ensure the utmost efficiency of the State Council.

2. Practicing the Premier Responsibility System within the State Council

The premier is the sole supreme leader of the State Council, while the other members of the State Council serve as assistants to the premier and are responsible only to him. The vice-premiers and state councilors assist in the work of the premier. They do not share power with the premier. The secretary-general, ministers in charge of the various ministries and commissions, and the auditor-general are each responsible for their share of work within the State Council and responsible for the premier.

Departments under the State Council report on their work, and the State Council shall make decisions accordingly.

3. The Premier Enjoys Decision-making Power in the Work of the State Council

The premier has the final say on the work of the State Council. The Organic Law of the State Council stipulates that discussions of the plenary meetings and executive meetings of the State Council have to be held before decisions are made for major issues concerning the State Council. But this law does not state clearly the relationship between the "discussion" and the final decision. So, under the premier responsibility system, these meetings actually do not produce final decisions, but just serve for advice and consultation. Therefore, the discussions and the opinions of the majority do not affect the power of the premier to make final decisions.

4. Power to Appoint and Remove Component Members of the State Council, and to Nominate the Other Working Personnel of the State Council

The premier has the power to submit the names of candidates for vice-premiers, state councilors, ministers in charge of the ministries and commissions, auditor-general and secretary general for appointment, and suggest removals to the NPC and its Standing Committee.

5. Power to Sign Decisions, Orders, and Administrative Laws and Regulations

Decisions, orders, and administrative laws and regulations, proposals submitted to the NPC and its Standing Committee, and appointment and removal of administrative personnel can only have legal force when they are signed by the premier.

II. Meeting System

Besides the premier responsibility system, the Constitution and the law also stipulate that important issues of the State Council have to be discussed in meetings. But the law does not prescribe the scope of the authority of the State Council meetings. This means that when decisions made at the meetings do not accord with those of the premier, it is unclear which side shall prevail.

One reason for this may be that the principle of democratic centralism has to be carried out in form, especially in the organs practicing the leader responsibility system. Another reason may be that the State Council practiced a committee system[3] before the Constitution stipulated that the State Council shall practice the premier responsibility system in 1982. Various meetings were held under the committee responsibility system. The members of the State Council took the responsibility of leadership, and made policy decisions together with the premier under the committee responsibility system. So the law still follows the old meeting system to a certain extent. So we can see that there can be conflicts in the practice of both the premier responsibility system and the meeting system on important issues.

1. The Plenary Meeting of the State Council

The plenary meeting of the State Council is composed of all component members of the State Council, presided over by the premier.

The plenary meetings generally discuss major issues and important issues involving more than one departments.

A plenary meeting is held every two or three months.

2. The Executive Meeting of the State Council

The executive meetings of the State Council are to be attended by the premier, vice-premiers, state councilors and the secretary-general of the State Council.

The executive meetings discuss important events related to the work of the State Council, bills to be submitted to the NPC, administrative laws and regulations to be issued, and important matters submitted by the various departments under it and local governments.

An executive meeting of the State Council is held once a month.

3. Work Meeting of the Premier

The premier convenes and presides over work meetings (or entrusts a vice-premier to do so), to discuss important problems of the daily work of the State Council.

Work meetings are held irregularly.

III. The Composition of the State Council

The State Council is composed of the premier, vice-premiers, state councilors, ministers in charge of the various ministries and commissions, the auditor-general and the secretary-general.

The term of office of the State Council is five years — the same as that of the National People's Congress.

The premier, vice-premiers and state councilors shall serve no more than two consecutive terms.

Vice-premiers, state councilors, the secretary-general, ministers in charge of the ministries and commissions and the auditor-general are responsible to the premier.

1. The Premier of the State Council

The premier can only be nominated by the president of the People's Republic of China and endorsed by the NPC. The president appoints and removes the premier.

The law does not stipulate the principle and procedure for the president to nominate a candidate for premier, or that the candidate nominated by the president is the only candidate. Moreover, the way the NPC endorses the premier is also not stipulated. Nor does the law stipulate how a new candidate for premier may be put forward if the candidate nominated by the president is rejected by the NPC.

The premier usually is the No. two or three leader of the Party Central Committee and an NPC deputy.

The premier of the State Council can be removed by the NPC and the president of the state. But the law does not stipulate the conditions for the removal of the premier. The president of the state usually signs and issues decisions and laws in accordance with the decisions of the NPC. So, in fact, the president only issues the order for the removal of the premier. Since the premier is nominated by the president and decided by the NPC, the president has the responsibility no less than the NPC for the removal of the premier. Does the president have to sign and issue the document for the removal of the premier after the NPC adopts it? If the president refuses to sign the document, is the decision to remove the premier still of legal validity?

The Constitution and laws do not stipulate the procedure and conditions for the resignation of the premier. The premier responsibility system complicates the relationship between the State Council and the premier. If the NPC rejects a budget put forward by the premier, shall the latter resign? If he resists resignation in such circumstances, the premier responsibility system will be undermined.

2. The Vice-Premiers of the State Council and State Councilors

The vice-premiers of the State Council and state councilors are appointed by the NPC after nomination by the premier.

The vice-premiers assist the premier in his or her work.

The state councilors are in charge of certain items of important work, and conduct activities with foreign countries on behalf of the State Council that the premier or the executive meetings of the State Council entrust to them.

The Constitution and laws do not stipulate the number of vice-premiers.

Because the State Council is an unwieldy organization and there are many affairs to be handled, each of the vice-premiers, in fact, serves as an intermediary between the premier on the one hand and the various ministries and commissions on the other, and is charged with the task to oversee the work of one or several ministries and commissions.

The powers and work relationships between the state councilors and vice-premiers are also indistinct. On the one hand, the state councilors are on the same level as the vice-premiers, being in charge of work entrusted to them by the premier or the executive meetings of the State Council. On the other, it seems that the state councilors are under the leadership of the vice-premiers.

3. The Ministers in Charge of Ministries and Commissions, the Secretary-General and the Auditor-General

The NPC appoints the ministers in charge of the ministries and commissions, the secretary-general and the auditor-general based on the nomination by the premier. When the NPC is not in session, its Standing Committee handles the appointments.

The secretary-general is the head of the General Office of the State Council, and assists the leaders of the State Council in their daily work.

The auditor-general supervises the financial revenues and expenditures of the state, and is in charge of the national auditing work under the leadership of the premier. He or she also audits and supervises the central budget performance, and reports the auditing results to the premier.

The ministries and commissions practice the minister responsibility system.

Ministers in charge of the ministries or commissions of the State Council are responsible for the work of their respective departments, and they convene and preside over all meetings of the ministries and commissions to discuss and decide on major issues in the work of their respective departments. They sign important reports to the State Council and higher-level government departments, and issue orders and directives from them.

Each ministry and commission has one minister, and two to four deputy ministers. Each commission has one minister, two to four deputy ministers and five to ten committee members.

Section 3 The Main Departments of the State Council

I. Types of Departments

The component departments of the State Council include the General Office, the ministries and commissions of the State Council, organizations directly under the State Council, administrative offices of the State Council, state bureaus under the ministries and commissions, coordination departments and others.

The General Office of the State Council assists the leaders of the State Council in handling their daily work.

The various component departments of the State Council carry out the basic administrative functions of the State Council in accordance with the law. They include the various ministries and commissions, the Bank of China and the National Audit Office. They independently exercise specially designated state administrative power, lead and manage relevant administrative affairs, and issue orders, directives and regulations within the jurisdiction of their respective departments. After the Sixth National People's Congress in 2003, the State Council has the following ministries and commissions: Ministry of Foreign Affairs, Ministry of National Defense, State Development Planning Commission, State Economic and Trade Commission, Ministry of Education, Ministry of Science and Technology, Commission of Science, Technology and Industry for National Defense, State Ethnic Affairs Commission, Ministry of Public Security, Ministry of State Security, Ministry of Supervision, Ministry of Civil Affairs, Ministry of Justice, Ministry of Finance, Ministry of Personnel, Ministry of Labor and Social Security, Ministry of Land and Resources, Ministry of Construction, Ministry of Railways, Ministry of Communications, Ministry of the Information Industry, Ministry of Water Resources, Ministry of Agriculture, Ministry of Foreign Trade and Economic Cooperation, Ministry of Culture, Ministry of Public Health, State Family Planning Commission, People's Bank of China and Auditing Administration of the People's Republic of China.

The organizations directly under the State Council have independent administrative functions, are in charge of special tasks and can issue administrative regulations and measures and standard documents, within the limits of their authority. The departments include: General Administration of Customs, State Environmental Protection Administration, State Administration of Taxation, General Administration of Civil Aviation of China, State Physical Culture Administration (State General Administration of Sports), State Statistics Bureau, State Administration of Industry and Commerce, State Press and Publication Administration (State General Administration of Press and Publication), State Forestry Bureau, State Drug Administration, State Bureau of Religious Affairs, Counselors' Office of the State Council, Government Offices Administration of the State Council, National Tourism Administration, State Intellectual Property Office, State Bureau of Quality Supervision, Inspection and Quarantine, and State Administration of Radio, Film and Television.

The administrative offices of the State Council assist the premier to handle special tasks, and do not have independent administrative functions. They are only responsible for investigation and analysis, and for handling specific work entrusted to them by the State Council. The offices are as follows: Foreign Affairs Office, Overseas Chinese Affairs Office, Legislative Affairs Office, Economic Restructuring Office and Research Office of the State Council.

State bureaus under ministries and commissions are in charge of specially designated business, and exercise administrative functions therein. They include: State Bureau of Production Safety Supervision (under the State Economic and Trade Commission, also known as State Bureau of Coal Mine Safety Supervision), State Tobacco Monopoly Bureau (under the State Economic and Trade Commission), State Grain Reserve Administration (under the State Development Planning Commission), State Bureau of Foreign Experts Affairs (under the Ministry of Personnel), State Oceanic Administration (under the Ministry of Land and Resources), State Bureau of Surveying and Mapping (under the Ministry of Land and Resources), State Posts and Telecommunications Bureau (under the Ministry of the Information Industry), State Cultural Relics Bureau (under the Ministry of Culture) and State Administration of Traditional Chinese Medicine and Pharmacy (under the Ministry of Public Health).

The coordination departments of the State Council are responsible for organizing and coordinating major events involving more than one departments of the State Council, after discussion with the State Council. In special and urgent circumstances, the coordination departments may, with the agreement of the State Council, enact interim administrative measures. The coordinating and non-permanent departments are as follows: State National Defense Mobilization Committee (work done by the State Development Planning Commission, Headquarters of the General Staff and General Logistics Department of the PLA), Special Committee of the Central Military Commission of the State Council (work done by the Commission of Science, Technology and Industry for National Defense), State Frontier Committee (work done by the Headquarters of the General Staff of the PLA), National Patriotic Sanitation Campaign Committee (work done by the Ministry of Public Health), National Afforestation Committee (work done by the State Forestry Bureau), Academic Degrees Committee of the State Council (special office established by the Ministry of Education), State Headquarters for Flood Prevention and Drought Resistance (work done by a special office under the Ministry of Water Resources), Coordination Committee for Work with Women and Children of the State Council (work done by the All-China Women's Federation), National Leading Group for Supporting the Army and Giving Preferential Treatment to Their Dependents and Supporting the Government and Cherishing the People (work done by the Ministry of Civil Affairs and the General Political Department of the PLA), the Three Gorges Project Construction Committee of the State Council (a special office established), Coordination Committee for the Disabled of the State Council (work done by the China Federation of the Disabled), Leading Group for Helping the Poor of the State Council (special office established by the Ministry of Agriculture), Tariff and Tax Regulations Committee of the State Council (work done by the Ministry of Finance), China National Disaster Reduction Ten-Year Committee (work done by the Ministry of Civil Affairs), Leading Group for Science, Technology and Education of the State Council (office established by the General Office of the State Council), State Leading Group for the Carrying Out the "Convention on the Prohibition of Chemical Weapons" (work done by the State Economic and Trade Commission), Leading Group for Settling Ex-Servicemen under the State Council (work done by the Ministry of Personnel), State Economic Restructuring Committee (work done by the Office for Economic Restructuring), and Office for Rectifying Malpractice in Various Sectors (work done by the Ministry of Supervision).

II. Establishment and Management of Organs of the State Council

The setting up, dissolving or amalgamating of departments of the State Council shall be decided on by the NPC after discussion of the plan drawn up by the organ in charge of set-up of the State Council and endorsed by an executive meeting of the State Council. If the NPC is not in session, it shall be submitted to the Standing Committee of the NPC to decide.

The setting up, dissolving or amalgamating of departments directly under the State Council, offices under the State Council and state administrative bodies administered by the State Council shall be decided by the State Council after a plan has been drawn up by the organ in charge of the set-up of the State Council.

The setting up, dissolving or amalgamating of coordinating and non-permanent departments shall be decided by the State Council after a plan has been drawn up by the organ.

When setting up coordinating and non-permanent departments, the specific departments undertaking any specially assigned tasks shall be clarified. The conditions and time for dissolution shall be stated clearly for non-permanent departments set up for the specially assigned tasks.

The setting up of coordinating or non-permanent departments shall be strictly controlled. Such departments shall not be set up if the work can be done or the problems can be solved by the existing departments.

The adjustment of the functions of established administrative organs of the State Council shall be decided by the State Council after a plan has been drawn up by the organ in charge of the set-up of the State Council.

The setting up, dissolving and amalgamating of departments of the administrative organs of the State Council shall be examined and checked by the organ in charge of the set-up of the State Council and approved by the State Council.

The setting up, dissolving and amalgamating of divisions of the administrative organs of the State Council shall be decided by the respective administrative organs in accordance with the regulations of the state, and reported to the organ in charge of the set-up of the State Council for the record each year.

The size of the administrative organs of the State Council is fixed when they are set up. Any plan to increase and reduce the number of departments in any of the ministries, commissions or offices of the State Council has to be examined and verified by the organ in charge of the set-up of the State Council, and then reported to the State Council for approval.

The number of leaders of the General Office of the State Council, the ministries and commissions, organizations directly under the State Council and administrative offices under the State Council shall be decided according to the Organic Law of the State Council. The number of the leaders of state administrative organs under the ministries and commissions shall be decided by referring to the Organic Law of the State Council.

The departments under the General Office of the State Council, the ministries and commissions, organizations directly under the State Council and administrative offices under the State Council shall have one head and two deputy heads. The departments of the state administrative organs under the ministries and commissions shall have one head and two deputy heads or one head and one deputy head, in view of the needs of work.

Section 4　Major Patterns of Administration of the State Council

The current Constitution and law do not clearly and specifically stipulate the patterns and means of administration to be used by the State Council in exercising administrative leadership. Generally speaking, the State Council theoretically enjoys wide and overall administrative power as it is the highest organ of state administration under the NPC system. Owing to the influence of the political and military power systems the CPC adopted before it seized national political power, it seems that the highest organ of state administration may adopt any kind of administrative patterns and means — even the means of military orders. But now the administrative leadership of the country mainly depends on policies, not law, as the enactment of laws and building of the legal system lag behind the development of the situation. So, on many occasions, the patterns and means of administration of the State Council have been adopted randomly, and its power has remained undefined. Therefore, the State Council may adopt any kind of administrative means.

In recent years, more emphasis has been put on improving the legal system and on running the country according to law. This has limited the randomness of the administrative patterns adopted by the State Council to a certain extent, and the trend of governing the country according to law is gaining momentum. At present, the major administrative methods adopted by the State Council are as follows: Participating in the enactment of laws, administrative legislation, and working out and carrying out national economic and social development plans and the state budgets, issuing direct administrative orders, collecting information and asking the local governments to report to it on their work, auditing work and administrative supervision, enforcing management of the various industries, making the ministries and commissions get in direct contact with the enterprises, allocating funds for special projects, and establishing representative offices.

I. Participating in the Enactment of Laws

According to the Constitution of the People's Republic of China, legislative power shall be exercised comprehensively by the NPC and its Standing Committee. Although in principle the State Council does not enjoy legislative power, it has the power to put forward legislative bills, enact laws as entrusted to it by the NPC and exercise special adjudication powers.

Legislative power itself is not administrative power, but the administrative organs may take part in some legislative activities. So, participation in legislative activities by the State Council reflects, to a certain extent, its administrative purpose. More importantly, it guarantees the State Council can gain the administrative capability it desires.

First of all, the State Council enjoys the power to put forward legislative bills. During a session of the NPC, the State Council may put forward legislative bills to the NPC. If the NPC is not in session, the State Council may put forward such bills to its Standing Committee. Having been read by the Standing Committee, the bills shall be submitted to the NPC for examination, and the Standing Committee or the State Council shall be responsible for giving explanations to the NPC. In fact, many of the laws enacted and revised by the NPC or its Standing Committee are drafted by the State Council or put forward to the legislative organ by the State Council after consultation with other relevant departments of the NPC. This means that the State Council is not only the main state organ putting forward drafts of laws, but also, in a sense, a law maker. In the process of making laws, the legislative and administrative organs cooperate with each other closely, thus preventing, to some extent, the overstepping of the boundaries of state organs in the division of legislative power.

Second, the State Council also enjoys legislative power as the NPC entrusts to it. The NPC and its Standing Committee may empower the State Council, in line with practical needs, to draw up administrative regulations (excluding criminal laws, deprivation of political rights and freedoms, and matters concerning the judicial system). In fact, there is a wide range of matters of legislation that can be entrusted to the State Council by the NPC and its Standing Committee. These include laws related to state sovereignty; the election, organization and functions of governments, courts of justice and procuratorates at all levels; the system of regional autonomy of ethnic minorities, special administrative regions, self-government organizations of the masses at the grassroots level; acquisition of non-state property; the basic system of civil affairs; basic economic system and basic systems of finance, taxation, customs, banking and foreign trade, as well as some other matters of which the laws must be enacted by the NPC and its Standing Committee. So, we can say that the State Council enjoys more legislative power than any other administrative organs.

Third, the State Council has the power to demand the legislative organ to give explanation to relevant legislation, because the Legislation Law of the People's Republic of China stipulates that when the stipulations of a law need to be further explained or a new situation occurs after the law has been worked out, the State Council and state organs of central and local governments may ask the Standing Committee of the NPC to give explanations to it.

Fourth, the State Council has the power to rule upon some legal problems. The Legislation Law stipulates that when the regulations adopted by a state department are not in conformity with a regional law on the same matter, and people are not certain which one shall be followed, the judgment of the State Council shall prevail. If the State Council thinks that the regional law applies, the regional law shall be followed in the locality. If the departmental regulations apply, the State Council shall submit the matter to the Standing Committee of the NPC for a decision. This means that if some local laws and regulations conflict with the regulations of the State Council, the State Council has the right to rule on the matter or partly rule on the matter. This in fact represents an extension of the legislative power of the State Council.

The above-mentioned legislative powers enjoyed by the State Council indicate that the State Council enjoys an important and outstanding position in state legislation.

II. Administrative Legislation

Administrative legislation is an important administrative means employed by the State Council. The Constitution stipulates that the State Council has the power to "adopt administrative measures, enact administrative rules and regulations and issue decisions and orders in accordance with the Constitution and the law,"[4] and the ministries and commissions under the State Council have the power to "issue orders, directives and regulations within the jurisdiction of their respective departments and in accordance with the law and the administrative rules and regulations, decisions and orders issued by the State Council."[5] The rules and regulations as well as decisions and orders enacted by the State Council and orders, directives and regulations issued by the ministries and commissions are all administrative legislation. The Legislation Law of the People's Republic of China stipulates that the administrative rules enacted by the State Council in accordance with the Constitution and the law may include the following: administrative regulations needed in carrying out the law, and the functions and powers of the State Council as stipulated in Article 89 of the Constitution of the People's Republic of China.[6] The ministries and commissions, the People's Bank of China, National Audit Office and other administrative organizations directly under the State Council may issue regulations within the jurisdiction of their respective departments and in accordance with the law and the administrative rules and regulations, and decisions and orders issued by the State Council. If the regulation involves two or more departments of the State Council, the regulation shall be formulated by the State Council or shall be worked out together by the departments of the State Council.

The above stipulations show that the administrative legislation of the State Council falls into two categories: First, the administrative rules formulated by the State Council which are only secondary to the law in legal force. Second, the regulations formulated by the various departments under the State Council, which are generally called "regulations," "measures" or "rules for implementation."

The administrative rules and regulations formulated by the State Council are authoritative and effective. To ensure the normal operation of the administrative power of the state these rules and regulations are of universal binding force on all administrative organs, enterprises, institutions, social organizations and citizens of the country. As the administrative rules and regulations are of legal binding force, they can only be canceled by the legislative body. Any other state organ cannot stand against and annul them. In this way the role of the State Council in legislative and judicial work is strengthened and the powerful status of the State Council in the administration of the state is protected.

From the perspective of administrative legislation, not only does the State Council hold an important position in the national administrative system; the ministries and commissions under the State Council also enjoy priority over local governments. Although the Legislation Law of China stipulates that the administrative regulations formulated by the departments under the State Council have the same legal force as the administrative regulations formulated by the local governments, it also stipulates that when regulations made by the departments under the State Council are in conflict with regulations formulated by local governments, the matter shall be decided by the State Council. The Legislation Law also stipulates that when regulations formulated by local governments conflict with regulations of a department under the State Council, the matter shall be submitted to the State Council. If the State Council holds that the local regulations apply, they shall be applied in relevant locality. If the State Council thinks that the department regulations apply, it shall submit the matter to the Standing Committee of the NPC for a decision.

The administrative regulations are, generally speaking, simple, easy and rapid to implement. In line with the Interim Provisions for the Formulation of Administrative Regulations issued on April 21, 1987, the various departments under the State Council should put forward, separately, their five-year plans and annual plans on the enactment of administrative regulations. On the basis of these plans, the Bureau of Legislative Affairs under the State Council shall draft an overall plan for the entire State Council after studying these plans, and submit it to the State Council. Again, the Bureau of Legislative Affairs under the State Council shall work out a five-year and annual guiding plan for the enactment of administrative regulations in line with various specific tasks listed in the five-year plan for national economic and social development, and report it to the State Council for approval. Once these plans are approved by the State Council, the Bureau of Legislative Affairs will be responsible for the organizational and supervisory work to see to it that these plans are implemented. The administrative regulations listed in the five-year and annual plans shall be drafted by the various departments of the State Council. If any important administrative regulations are closely related to the work of more than one departments, the drafting shall be the responsibility of the Bureau of Legislative Affairs or a major department of the State Council. Opinions shall be collected and consultation with relevant departments shall be made when drafting the administrative regulations. If consensus on some issues cannot be reached after consultation, explanations shall be given when the draft of the regulations in question is submitted. When the draft of the regulations is completed and signed by the responsible personnel, the drafting department shall submit it, together with relevant materials, to the State Council for approval. If rules for implementation of the regulations are needed, a draft of the rules shall also be attached. The draft of the administrative regulations is first examined by the Bureau of Legislative Affairs, and then reported to the State Council for examination. After examination, it is submitted to an executive meeting of the State Council or the premier of the State Council for approval. The document is then issued by the State Council or the competent department of the State Council with the approval of the State Council. A communiqué of the State Council of the People's Republic of China shall be published when the administrative regulations are issued. Foreign-language versions of the administrative regulations are examined and approved by the Bureau of Legislative Affairs. The rules for the implementation of the regulations shall also be issued at the same time or immediately after the issuing of the regulations, and the date of the rules coming into force shall be the same as that of the regulations.

III. Drawing Up and Implementing the National Economic and Social Development Plan and State Budget

To draw up and carry out of the national economic and social development plans and state budgets are an important aspect for the state organ — the State Council — to exercise its administrative functions.

According to the stipulations of the Budget Law of the People's Republic of China, the State Council is responsible for reporting to the NPC the central and local budget plans; for gathering the budget plans of the provinces, autonomous regions and municipalities directly under the central government and reporting them to the Standing Committee of the NPC for the record; for organizing the central departments and local governments to implement the budgets; for deciding on the utilization of the reserve funds of the central government; for working out adjustment plans for the central budgets; for overseeing the implementation of the budgets by the central and local governments; for changing or canceling unsuitable decisions and orders concerning the budgets and final accounts of central government departments and local governments; and for reporting to the NPC and its Standing Committee on the implementation of the budgets by the central departments and local governments. The financial department of the State Council is responsible for organizing the performance of the central and local budgets and for reporting regularly to the State Council on the performance of the central and local budgets. The governments of the provinces, autonomous regions and municipalities directly under the central government report their overall budget plans to the State Council for examination in the time prescribed by the State Council. The State Council and the local governments above the county level submit the plans to the standing committees at the same level for examination and approval when they think that the budget plans submitted by lower-level governments conflict with laws or administrative regulations, or are not appropriate. The draft of the final accounts shall be worked out after the budget year by governments at all levels, and by departments and units of the State Council, in the prescribed time. The specific work of drawing up final accounts shall be arranged by the Ministry of Finance in the State Council.

In line with the stipulations of the Regulations on the Implementation of the Budget Law of the People's Republic of China, before November 10 each year the State Council shall give instructions to the provinces, autonomous regions and municipalities directly under the central government, and departments under the central governments, for drawing up of the budget draft for the following year, and lay down the principles and specific requirements. The State Council has the power to decide the specific methods for the division, return and subsidy of the income and expenditure budget among the central government and the governments of the provinces, autonomous regions and municipalities directly under the central government. The Ministry of Finance has the power to gather the budget drafts by the central government departments and the local governments. The governments of the provinces, autonomous regions and municipalities directly under the central government put forward their own requirements when making budget drafts, in line with the instructions of the State Council and the arrangements of the Ministry of Finance. The total budget drafts of the financial departments of the governments of the provinces, autonomous regions and municipalities directly under the central government must be reported to the Ministry of Finance before January 10 of the next year, after examination and approval by the governments at the corresponding levels. The financial departments of the provincial, autonomous regional and municipal governments shall report their respective budget performances to the Ministry of Finance in accordance with the following deadlines and methods: (1) Ten-day report made in accordance with the regulations of the Ministry of Finance on budgetary revenues and expenditures shall be submitted to the Ministry of Finance within three days after ending of each ten-day period; (2) Monthly report made in accordance with the regulations of the Ministry of Finance on budgetary revenues and expenditures shall be submitted to the Ministry of Finance within five days after the ending of each month; (3) Written materials on the performance of budgetary revenues and expenditures shall be submitted to the Ministry. of Finance ten days after the ending of each month, and a written analysis on the three-month performance of budgetary revenues and expenditures shall be submitted to the Ministry of Finance within ten days after the ending of each three-month period; (4) Annual final accounts of revenue and expenditure shall be done in accordance with the Budget Law and relevant regulations. The State Council has the power to supervise the performance of the budgets of governments of provinces, autonomous regions and municipalities directly under the central government, and halts practices in budgetary performance going against state law, administrative regulations and policies. The governments of provinces, autonomous regions and municipalities directly under the central governments shall provide the necessary materials in time and report exactly how things stand. They shall strictly carry out the decisions of the State Council and report the implementation results in time.

IV. Direct Orders

The Constitution stipulates that the State Council exercises the power to adopt administrative measures, enact administrative rules and regulations and issue decisions and orders in accordance with the Constitution and the law.

In a broad sense, there is no essential difference between adopting administrative measures and issuing administrative orders and administration legislation. But there is still a great difference between administrative measures and orders and administrative legislation, when the legal system is not perfect and policies are often substituted for laws. The routine work of the State Council is often manifested in enacting a large number of administrative measures and issuing a lot of administrative orders. The governments of the provinces, autonomous regions and municipalities are directly under the leadership of the State Council. As the Constitution also stipulates that the State Council exercises leadership over the work of local organs of state administration at all levels throughout the country, the State Council not only can issue orders directly to the governments of the provinces, autonomous regions and municipalities, but also to local governments at any level without the need to notify the government of the next-higher level.

V. Collecting Information and Requiring Local Governments to Report on Their Work

Timely collecting information is a necessary means for the State Council to perform its administrative functions. There are two channels for the State Council to gather information: first, through the State Statistics Bureau and its investigation organizations set up throughout the country; and second, through reports to the State Council from local governments.

The tasks of the State Statistics Bureau are to organize and manage national statistics and investigation projects; to examine and approve the statistical and investigation plans of different regions and departments; to study and put forward general survey plans on the national conditions and strength, and do organizational work for the implementation of such plans when they are approved; to organize social and economic investigations of different regions and departments in a unified way and sort out basic national statistical materials; to make analysis and prediction and carry out supervision concerning national economic and social development, and scientific and technological progress, and supply statistical information and consultation to the CPC Central Committee, the State Council and other relevant departments; to check, manage and issue basic national statistics; and to establish, improve and manage the state statistical information automation system and state statistics bank. As state organ exercising the administrative functions related to statistical information, the State Statistics Bureau gathers information from direct investigation organizations all over the country. The investigation organizations include rural social and economic investigation teams, urban social and economic investigation teams and enterprise investigation teams.

The second channel for the State Council to acquire information is to ask the local governments to report to it on major events in time. The Notice on Improving the System of Timely Information Reports from Governments to the General Office of the State Council issued by the General Office of the State Council on December 14, 1999 demands that local governments at all levels report, as soon as possible, major unexpected incidents, important social trends, disasters and epidemic diseases, and other emergent events to the State Council, while making efforts to handle them in a timely and proper manner. They have to closely follow the progress of the events and report on the situation continually. The main responsible persons of the different regions and departments are responsible for forwarding information on major emergent events to the State Council. The General Office of the State Council will establish a circulation system on emergent important information and gather and analyze regularly such information from local governments and departments. Local governments and departments that have done a good job shall be cited, while those that delayed or failed to report the emergent and important information, or cover up something shall be criticized and, if serious damage has been caused, the responsibility shall be investigated. The governments of the provinces, autonomous regions and municipalities shall submit their work reports during January to March and July to September of each year.

VI. Auditing and Administrative Supervision

The National Audit Office is under the direct leadership of the premier. It supervises by means of auditing the revenue and expenditure of all departments under the State Council and of the local governments at all levels, and is responsible for supervising their auditing work. The local auditing departments shall carry out the decisions and regulations on auditing work drawn up by the National Audit Office. If the directives or decisions made by local auditing departments are different from those of the National Audit Office, the latter shall prevail. Local auditing departments shall carry out conscientiously the auditing work plan, national industry auditing or special auditing jobs assigned or entrusted to them by the National Audit Office. The auditing work, major breaches of discipline and other relevant documents and materials of the auditing offices of provinces, autonomous regions and municipalities shall be submitted promptly to the National Audit Office. The latter is authorized to correct all incorrect auditing conclusions and decisions made by local auditing departments. Local auditing departments shall report the decisions concerning the revenue and expenditures of their governments and special auditing jobs entrusted to them by the National Audit Office to the latter for the record, and decisions on major auditing jobs shall be approved by the National Audit Office. The appointment, removal and transfer, and disciplinary punishment for directors and deputy directors of auditing offices of provinces, autonomous regions and municipalities require approval in advance from the National Audit Office.

The National Audit Office is responsible for checking the budgetary performance and final accounting of the provincial governments; for organizing the auditing of the accounts of local Party and government leaders; for handling appeals for the reconsideration of auditing decisions; for providing leadership to provincial-level auditing organizations, and appointing and removing the responsible personnel of provincial-level auditing organizations together with the provincial governments; for managing the offices of local auditing commissioners; for exercising supervision over large state enterprises and key construction projects through auditing in cooperation with auditing commissioners; and for exercising supervision over other state enterprises and state construction projects through auditing.

The local offices of auditing commissioners forms an auditing system directly under the National Audit Office that is specially responsible for the auditing of local governments and their officials. At present, 16 auditing commissioners' offices have been set up in Beijing, Tianjin, Taiyuan, Harbin, Shanghai, Nanjing, Wuhan, Guangzhou, Zhengzhou, Ji'nan, Xi'an, Lanzhou, Kunming, Chengdu, Changsha and Shenzhen, respectively. The auditing commissioners supervise the local governments with the authorization of the National Audit Office, to which they are directly responsible. Administrative supervision is another way for the State Council to ensure the efficacy of its administrative leadership. The Ministry of Supervision is in charge of administrative supervision throughout the country. It supervises the cadres appointed by the State

Council and its various departments, as well as the governments of the provinces, autonomous regions and municipalities and their principal leaders in their implementation of state laws, policies and regulations, the national economic and social development plan as well as the decisions and orders issued by the State Council. It investigates and corrects their violations of laws and discipline. The Ministry of Supervision exercises leadership over the work of supervision departments at lower levels, by planning, drafting related regulations, working principles, policies and rules, conducting macro instruction as regards the work of supervision departments; inspecting the work of supervision departments at lower levels; examining and approving appointments and transfers of heads and deputy heads of the supervision departments at the lower levels; etc.

VII. Administration of Various Industries and Making the Ministries and Commissions in Contact with Enterprises

A system of separating the functions of the government from enterprise management has been established since the government structural reform started in 1998, which has brought about a fundamental change to the government's management over enterprises, which is manifested in the following two aspects. First, the government no longer manages the enterprises directly, thus weakening the function of the government over the enterprises; second, the form and link of government control over enterprises have been changed, with the government still exercising a certain amount of control. Since the reform started, some industrial economic management departments, and administrative corporations and associations have been established. They are no longer responsible for examining and approving investment projects and approving the function of companies. They no longer assign production and distribution quotas or profits and losses quotas. These departments, corporations and associations are mainly responsible for working out the industry development plans and industry policies, thus changing the former practice of government managing the enterprises to managing the industries. This is a significant change. Three years later, in 2001, the State Council dismantled most of the state bureaus under the State Economic and Trade Commission. The functions of these bureaus were given to the State Economic and Trade Commission, while the professional management functions were turned to the industry associations established in the wake of the introduction of the reform. At present, except for a few government departments, such as the State Economic and Trade Commission, which still exercise direct management over enterprises, the State Council mainly exercises management over enterprises through the industry associations.

Industry administration is mainly exercised by ministries and commissions or industry associations entrusted by ministries and commissions. Take the State Economic and Trade Commission as an example. Before the reform started, in 1998, the state bureaus under it administered or were otherwise connected with nearly 300 industry associations and each association also administered and was connected with many enterprises. Since the abolition of the bureaus, the State Economic and Trade Commission is responsible for the administration of or liaison with these associations.

According to the regulations in the Opinions on Management of Trade Associations under the State Economic and Trade Commission, the commission now directly manages 15 industry associations (hereinafter referred to as "directly managed associations").In addition, it has entrusted the management of some other associations to these directly managed associations (hereinafter referred to as "indirectly managed associations"). These two kinds of associations have equal legal person status, and they undertake civil liability independently, and the State Economic and Trade Commission is the higher authority for both kinds of associations. The directly managed associations of the commission shall not overstep their authority or interfere with the lawful business activities of the indirectly managed associations as prescribed in the charters of the latter. So the enterprises, which used to be managed by the state bureaus under the State Economic and Trade Commission, are now managed by the various types of industry associations. Therefore, they are still linked with the government, in one way or another.

The State Economic and Trade Commission mainly instructs the associations to conduct their business activities in accordance with the stipulations prescribed in their respective charters; guides their reform, readjustment and development, and is responsible for the examination of their applications to set up new business, the related registration matters and the annual check of their businesses; sees to it that the associations abide by the law and relevant regulations and policies, and aids the law-enforcement departments to deal with any illegal activities of the associations; guides their personnel and foreign affairs, and exercises supervision over their finances and management of state assets; and undertakes other responsibilities assigned by the competent authorities.

The obligations of the associations directly under the State Economic and Trade Commission are as follows: In line with arrangements made by the commission, the directly managed associations guide the indirectly managed associations to do business in accordance with the stipulations as prescribed in their respective charters; relate to them the documents and policies of the State Economic and Trade Commission; exercise supervision over their implementation of the law and related state regulations and policies; assist the law-enforcement departments in their investigations of any illegal activities of the indirectly managed associations; and put forward proposals for the latter's reform, readjustment and development. They examine the applications filed by the indirectly managed associations to set up new businesses, oversee their registration and make preliminary examination of their reports for annual checks. In accordance with the principles that the Party exercises control over cadres and democratic centralism, leading cadres of the indirectly managed associations are to be recommend by the directly managed associations through collective discussions at their Party committees or standing committees. The directly managed associations are responsible for appointments and removals of the leaders of the institutions under them. Those directly managed associations that are given the power to handle foreign affairs also examine and approve or reject applications to go abroad for business trips (except ministerial leading cadres) from their own staff and staff of the indirectly managed associations put under them; they can also invite delegations of foreign mass organizations and government officials under the ministerial level to China.

Besides management of the industries, the State Council also holds control over a few large-scale enterprises through the ministries and commissions. At present, the large-scale enterprises put under the control of the State Economic and Trade Commission are the State Electric Power Corporation, China National Offshore Oil Corporation and China National Nonferrous Metals Corporation. The large-scale enterprises under the People's Bank of China are the China Trust and Investment Corporation and China Ever bright Stock Company. General managers and deputy general managers of these large companies under the ministries and commissions are appointed and removed by the State Council and managed by the CPC Central Committee.

VIII. Special-Purpose Allocations

Special-purpose allocations to local governments by the central government refer to special funds allocated to local governments to subsidize the accomplishment of specific macro goals from the central finance. These funds serve as a major means for the central government to carry out its macro policies, thus also an important administrative means adopted by the State Council.

Why do we say these funds serve as an important administrative means? It is because, first, the special funds are allocated according to the policies, regulations and administrative intentions of the CPC Central Committee and the State Council, thus directly mirror the administrative purpose of the central government and, second, the special funds are an important instrument for the State Council to carry out its macro policies guidance and ensure its control over the various trades and departments. Through the special funds, the State Council can guide the local governments to spend money according to the purpose of the central government and ensure the input of funds in key projects. For example, to encourage the local governments to increase grain production, a special grain production risk fund was established by the State Council in 1994, with 3.36 billion yuan coming from the central finance. In addition, the local governments were also asked to provide the rest of the funds at a ratio of 1:1.1. A special account was opened for the fund.

The special funds feature a strong administrative function. The recipients and amount of the special funds are decided by the Ministry of Finance in line with the requirements of macro control and the actual annual budget of the central government. Requests for the special funds from the financial departments (bureaus) of the provinces, autonomous regions and municipalities directly under the central government or cities with independent budgetary status shall be discussed and examined by the Ministry of Finance. If necessary, investigations shall be made by the ministry or local commissioners' offices set up by the ministry.

After receiving a special fund from the Ministry of Finance, the financial department (bureau) of a province, autonomous region, municipality or city with independent budgetary status must distribute the money to the lower-level governments in line with the stipulations for the use of the money by the Ministry of Finance. The money must in no way be misappropriated or used for other purposes. The headings of the budgetary expenditure cannot be changed.

IX. Establishment of Representative Offices

Setting up representative offices in the localities is an important means adopted by the State Council to see to it that its macro regulation and control are strengthened and the administrative laws and regulations are enforced. More such offices have been set up in recent years.

Financial supervision commissioners' offices are set up by the Ministry of Finance in the provinces, autonomous regions (except Tibet) and municipalities directly under the central government or cities with independent budgetary status. Such sub-offices are also set up by the supervision commissioners' offices in cities (prefectures) with the approval of the Ministry of Finance. Both kinds of the offices are to mainly exercise supervision representing the central financial department.

In order to strengthen its macroeconomic control, the People's Bank of China has restructured its management system since October 1998. The branch banks set up in the provinces, autonomous regions and municipalities were closed down, and relocated to nine major cities (Tianjin, Shenyang, Shanghai, Nanjing, Ji'nan, Wuhan, Guangzhou, Chengdu and Xi'an). These nine branches serve as the representative offices of the People's Bank of China.

According to the Auditing Law of the People's Republic of China, adopted on August 31, 1994, the auditing department under the central government (the National Audit Office of the State Council) may establish auditing commissioners' offices throughout the country in line with the requirements of the auditing work. Within the limits of authority empowered by the auditing department of the central government, these offices may conduct auditing work according to the law. The State Council may send special auditing commissioners to and set up special auditing commissioners' offices in the provinces, autonomous regions and municipalities directly under the central government. The auditing commissioners may carry out auditing and supervisory work within the scope of authority delegated to them by the National Audit Office, and they are responsible directly to the National Audit Office. Bureau-level officials are appointed as special auditing commissioners by the National Audit Office. Offices set up under the leadership of the special auditing commissioners are to handle the day-to-day auditing work.

Special inspectors are dispatched by the State Council to represent the state in exercising supervision over the financial affairs and leading members of state enterprises. Special inspectors' offices may set up, with one head and several assistants, to carry out the work. The special inspector responsibility system is practiced. Officials at the vice-ministerial level are selected to serve as the special inspectors, while official at the department or division levels are picked to serve as their assistants.

X. Vertical Administration

Under the planned economy system, the administration of the central government over state affairs and the local governments was usually manifested in a vertical mode, that is, through direct control and administrative orders. But since the start of the reform, great changes have taken place in the relations between the central government and the local governments, and the scope of vertical administration has been greatly narrowed.

Now, vertical administration still applies to departments that are strongly influenced by the market and do not have a pronounced political function. This is because officials of such departments tend to ignore the orders of the central government, and act as they think fit. Departments of a decidedly political nature tend to act as one with the central government, and therefore do not require strict control.

The degree of vertical administration varies with different departments. The most strict vertical management is enforced over the customs. The General Administration of Customs vertically administers the customs offices throughout the country. Such administration covers every aspect — their organizational setup, size of staff, salaries and welfare, education and training, as well as the appointment and removal of cadres.

The state taxation departments are the next most strictly controlled. In line with the regulations on the functions of the State Taxation Administration following the structural reform in 1998, the State Administration of Taxation exercises vertical management of state taxation departments throughout the country, including personnel and salary affairs, organizational setup and funds. In cooperation with the provincial governments, it exercises leadership over the directors and deputy directors of provincial state taxation bureaus and puts forward proposals for the appointment and removal of directors of the provincial state taxation bureaus.

Vertical administration is also exercised in state quality supervision, inspection and quarantine departments, but it covers only entry-exit inspection and quarantine.

The State Administration of Industry and Commerce exercises certain administrative powers over provincial departments of industry and commerce. The bureaus of industry and commerce of prefectures (prefecture-level cities) and counties (county-level cities) are, as representative offices of the provincial bureaus of industry and commerce, directly under the higher-level bureaus of industry and commerce. The organizational setup and number of official of the province-level bureaus of industry and commerce are decided and managed by the personnel departments of the provincial governments, and the organizational setup of the bureaus of industry and commerce (including offices of industry and commerce) of the prefectures, cities and counties, and the numbers of their leaders are decided and managed by both the personnel departments and bureaus of industry and commerce of the provinces. The directors and deputy directors of the provincial bureaus of industry and commerce are under the leadership of both the State Council and the provincial governments, mainly the latter. The directors and deputy directors of bureaus of industry and commerce of the prefectures, cities and counties are decided by the Party committees of the industry and commerce bureaus at the next higher level after consultation with the local Party committees. In addition, some ministries and commissions of the State Council exercise vertical administration over the appointment and removal of the leaders of the departments under them. For example, the Ministry of Land and Resources has the right to veto the appointment or removal of the main leaders of provincial departments of land and resources. That is to say, the appointment and removal of such officials must be approved by the Ministry of Land and Resources.

Notes:

[1] *Constitution of the People's Republic of China*, Fourth edition (with Chinese text). Beijing: Foreign Languages Press, 1999, p. 39.

[2] Ibid. p. 40.

[3] In the period 1949-1954, major policy decisions were made through discussion by the Government Administrative Council, and some resolutions and orders issued by the Government Administrative Council were signed by the premier and leaders of the de-

partments of the State Council. From 1954 to 1975, major resolutions and orders made by the State Council had to be adopted by plenary meetings of the State Council.

[4] *Constitution of the People's Republic of China*, Fourth edition (with Chinese text). Beijing: Foreign Languages Press, 1999, p. 40.

[5] *Constitution of the People's Republic of China*, Fourth edition (with Chinese text). Beijing: Foreign Languages Press, 1999, p. 42.

[6] *Constitution of the People's Republic of China*, Fourth edition (with Chinese text). Beijing: Foreign Languages Press, 1999, pp. 40-42.

Chapter Five

COURTS AND PROCURATORATES

In accordance with the Constitution, the state power of the People's Republic of China is shared by the administrative, judicial and procuratorial organs under the people's congresses. The courts and procuratorates are the organs which exercise the judicial power and procuratorial power of the state. The courts are the judicial organs of the state, and the procuratorates are the legal supervision organs of the state.

Because the People's Republic of China does not practice the political system of separation of powers, the division of the legislative, executive and judicial powers is not very strict. Although the legislative, executive and judicial powers are allocated to the respective organs, there is, in fact, a certain degree of mixing and overlapping among them. In concrete terms, the judicial power, for instance, is shared by the legislative and executive organs of the state, the courts, procuratorates and other judicial organizations, and even organs of the Communist Party of China. The judicial organs refer not only to the courts and procuratorates, but also to the public security, state security and judicial administration organs, investigation committees of people's congresses on specific issues and other organs having the relevant authority and functions. Therefore, strictly speaking, the courts and procuratorates are organs only for exercising judicial power and legal supervision in the whole judicial structural system.

Section 1 Judicial Organs

I. The System, Functions and Powers of the Judicial Organs

1. The System of Judicial Organs

The judicial organs of the People's Republic of China are composed of the Supreme People's Court, the people's courts at various local levels and military courts. The judicial work of all these courts is subject to supervision by the Supreme People's Court. The local courts are established on the basis of the country's regional administrative division and the special courts are established as needed.

The courts at various local levels are divided into grassroots courts, intermediate courts and high courts.

2. The Functions and Powers of the Grassroots Courts and Tribunals

In accordance with the Organic Law of the People's Courts of the People's Republic of China, the grassroots courts include the county courts, autonomous county courts, the courts of the cities not divided into districts, and the courts of the districts directly under municipal governments. Their main functions and powers are:

(1) To hear criminal, civil and administrative cases of first instance, except cases prescribed otherwise by law. If a case is considered as important enough to be heard by a higher court, it may request that the case be transferred to the higher court for hearing.

(2) To handle civil disputes and minor criminal offenses for which no hearing is needed.

(3) To give guidance to the work of the people's mediation committees.

Besides, people's tribunals are established under the grassroots courts as their representative agencies for the convenience of handling complaints from the people. But the people's tribunals are not trial courts; their functions and powers are limited only to hearing ordinary civil disputes and minor criminal offenses, giving guidance to the work of the people's mediation committees, giving publicity to the legal system, and handling petitions and receiving visits from the people. In spite of all this, it is stipulated in the law that the judgment or verdict passed by a people's tribunal is the judgment or verdict of a grassroots court.

3. The Functions and Powers of the Intermediate Courts

The intermediate courts include the intermediate courts established on the basis of the prefectures in the provinces and autonomous regions, the intermediate courts established in the municipalities directly under the central government and the intermediate courts in the cities directly under the provincial and autonomous regional governments and in the autonomous prefectures. Their functions and powers are mainly as follows:

(1) To hear cases of first instance under their jurisdiction as specified by law. In accordance with the stipulations of the Criminal Procedure Law, the criminal cases of first instance under the jurisdiction of the intermediate courts are: offences against national security, ordinary crimes that may bring sentences of life imprisonment or death, and crimes committed by foreigners or crimes committed by Chinese citizens by infringing on the legitimate rights and interests of foreigners. In accordance with the stipulations of the Civil Procedure Law, the civil cases under the jurisdiction of the intermediate courts are major cases involving foreigners, cases with major influence in the areas under their jurisdiction, and cases under the jurisdiction of the intermediate courts at the instruction of the supreme court.

In accordance with the stipulations of the Administrative Procedure Law, the administrative cases of first instance under the jurisdiction of the intermediate courts are: cases involving patent rights, cases handled by the customs, cases running counter to specific administrative acts of the people's government of a province, autonomous region or municipality directly under the central government, and cases of major importance and complexity in areas under their jurisdiction.

(2) To hear cases of first instance transferred from grassroots courts.

(3) To hear cases of appeal or protest against judgments or verdicts passed by grassroots courts.

If a criminal, civil or administrative case accepted by an intermediate court is considered to be important enough to be heard by a higher court, it may request that the case be transferred to a higher court for hearing.

(4) To supervise the work of the grassroots courts in the area under its jurisdiction. If a legally effective judgment or verdict made by a grassroots court is found to be wrong, it has the right to hear the case by itself or instruct the grassroots court to rehear it.

4. The Functions and Powers of the High Court

In accordance with the Organic Law of the People's Courts of the People's Republic of China, the functions and powers of the high court are mainly: To hear major and complex criminal, civil and administrative cases of first instance under its jurisdiction as specified by law, cases of first instance transferred from lower courts, cases of appeal or protest against judgments or verdicts passed by lower courts (the high court in the area where a maritime court is located has the right to hear an appeal against a judgment or verdict passed by the maritime court); to hear cases of protest brought up by the procuratorate in accordance with the procedure of adjudication and supervision; to recheck criminal cases of first instance involving a sentence of death processed by an intermediate court, in which no appeal has been lodged (including reporting to the Supreme People's Court for approval judgments they agree with, and sending back to the original courts for rehearing judgments they disagree with); to check cases in which the intermediate courts have handed down death sentences with a two-year suspension; to examine and rule on death sentences upon authorization by the Supreme People's Court; and to supervise the work of the courts at lower levels in the area under its jurisdiction. If a legally effective judgment or verdict made by a lower court is found to be wrong, it has the right to hear the case by itself or instruct the lower court to rehear it.

5. The Functions and Powers of the Major Special Courts

The Organic Law of the People's Courts does not enumerate the types of special courts. The special courts refer to the courts established at specific departments to hear specific cases as actual needs arise. Now, the major special courts include the military courts, maritime courts and railway transport courts.

The military courts are divided into three levels: the grassroots military courts, the military courts established at the military area commands and the services and arms of the armed forces, and the Military Court of the Chinese People's Liberation Army.

The Military Court of the Chinese People's Liberation Army is the highest military court. Its functions and powers are: to hear cases of first instance involving crimes committed by division commanders and higher, to hear criminal cases involving foreigners, to hear cases authorized or designated by the Supreme People's Court and other criminal cases of first instance which it deems should be handled by itself, and to hear cases of second instance, reexamine death sentence cases and hear retrial cases.

The military courts at the military area commands and the services and arms of the armed forces include the military courts established at all military area commands, the military courts of the navy and the air force, the military court of the Second Artillery Force, and the military court of the organizations directly under the general headquarters of the People's

Liberation Army. Their functions and powers are: to hear cases of first instance involving crimes committed by deputy division commanders and regimental commanders, to hear cases which may involve a sentence of death and cases authorized or designated by the higher military court, and to hear cases of appeal and protest.

The grassroots courts include the military courts established at the army-unit level of the ground forces, military courts at the provincial military commands, military courts at the naval fleets, military courts of the air force at the military area commands, and the military court of the organizations directly under the general headquarters of the Chinese People's Liberation Army stationed in Beijing. Their functions and powers are to hear cases of first instance involving crimes committed by battalion commanders and officers of lower ranks which may involve a sentence of life imprisonment or lighter penalties, and cases of first instance authorized or designated by the higher military courts.

The maritime court is a special court established to exercise maritime judicial jurisdiction, and especially to hear maritime cases of first instance. The Supreme People's Court issued the Certain Provisions Concerning the Types of Cases to Be Heard by the Maritime Court" on August 9, 2001, which stipulates that the maritime court hears maritime cases among Chinese legal persons or citizens, between Chinese legal persons or citizens and legal persons or citizens of foreign countries and the Hong Kong, Macao and Taiwan regions of China, and among legal persons or citizens of foreign countries and the Hong Kong, Macao and Taiwan regions.

The Railway Transport Courts are special courts established along the railway lines and mainly hears the following cases:

(1) Criminal cases occurring along a railway line investigated by a railway public security organ and prosecuted by a railway procuratorate.

(2) Economic disputes. In accordance with the stipulations of the Supreme People's Court, there are 12 categories of cases in this respect, including: disputes arising from railway freight transport contracts, disputes arising from international railway through transport contracts, economic disputes between different railway transport organizations, infringement disputes arising from damage done to the railways by violation of the railway security regulations, and infringement cases involving personal and property damages caused by train movement and dispatch when the plaintiff files a suit with a the railway transport court.

6. The Functions and Powers of the Supreme Court

The Supreme People's Court is the supreme judicial organ of the state, and exercises the highest judicial power of the state. At the same time, it supervises the work of the local courts at all levels as well as the special courts. The Supreme People's Court exercises the following functions and powers:

(1) Exercising supervision over the work of the local courts at all levels and the special courts. If a legally effective judgment or verdict made by a local court at any level or by a special court is found to be wrong, it has the right to hear the case again by itself or instruct the lower court to rehear the case.

(2) Hearing cases of first instance under its jurisdiction as specified by law and which it deems should be heard by it. The Criminal Procedure Law stipulates that criminal cases of first instance under its jurisdiction are major criminal cases of national nature. The Civil Procedure Law stipulates that civil cases of first instance and economic dispute cases under its jurisdiction are major cases that produce a nationwide impact. The Administrative Procedure Law stipulates that administrative cases of first instance under its jurisdiction are major and complex cases of national significance.

(3) Hearing appeals and protests against judgments or verdicts made by high courts and special courts, and protests lodged by the Supreme People's Procuratorate in accordance with the procedure for adjudication supervision.

(4) Examining and ruling on cases in which a death sentence has been passed.

(5) Making judicial interpretations, namely, making interpretations on questions of how a court applies laws and decrees in the course of hearing a case.

(6) Directing and managing matters concerning the judicial and administrative work of the courts at all levels throughout the country.

II. The Organizational Setup of the Judicial Organs

1. The Setup of the Supreme Court

In accordance with the stipulations of the Organic Law of the People's Courts of the People's Republic of China, "the Supreme Court is composed of the president, vice-presidents, chief judges, deputy chief judges and judges. The candidate for the president of the Supreme People's Court is nominated by the presidium of the National People's Congress and elected by the National People's Congress. The president of the Supreme People's Court is responsible and reports on his work to the National People's Congress. The term of office of the president is five years, and he shall serve no more than two consecutive terms. The vice-presidents, chief judges, deputy chief judges and judges are nominated by the president of the Supreme People's Court, and appointed or removed by the Standing Committee of the National People's Congress.

Under the Supreme People's Court are the following organs:

(1) Organs of Registration, Adjudication Execution and Adjudication Supervision

The establishment of a registration division for putting cases on file and an adjudication supervision division for supervision over adjudication is intended to achieve the "three separations," that is, separation of registration from adjudication, separation of adjudication from execution, and separation of adjudication from supervision.

The registration division is responsible for registering cases and assigning them to judges in sequence. It is also responsible for controlling the time-limit flow chart for the adjudication of all categories of cases heard in the court, so as to separate the registration procedure from the court hearing procedure, to prevent or reduce contacts between the judges and the parties involved out of court, and to strengthen control over the time limit for adjudication, and help to improve the efficiency of handling cases.

The execution office is responsible for executing the decisions of the court.

The adjudication supervision division is responsible for hearing appeals against effective judgments made by the court and some effective criminal or civil judgments made by lower courts. The purpose is to separate the procedures for the first and second instances from the retrial procedure, so that the judges of the original court do not retry their own cases, and properly protect the legitimate rights and interests of the parties involved.

(2) Organs of Criminal Justice

There are two criminal tribunals. They are responsible for hearing major criminal cases. The No. 2 criminal tribunal is responsible for hearing (or examining) and handling appeals lodged with the Supreme People's Court by the parties concerned, defendants, their families or other citizens against legally effective judgments or verdicts, and correcting the possible mistakes occurring in the course of the trials in good time.

In order to strengthen the work of hearing economic criminal cases, special adjudication divisions are set up inside the above two tribunals respectively for hearing economic criminal cases.

(3) Organs of Civil Justice

There are four tribunals for civil justice.

The No. 1 tribunal is responsible for hearing cases involving marital and family, personal property and real estate contract disputes.

The No. 2 tribunal is responsible for hearing cases involving disputes arising from contracts of all types and infringements between legal persons, and between legal persons and other economic organizations.

The No. 3 tribunal is responsible for hearing intellectual property cases.

The No. 4 tribunal is responsible for hearing maritime cases.

(4) Administrative Court

The administrative court is responsible for hearing cases involving administrative actions taken by central organs of the state.

Apart from the above organs, the Supreme People's Court also has a judicial committee that is actually responsible for directing the judicial work of the whole court. The judicial committee of the Supreme People's Court is set up in accordance with the principle of leadership based on democratic centralism. Therefore, it serves as the leading group of the Supreme People's Court, not an organ for the enforcement of the law. The task of the judicial committee is to sum up experience in judicial work, and discuss major or difficult cases and other problems related to judicial work. The president of the Supreme People's Court presides over the meetings of the judicial committee, the members of which are appointed or removed by the Standing Committee of the National People's Congress upon the recommendation of the president of the Supreme People's Court. The credentials for the members of the judicial committee are limited only to the president, vice-presidents, chief judges, deputy chief judges and judges of the court. The judicial committee is a unique form of leadership over adjudication in China.

2. The Setup of Local Courts

The local courts in the People's Republic of China are divided into three levels, on the basis of administrative division: grassroots courts, intermediate courts and high courts.

(1) Grassroots Courts

The grassroots courts include county courts, city courts, autonomous county courts and courts in the districts directly under the municipal governments. Generally speaking, the grassroots courts are homologous to the county-level administrative division. Besides, grassroots courts are also established at the large reform-through-labor farms in some regions with special permission of the state. For example, Hubei Province has a grassroots court at the Shayang Reform-through-labor Farm, which is directly under the guidance and supervision of the intermediate court of Jingzhou Prefecture.

A grassroots court is composed of the president, vice-president(s) and judges of the court. Its internal organs include a judicial committee, a criminal tribunal, a tribunal for civil cases, a tribunal for economic cases and a tribunal for administrative offenses. All the tribunals have chief judges and deputy chief judges. The other organs include the division for execution, correspondence and visitation section, personnel section, general office (including investigation and research, judicial statistics and medico-legal expertise section).

The president of the grassroots court is elected by the people's congress at the corresponding level. Its vice-presidents, chief judges, deputy chief judges and judges are appointed or removed by the standing committee of the people's congress at the same level. All of them serve for a term of three years.

Under Article 20 of the Organic Law of the People's Courts, a people's tribunal is established for every two to three townships, or a population of around 50,000, in the rural areas of the Chinese mainland. It is a component part, and a representative organ, of the grassroots court. Its judgment or verdict is at the same time the judgment or verdict of the grassroots court. Each people's tribunal has at least three judges and one clerk.

(2) Intermediate Courts

The intermediate courts include the intermediate courts established in the prefectures of the various provinces and autonomous regions, the intermediate courts established in the municipalities directly under the central government, the intermediate courts in the cities directly under the governments of the provinces and autonomous regions, and the intermediate courts in the autonomous prefectures. The intermediate courts are homologous to the administrative division at the prefectural level or at the level of a city divided into districts.

The intermediate court is composed of the president, vice-presidents, chief judges, deputy chief judges and judges of the court. Its internal organs include a judicial committee, a division for registration, No. 1 criminal tribunal (for hearing criminal cases of first instance), No. 2 criminal tribunal (for hearing criminal cases of appeal or protest), No. 3 criminal tribunal (for hearing protest cases brought up according to the adjudication supervision procedure), No. 1 civil tribunal (for hearing civil cases of first instance), No. 2 civil tribunal (for hearing civil cases of appeal), an economic tribunal, a tribunal for hearing administrative cases, a tribunal of execution, adjudication supervision division, general office, political department, supervision office, investigation and research office, personnel department, judicial administration department, medical jurisprudence center, clerks section and judicial police squad. All the divisions have chief judges and deputy chief judges or other chiefs with homologous titles.

The president of the intermediate court in a city directly under the government of a province and autonomous region, or of an intermediate court in an autonomous prefecture, is elected by the people's congress at the corresponding level. Its vice-president(s), chief judges, deputy chief judges and judges are appointed or removed by the standing committee of the people's congress at the same level. The president, vice-president(s), chief judges, deputy chief judges and judges of the intermediate court, established on the prefectural basis in a province or autonomous region or by an intermediate court established in a municipality directly under the central government, are appointed by the standing committee of the people's congress of the province, autonomous region or municipality for a term of five years, and are removed by the same committee.

(3) High Courts

The high courts include the high court of a province, the high court of an autonomous region and the high court of a municipality directly under the central government. They are homologous to the administrative division of the relevant province, autonomous region and municipality.

The high court is composed of the president, vice-president(s), chief judges, deputy chief judges and judges. Its internal organs include a judicial committee, No. 1 criminal tribunal (for hearing criminal cases of first instance), No. 2 criminal tribunal (for hearing cases of criminal appeal and protest), No. 3 criminal tribunal (for hearing cases of criminal protest brought up according to the adjudication supervision procedure), a civil tribunal, an economic tribunal, an administrative tribunal, a general office (including sections handling correspondence, visitation, secretariat and archives), a political division, a policy research division (including a section handling the collection of judicial statistics), and a division for judicial administration.

The president of the high court is elected by the people's congress of the relevant province, autonomous region or municipality. Its vice-president(s), chief judges, deputy chief judges and judges are appointed or removed by the standing committee of the people's congress at the same level. They all serve for a term of five years.

3. The Setup of the Special Courts

The special courts are a component part of the court system. They and the local courts at all levels jointly exercise the judicial power of the state. However, the special courts are distinguished from the local courts mainly in the following aspects:

(1) A special court is a judicial organ established for a specific organization (a railway administration, for example) or to hear cases of a specific type (maritime cases, for example) while a local court is a judicial organ established on the basis of the administrative division.

(2) A case under the jurisdiction of the special court is different from that heard by a local court in nature, and the cases it handles are strictly restricted.

(3) The establishment of the special court and the appointment and removal of its personnel are different from those of the local courts. For example, the president of a military court is not elected by the people's congress, but appointed by the Supreme People's Court and the Central Military Commission.

However, both the ordinary courts and the special courts are component parts of the single judicial system. They must apply the same laws of the state and their adjudication must be subject to supervision by the Supreme People's Court.

The Setup of Military Courts

(1) The Establishment of Military Courts

A military court is a special judicial organ that exercises the judicial power of the state inside the Chinese People's Liberation Army. It joins the Military Procuratorate and the Military Security Department to form the military judicial system.

The military courts are divided into three levels: the Military Court of the Chinese People's Liberation Army; the military courts established in the military area commands and the services of the armed forces, including the military courts established in all military area commands, the military courts of the navy and the air force, and the military court of the organizations directly under the general headquarters of the People's Liberation Army; and the grassroots military courts, including the military courts established at the army unit level, the military courts in the provincial military commands, the military courts of the naval fleets and the military courts of the air force in the military area commands.

In accordance with Article 127 of the Constitution of the People's Republic of China, the military courts are subject to supervision by the Supreme People's Court.

(2) The Internal Organs of the Military Courts

The Military Court of the Chinese People's Liberation Army has a president and a vice-president. It has two tribunals, each of which has a chief judge, a deputy chief judge, several judges and clerks. The military courts in the military area commands and the various services of the armed forces and the grassroots courts each have a president, several judges and clerks. The establishment and dismantling of a military court and its size of personnel are decided on by the Central Military Commission of the People's Republic of China. The military courts at all levels are established on the basis of the organizational system of the armed forces, and their size of personnel is included in the array of the political organ (political department) at the same level.

Judicial committees are established in the military courts at all levels to discuss major and difficult cases and other questions related to adjudication. The meetings of the judicial committee are presided over by the president. The procurator-general of the military procuratorate at the same level may also attend the meetings as a non-voting member.

(3) Establishment of the Military Courts and Their Responsibilities

The military courts at all levels are responsible to the political departments of the armed forces. Apart from that the Standing Committee of the National People's Congress appoints or removes the president of the military court of the Chinese People's Liberation Army, as prescribed in Clause 11 in Article 67 of the Constitution, all other cadres of the military courts at all levels are appointed or removed by the army.

The Setup of Maritime Courts

The maritime courts are special courts established in the mid-1980's to hear maritime cases to meet the needs of the development of maritime transport and foreign trade. Maritime courts are established at the port cities of Guangzhou, Shanghai, Wuhan, Qingdao, Tianjin and Dalian.

A maritime court has a president, vice-presidents, chief judges, deputy chief judges and judges. The standing committee of the people's congress of the city where the maritime court is located appoints or removes the president of the maritime court upon the nomination by the chairman of the standing committee of the municipal people's congress. It also appoints or removes the vice-presidents, chief judges, deputy chief judges and judges of the maritime court at the recommendation of the president of the maritime court.

The maritime court has a maritime tribunal and a tribunal in charge of maritime trade, a research office and a general office.

The work of the maritime court is subject to supervision by the high court in the city where the maritime court is located.

The Setup of Railway Transport Courts

Railway transport courts are special courts set up to adjudicate civil and criminal cases occurring along the railway lines and inside the railway system. They are divided into two levels, namely, the intermediate railway transport courts established at the railway administrations, and the grassroots courts established at the railway sub-administrations. The work of the intermediate railway transport courts are subject to supervision by the high courts in the cities where these courts are located.

The standing committee of the people's congress of the city where a railway transport court is located appoints or removes the president of the railway transport court upon nomination by the chairman of the standing committee of the people's congress. It also appoints or removes the vice-presidents, chief judges, deputy chief judges and judges of the railway transport court at the recommendation of the president of the railway transport court.

The railway transport court has a criminal tribunal, an economic tribunal, a civil tribunal, and a general office.

The Setup of Forestry Courts

Forestry courts are special courts set up to hear cases involving the destruction of forest resources, cases of accidents due to serious negligence of duty, and cases involving foreigners.

The forestry courts include the grassroots forestry courts (people's tribunals in the forest areas) and intermediate forestry courts (forestry tribunals established at intermediate courts) and the forestry tribunals established in high courts.

The grassroots forestry courts are usually established at the places where the forestry bureaus (including the bureaus for the water transport of timber) are located in certain specific forest areas. The intermediate forestry courts are usually established in places where the prefectural (league) forest administrations are located or in areas where the state-owned forests are concentrated and linked together. In other regions with abundant forest resources, a certain number of judges are added to the local courts at the provincial (autonomous regional), prefectural (league) and county (banner) levels to specially look after cases occurring in the forest areas, or a grassroots court establishes a people's tribunal on a major state forest farm or in a forest area as needs arise. Forestry tribunals are established in the intermediate courts of the prefectures where there are more forests and in the high courts of the provinces and autonomous regions where there are more forestry courts to hear forest-related cases.

Section 2 The Procuratorial Organs

I. The System, Functions and Powers of the Procuratorial Organs

1. The System of the Procuratorial Organs

The system of the procuratorial organs of China covers the Supreme People's Procuratorate and local people's procuratorates at all levels, as well as the military procuratorates and other special procuratorates.

The local procuratorates include: the procuratorate of a province, autonomous region or municipality directly under the central government, the branch procuratorate of a province, autonomous region or a municipality directly under the central government, the procuratorate of an autonomous prefecture or a city directly under the provincial government, and the procuratorate of a county, a city, an autonomous county or a district directly under the city government.

The procuratorate at the provincial level or at the county level may establish a procuratorate as its representative organ in an industrial or mining area, a reclamation farm or a forest area, in line with actual needs, upon approval by the standing committee of the people's congress at the corresponding level.

2. The Main Functions and Powers of the Procuratorial Organs

The task of the procuratorates at all levels is: to exercise procuratorial power over cases of treason, cases of splitting the country and major cases of grave disruption of the implementation of policies and laws, and unification of local and government decrees; to investigate the criminal cases it handles directly; to examine the cases investigated by public security organs and state security organs to decide whether to make arrests, prosecute or exempt from prosecution; to supervise the legality of the investigative activities of the public security organs; to conduct and support the public prosecution of criminal cases; to supervise the legality of the judicial activities of the courts; and to supervise the execution of the judgments and verdicts and the legality of the activities of prisons, houses of detention and organs of reform through labor.

The specific functions and powers of a county-level procuratorate are: to supervise the state functionaries in the areas of its jurisdiction, to investigate and conduct public prosecution of offenders; to exercise legal supervision over the process of investigation made by county public security organs and state security organs and to stop the violations of law discovered, and to prosecute in court if the violations are grave; to examine requests for the approval of arrests and prosecutions made by county public security bureaus to decide whether to make arrests and approve the prosecutions; to conduct public prosecutions in grassroots courts; to make protests against judgments and verdicts considered erroneous made by grassroots courts; to supervise the execution of the judgments and verdicts on criminal cases made by county-level judicial and administrative organs; and to exercise legal supervision over the civil and administrative actions of the grassroots courts.

The specific functions and powers of a prefecture-level procuratorate are: to supervise state functionaries in the areas under its jurisdiction; to exercise supervision over the investigative activities carried out in its area of jurisdiction by prefecture-level public security organs and state security organs; to participate in actions against criminal cases of first instance under the jurisdiction of the intermediate court; to exercise legal supervision over the judicial activities of the intermediate court in handling civil cases and administrative cases; to make protests to the intermediate court in accordance with the procedure for adjudication supervision if it finds a legally effective judgment or verdict made on a criminal case by a grassroots court to be erroneous.

A provincial procuratorate has the power to supervise the state functionaries in the area under its jurisdiction; to exercise supervision over the investigative activities of provincial public security organs and state security organs; to participate in court actions against the criminal cases of first instance under the jurisdiction of the high courts; to supervise the judicial activities of the high courts in handling civil cases and administrative cases; to make protests in accordance with the procedure for adjudication supervision to the lower courts if it finds legally effective judgments or verdicts made on criminal cases by them to be erroneous; and to exercise legal supervision over the execution of judgments or verdicts against criminal offenders in prisons, houses of detention and organs of reform through labor under the jurisdiction of the judicial organs of the province.

The main task of the Supreme People's Procuratorate is to guide the local procuratorates at all levels and special procuratorates to exercise legal supervision in accordance with the law, and guarantee the harmony and correct implementation of the state laws. Its specific functions and powers are: to direct the work of the local and special procuratorates at all levels; to determine the guiding principles for the procuratorial work and make arrangements for procuratorial work; investigate cases of corruption and bribery, cases of infringement on citizens' democratic rights, cases of dereliction of duty and other criminal cases it deems it necessary to handle directly in accordance with the law; to direct the investigative work of the local procuratorates at all levels and the special procuratorates, to examine and approve arrests, and conduct public prosecutions against major criminal cases; to lead the local procuratorates at all levels and the special procuratorates to examine and approve arrests and prosecute criminal cases; to lead the local procuratorates and the special procuratorates in their work to exercise legal supervision over civil and economic adjudication, and administrative actions; to make protests to the Supreme People's Court in accordance with the law against legally effective judgments or verdicts made by courts at all levels it deems to be erroneous; to examine the decisions made by the local procuratorates and the special procuratorates in exercising their procuratorial powers and correct erroneous decisions; to handle charges, appeals and complaints made by the citizens; to accept reports on bribery and corruption, and direct the reporting work of the procuratorial organs of the whole country; to map out the program for the restructuring of the procuratorial organs and organize for the implementation of the program after approval by the competent authority; to plan and guide the procuratorial technical work and the work of inspection, examination and identification of physical evidence by the procuratorial organs of the whole country; to make judicial interpretations on the concrete application of the laws in the course of procuratorial work; to formulate regulations, detailed rules and stipulations concerning procuratorial work; to be responsible for the ideological and political work, and training of personnel in the procuratorial organs; to direct the work of the local procuratorates and the special procuratorates in exercising supervision over the procurators; to formulate rules for the clerks; to cooperate with the provincial committees of the Communist Party of China in supervising and appraising the procurators-general and deputy procurators-general of the procuratorates of the provinces, autonomous regions and municipalities directly under the central government, and make recommendations to the NPC Standing Committee to approve or reject the appointment or removal of the procurators-general of the procuratorates of the provinces, autonomous regions and municipalities directly under the central government, and make recommendations to the NPC Standing Committee in making decisions on the appointment or removal of procurators-general of the special procuratorates; to make suggestions to the NPC Standing Committee for replacing the procurators-general, deputy procurators-general and members of the procuratorial committees of the lower procuratorates; to cooperate with the competent departments in controlling the organizational setup and size of staff of the procuratorates; to organize and give guidance to the educational and training work for cadres in the procuratorial system; to plan and give guidance to the planning, financial and equipment work of the procuratorial organs of the whole country; to organize exchanges between the procuratorates and their foreign counterparts, and seek international judicial assistance; to examine and approve cooperation in the investigation of individual cases with public prosecution organizations in the Hong Kong, Macao and

Taiwan regions; and to be responsible for other matters that the Supreme People's Procuratorate shall handle.

3. The Types of Cases to Be Filed to the Procuratorates for Investigation and Prosecution

Apart from handling cases turned in from the public security and state security organs, the procuratorates may also directly start investigations into certain cases. The cases that can be directly handled by the procuratorates include:

(1) Cases of Bribery and Corruption

Such cases include cases of bribery, cases of corruption, cases of embezzlement of public funds, cases of concealing overseas deposits, and cases of dividing up state assets or confiscated property privately.

(2) Cases of Neglect of Duty

These include cases of abuse of power, cases of neglect of duty, cases of fraudulence for self gains by functionaries of state organs, cases of disclosing state secrets intentionally or negligently, cases of unjustified prosecution and judgment (including those in civil and administrative adjudication), cases of unjustified release of criminals in custody, cases of negligence of duty leading to the escape of criminals in custody, cases of commutation, parole or release of law offenders from custody for self gains, cases of failure to hand over criminal cases for self gains, cases of exempt or reduction of tax payment for self gains, cases of selling invoices, countervailing and withholding tax payments and giving export rebates for self gains, cases of illegal issuing of export rebate receipts, cases of neglect of duty in signing and honoring contracts, cases of illegal issuing of tree-felling licenses, cases of neglect of duty in environmental monitoring and control, cases of neglect of duty in the prevention and treatment of infectious diseases, cases of illegal approval of requisition and occupation of land, cases of illegal sale of the right to use state-owned land at low prices, cases of connivance at smuggling, cases of misconduct or neglect of duty in the course of commodity inspection for self gains, cases of misconduct or neglect of duty in the course of animal and plant quarantine for self gains, cases of connivance at production and marketing of fake or inferior commodities, cases of illegally processing exit and entry certificates for people crossing national borders, cases of allowing people to cross national borders illegally, cases of failure to rescue or impeding the effort to rescue abducted women or children, cases of helping law offenders escape penalties, cases of misconduct in recruiting public servants or students for self gains, and cases of damage to or loss of valuable relics due to neglect of duty.

(3) Offences Committed by Functionaries of State Organs in Abusing Their Power

These include cases of illegal detention, cases of illegal search, cases of extorting confessions by torture, cases of taking evidence by force, cases of maltreating people under supervision and control, cases of retaliation, cases of frame-up and cases of undermining an election.

(4) Cases for Investigation upon Special Decisions

When a procuratorate deems it necessary to handle directly major cases of state functionaries abusing their powers, it can start the investigation upon a decision made by the procuratorate at the provincial level or above.

II. The Organizational Setup and Main Departments of the Procuratorial Organs

1. The Organizational Setup of the Procuratorial Organs

(1) The Organs of the Supreme People's Procuratorate

The Supreme People's Procuratorate has a procurator-general, deputy procurators-general and procurators. The procurator-general directs the work of the procuratorate. The procurator-general is elected or removed by the National People's Congress. The deputy procurators-general and procurators are appointed or removed by the Standing Committee of the National People's Congress on the recommendation of the procurator-general.

The Supreme People's Procuratorate has fifteen functional departments: the general office, the investigation and supervision department, public prosecution department, the anti-corruption and anti-bribery bureau, the procuratorial department in charge of cases of neglect of duty and infringement of right, the procuratorial department in charge of work in the prisons, the procuratorial department in charge of civil and administrative cases, the accusation procuratorial department (the reporting center of the Supreme People's Procuratorate), the criminal appeal procuratorial department, the railway transport procuratorial department, the department for the prevention of crimes committed by abusing power in hand, the law and policy research office, the supervision bureau, the foreign affairs bureau, and the planning, financial and equipment bureau.

In accordance with the Organic Law of the People's Procuratorates of the People's Republic of China, the Supreme People's Procuratorate establishes a procuratorial committee. The tasks of the procuratorial committee are to discuss and decide on major issues arising in the implementation of the laws and policies of the state as regards procuratorial work; to sum up experiences in procuratorial work and study new developments and new problems in procuratorial work; to discuss and adopt interpretations on the concrete application of the law in procuratorial work; to discuss and study rules, regulations and measures to be adopted in procuratorial work; to discuss matters concerning the registration of cases to be handled directly by the Supreme People's Procuratorate, decisions on arrests, transfer and prosecution of cases, requests for instructions from the procuratorates of provinces, autonomous regions and municipalities directly under the central government and the special procuratorates in accordance with stipulations in the law, and cases to which the procuratorates of provinces, autonomous regions and municipalities directly under the central government request the Supreme People's Procuratorate to make protests, and make corresponding decisions; to discuss and adopt motions to be submitted to the National People's Congress and its Standing Committee; to discuss and draft work reports to be submitted to the National People's Congress and its Standing Committee; and to discuss and decide on other matters that must be discussed by the procuratorial committee.

The Standing Committee of the National People's Congress appoints and removes the members of the procuratorial committee upon the recommendation of the procurator-general. Presided over by the procurator-general, the procuratorial committee discusses and decides on major cases and other major questions. The meeting of the procuratorial committee can be convened only when more than half of the committee members are present. It is convened once a week, and may be convened before or after the scheduled date when necessary.

The procuratorial committee practices democratic centralism, wherein the minority is subordinate to the majority. A decision on any question under discussion can be adopted only when more than half of the committee members agree. When a decision is to be made on a case or a matter under discussion, the president of the meeting shall take into account different views. If more than half of the members of the procuratorial committee are in agreement, a decision shall be made. The views of the minority can be filed for the record. As to a matter or case to be discussed, if the procuratorial committee deems it unnecessary for the committee to make a decision, it may instruct the department in charge to handle it. If the procurator-general does not agree with the majority on a major question, it can be reconsidered or handled in accordance with the stipulations of the relevant law. If there is a big difference of opinion among the members of the committee, it shall be discussed again. If the procurator-general does not agree with the majority, the matter may be submitted to the NPC Standing Committee for a decision. The matters decided by the procuratorial committee shall be turned to the department in charge and the procuratorates of the concerned provinces, autonomous regions and municipalities directly under the central government for implementation in the form of a circular on the decisions made by the committee meeting. The department in charge and the units concerned shall carry out the decisions made by the procuratorial committee. It they have any objection, they may request the procuratorial committee to reconsider the matter in accordance with the relevant procedure. The department in charge and the units shall inform the secretariat of the procuratorial committee on the implementation of the decisions. The secretariat of the procuratorial committee shall report to the procurator-general and the procuratorial committee on the implementation in good time.

(2) The Organs of the Local Procuratorial Organs at All Levels

a) The Setup of the Local Procuratorates at All Levels

The setup of a local procuratorate, like that of a local court, is homologous to the local administrative division. Generally speaking, where there is a court, there is a procuratorate. The procuratorate and the court established in the same administrative region are at the same level and have a common area under their jurisdiction.

The local procuratorates are divided into the procuratorates of the provinces, autonomous regions and municipalities directly under the central government, the branch procuratorates of the provinces, autonomous regions and municipalities directly under the central government and the procuratorates of the counties, cities, autonomous counties and districts directly under the city government. The provincial and county procuratorates may also establish procuratorates in industrial or mining areas, land-reclamation areas and forest areas as their representative organs.

b) The Organs of the Local Procuratorates at All Levels

In accordance with the stipulations of the Organic Law of the People's Procuratorates of the People's Republic of China, a procuratorate at any level has a procurator-general, deputy procurators-general and procurators, and establishes a procuratorial committee. The term of office of the procurator-general at all levels is the same as that of the people's congress at the corresponding level.

The procurators-general of the procuratorates of the provinces, autonomous regions and municipalities directly under the central government are elected or removed by the people's congress of the provinces, autonomous regions and municipalities directly under the central government, and the deputy procurators-general, members of the procuratorial committees and procurators of these procuratorates, and the procurators-general, deputy procurators-general, members of the procuratorial committees and procurators of their branch procuratorates are appointed or removed by the standing committees of the people's congresses upon the recommendation of the procurators-general of the procuratorates of the provinces, autonomous regions and municipalities directly under the central government. The appointments and removals of the procurators-general of the procuratorates of the provinces, autonomous regions and municipalities directly under the central government shall be reported to the procurator-general of the Supreme People's Procuratorate for approval by the Standing Committee of the National People's Congress.

The procurator-generals of the procuratorates of the autonomous prefectures, cities directly under the provincial governments, counties, cities and districts directly under the city governments are elected and removed by the people's congresses at the corresponding levels. The deputy procurators-general, members of the procuratorial committees, and procurators of the procuratorates are appointed or removed by the standing committees of the people's congresses at the corresponding levels upon the recommendation of the procurators-general. The appointments or removals of the procurators-general of the procuratorates of the autonomous prefectures, cities directly under the provincial governments, counties, cities and districts directly under the city governments shall be reported to the procurators-general of the higher procuratorates for approval by the standing committees of the people's congresses at the corresponding levels.

The procurators-general, deputy procurators-general, members of the procuratorial committees and procurators of the procuratorates established by provincial or county procuratorates in industrial or mining areas, land-reclamation areas and forest areas are appointed or removed by the standing committees of the people's congresses at the corresponding levels upon the recommendation of the procurators-general of the procuratorates which have established them.

The National People's Congress and the people's congresses of the provinces, autonomous regions and municipalities directly under the central government may replace the procurators-general, deputy procurators-general and members of the procuratorial committees of the lower procuratorates upon the recommendation of the procurators-general of the procuratorates at the corresponding levels.

The procuratorates at all levels may establish a number of procuratorial work organs.

There is a slight difference in the internal setup of the provincial procuratorates among different provinces, autonomous regions and municipalities. But, it is usually organized according to the division of work among the following links of work: examination for the approval of arrests, examination for prosecution, procuratorial work concerning violations of law and discipline, appeal and accusation, public prosecution of economic cases, prosecution of cases related to the prisons, and forestry cases. The internal organs of a provincial procuratorate usually include the No. 1 division for criminal cases, No, 2 division for criminal cases, the division handling investigation, accusation and appeal against acts in violation of law and discipline (sometimes divided into two sections), technical investigation division, logistics service and equipment division, general office (divided into three sections in charge of secretarial work, security and archives respectively), political department (in charge of the allocation of the procuratorial officials of the whole province, personnel, and political and ideological work), research office and schools.

The internal organs of the procuratorates at the prefectural level usually include a section for examination for approval of arrests, a section handling investigation, accusation and appeal against acts in violation of law and discipline, a section handling economic cases, a section handling cases related to prisons, a section in charge of personnel work and a general office.

The internal organs of the county procuratorates mainly include a section for examination for approval of arrests, a section for examination for prosecution, a section handling investigation, accusation and appeal against acts in violation of law and discipline, a section handling economic cases, and a section dealing with cases related to prisons.

The local procuratorates, like the Supreme People's Procuratorate, each establish a procuratorial committee. The procuratorial committee consists of the procurator-general, deputy procurators-general and some procurators. The number of members of the procuratorial committee is nine to fifteen for provincial procuratorial committees, seven to eleven for prefectural procuratorial committees, and five to nine for county procuratorial committees.

The procuratorial committees are the organs of power of the procuratorates at all levels. Presided over by the procurators-general, they discuss and decide on major legal cases and other major issues.

c) The Organs of the Special Procuratorates

The special procuratorates refer to the procuratorates established in specific fields of work and trades. These include mainly the military procuratorates and railway transport procuratorates, etc.

The military procuratorates are the organs of legal supervision established by the state in the People's Liberation Army. They include the Military Procuratorate of the Chinese People's Liberation Army (called the Military Procuratorate of the Supreme People's Procuratorate before 1965), the military procuratorates of the military area commands, the services of the armed forces, including the military procuratorates of the military area commands, the military procuratorate of the navy and the military procuratorate of the air force, and the grassroots military procuratorates, including the military procuratorates at the army group level, military procuratorates at the army unit level, the military procuratorates of the naval fleets and the military procuratorates of the air force in the military area commands.

Some of the military procuratorates are established on a regional basis, while others are established on a system basis. Concretely, the military procuratorates of the navy and air force (established at the headquarters of those services) and the grassroots military procuratorates (established at the headquarters of the naval fleets and the air force units under the military area commands) are all established on the command system. They handle criminal cases involving servicemen under the leadership of the higher military procuratorates. The grass-roots military procuratorates of the ground forces are established on a regional basis (usually in the provincial capital cities and municipalities directly under the central government). They are the representative organs of the military procuratorates of the military area commands, conduct their work under the leadership of the military procuratorates of the military area commands, and handle criminal cases involving servicemen of the ground forces in the areas under their jurisdiction.

The military procuratorates at all levels are organized on military principles. Their officials must be officers on active service. The procurator-general of the Military Procuratorate of the Chinese People's Liberation Army is appointed or removed by the NPC Standing Committee. The procurators-general and the members of the procuratorial committees of the military procuratorates at different levels are appointed or removed with the approval of the political departments of the PLA at the corresponding levels, but with the consent of the higher procuratorial organs.

The railway transport procuratorates are established at two levels: branch procuratorates are established at the railway administrations, and grassroots procuratorates are established at the railway sub-administrations.

The activities of the railway branch procuratorates are subject to the leadership of the procuratorates of the provinces, autonomous regions or municipalities directly under the central government where the headquarters locate. The size of staff of the branch procuratorates is included in the staff of the railway administrations at the same level.

2. The Main Work Departments of the Procuratorial Organs

The procuratorates establish internal organs in accordance with the provisions of the law, and on the basis of division of work between different links of the procuratorial work, that is, investigation, examination for arrests and examination for prosecution.

(1) The Department Handling Accusations and Appeals

It accepts and handles reports, accusations and complaints; hear confessions from offenders, accept appeals against a procuratorate's decisions not to approve arrests and prosecute, and other erroneous decisions; accept appeals against legally effective criminal judgments or verdicts passed by the court; etc.

(2) The Department against Corruption and Bribery

It investigates and handles cases of crime committed by functionaries of state organs, such as corruption, bribery, embezzlement of public funds, etc. by abusing their power.

(3) The Department Handling Cases of Negligence of Duty and Tort

It investigates and handles accusations of neglect of duty committed by functionaries of state organs and crimes they commit by abusing the power in hand, such as illegal detention, extorting confessions by torture, retaliation and frame-ups, illegal search, sorting evidence by violence, and undermining elections.

(4) The Department to Examine and Approve Arrests

It examines requests from public security organs, state security organs and the investigation department of the procuratorate for approval of arrests and decides whether to make the arrests. It also examines requests from public security organs, state security organs and the investigation department of the procuratorate for extension of the time duration for investigation and detention, decides whether to extend the time duration, and exercises supervision over the public security organs to see to it that their investigative activities are legal.

(5) Department of Examination and Prosecution

This department examines cases transferred to it by public security organs, state security organs and the investigation department of procuratorate for decisions on whether to pursue public prosecution or not, attends court hearings to support public prosecutions, exercises supervision over the judicial activities of the courts and protests erroneous criminal judgments or verdicts.

(6) Department Dealing with Cases Related to Prisons

This department supervises the execution of the criminal judgments or verdicts, and exercises control over the running of prisons; directly starts investigations into cases of maltreatment of prisoners, illegal release of criminals in custody, neglect of duty leading to the escape of criminals in custody, and illegal commutation, parole and execution of sentences for self gains; examines requests for arrest and prosecution of criminals serving non-jail sentences and persons undergoing reform through labor who have committed further offences.

(7) Department Handling Civil and Administrative Cases

This department is responsible to lodge protests, in accordance with the law, against legally effective civil and administrative judgments or verdicts passed by the courts which are found to be erroneous or to have violated legal procedure and which might have affected correct judgments or verdicts.

(8) Technical Department

This department conducts on-the-spot investigations, collects evidence related to cases, and makes scientific verification, examinations and verifications of evidence with technological means for other law-enforcing departments.

(9) Department for Discipline Inspection and Supervision

It accepts reports and accusations from people of all walks of life concerning violations of the law and discipline by procuratorial personnel who act *ultra vires*, extort confessions by torture, or go to entertainment invitations and accept bribes, and makes investigations into and handles such cases.

Section 3 Judges and Procurators

I. Judges

1. The Duties of a Judge

The duty of a judge is to hear cases with a collegiate panel or on his or her own, and to assume other duties as specified by law. Apart from hearing cases, the president, vice-presidents, members of the judicial committee, chief judge and deputy chief judges shall also perform duties compatible with their posts.

2. Qualifications of a Judge

A judge is a member of the judicial body which exercises the judicial power of the state in accordance with the law.

A judge must have the following qualifications: having the nationality of the People's Republic of China; having reached the age of 23; supporting the Constitution of the People's Republic of China; having sound political integrity and professional qualities and good conduct; having good health; having completed a four-year college course in law or having completed a four-year course in other studies but with a knowledge of the law and two years of work experience, or having acquired a bachelor degree in law and having one year of work experience, or having acquired a master degree or doctor degree in law.

A person lacking the above-mentioned qualifications shall receive training if he or she applies to be a judge. Following such training, the said person's qualifications shall be scrutinized according to the rules formulated by the Supreme People's Court.

Any person who has once received a criminal penalty or has once been discharged from public service is not permitted to be a judge.

Besides, in accordance with the stipulations of the Organic Law of the People's Courts of the People's Republic of China, the president or vice-president of a court, chief judge, deputy chief judges, judges, assistant judges and people's assessors must be citizens of the People's Republic of China with the right to elect and stand for election, have reached the age of 23 and have professional knowledge in law.

3. Appointment or Removal of a Judge

In accordance with the Law on Judges of the People's Republic of China, a judge is appointed or removed in accordance with the procedure for appointment and removal as specified in the Constitution and other laws.

The president of the Supreme People's Court is elected or removed by the National People's Congress; its vice-presidents, members of the judicial committee, chief judges, deputy chief judges and judges are appointed or removed by the Standing Committee of the National People's Congress upon the recommendation of the president.

The presidents of the local courts at all levels are elected or removed by the local people's congresses at the corresponding levels, and their vice-presidents, members of the judicial committees, chief judges, deputy chief judges and judges are appointed or removed by the standing committees of the people's congresses at the corresponding levels upon the recommendation of the presidents of those courts.

The presidents of the intermediate courts established in the provinces and autonomous regions on the basis of regional division and those established in the municipalities directly under the central government are appointed or removed by the standing committees of the provincial, autonomous regional and municipal people's congresses upon the nomination of the council of chairmen of these people's congresses. The vice-presidents, members of the judicial committees, chief judges, deputy chief judges and judges are appointed or removed by the standing committees of the provincial, autonomous regional and municipal people's congresses upon the recommendation of the presidents of the high courts in relevant provinces, autonomous regions and municipalities under the central government.

The presidents of the local courts at all levels established in places where ethnic minority autonomy is practiced are elected or removed by the people's congresses at all levels in these places. The vice-presidents, members of the judicial committees, chief judges, deputy chief judges and judges are appointed or removed by the standing committees of the people's congresses at the same levels upon the recommendation of the presidents of these courts. The assistant judges are appointed or removed by the presidents of the respective courts.

The procedure for the appointment or removal of the presidents, vice-presidents, members of the judicial committees, chief judges, deputy chief judges and judges of the military courts and other special courts are prescribed separately by the Standing Committee of the National People's Congress.

Preliminary judges and assistant judges shall be nominated from among people with the best qualifications for judges according to the criteria of combining political integrity and ability through public examinations and strict assessment.

Candidates for presidents, vice-presidents, members of the judicial committees, chief judges and deputy chief judges shall be selected from among people with the actual work experience and sound record.

In the case of a judge who has lost the nationality of the People's Republic of China, who has been transferred from a court, who has moved to other post and does not need to keep his or her post as a judge, who is regarded as incompetent, who is unable to perform his or her duty for reasons of poor health, who retires, resigns from his or her post or is dismissed, who is unable to continue to hold his post because of violation of discipline or law, or who must be removed for other reasons, the competent organ shall request his or her removal in accordance with the law.

A judge shall not be a member of the standing committee of a people's congress, nor take a post in an administrative and procuratorial organ, in an enterprise or institution, nor serve as a lawyer.

Judges are classified into twelve grades. The president of the Supreme People's Court is the chief justice, and the judges from Grade 2 to Grade 12 are classified as justice, senior judge, and judge.

4. Avoidance by a Judge

Judges who have a marital or affinal relations, or consanguineous relations within three generations shall not hold the following posts at the same time: president, vice-president, member of the judicial committee, chief judge, deputy chief judge and assistant judge of the same court; chief judge, deputy chief judge, judge and assistant judge of the same tribunal, and president or vice-president of the courts at two adjoining levels.

5. The Committee for the Evaluation of Judges

A court establishes a committee for the evaluation of its judges. The evaluation committee is composed of five to nine persons. The chairman of the committee is the president of the court. The committee's duty is to give guidance to the training, supervision and appraisal of the judges. The committee for the evaluation of judges of the Supreme People's Court organizes nationwide uniform examinations for judges and assistant judges of first trial.

6. Dismissal of Judges and Appeals against Dismissal

A judge can be dismissed if he or she is ascertained as not qualified for two years in a run at the annual appraisal, is incompetent for his or her present job and refuses to accept another job, is transferred to another job as a result of the readjustment of the judicial organs or staff reduction and refuses to accept a reasonable alternative, stays away from work without leave or exceeds a period of leave without justifiable reason by 15 successive days or by a total of 30 days in one year, fails to perform the duties of a judge and refuses to make correction after education.

A dismissed judge shall be removed from his or her post in accordance with the procedure as specified by the law.

If a judge refuses to accept dismissal, he or she may apply to the original organ that has taken the removal action for reconsideration within 30 days from the day he or she is informed of the decision, or has the right to appeal to the original organ's superior organ. The organ that accepts the appeal must handle it as specified, but during the period of reconsideration and appeal the execution of the decision will not be halted.

A judge has the right to bring lawsuit against any organ of the state and its staff for infringing on his or her rights.

Any administrative organ, public organization or individual interfering with the work of a judge handling a case in accordance with the law must be held responsible for the consequences.

A judge shall be held responsible for fabricated facts and false charge(s) in any lawsuit lodged by him or her.

If an action taken against a judge is wrong, it shall be corrected in time. If his or her reputation is injured, it shall be rehabilitated and an apology made. If there is any economic loss, compensation shall be paid. The responsibility of the person directly responsible for the action shall be investigated in accordance with the law.

II. Procurators

Procurators are personnel who exercise the procuratorial power of the state in accordance with the law.

1. The Duties of Procurators

The duties of procurators are to exercise legal supervision in accordance with the law, make public prosecutions on behalf of the state, investigate criminal cases directly handled by the procuratorates as specified by law, and perform other duties as specified by law.

Apart from performing their procuratorial duties, the procurators-general, vice procurators-general and members of the procuratorial committee shall also perform other duties compatible with their posts.

2. The Qualifications of a Procurator

A procurator must have the following qualifications: having the nationality of the People's Republic of China, having reached the age of 23, supporting the Constitution of the People's Republic of China, having sound political integrity and professional qualities and good conduct, having good health, having completed a four-year college education in law or a four-year course in other studies but with a knowledge of law and two years of work experience, or having acquired a bachelor degree in law and having one year of work experience, or having acquired a master degree or doctor degree in law.

The Law on Public Procurators of the People's Republic of China also specifies alternative conditions for personnel who do not have the above-mentioned qualifications but have actually taken posts as procurators. It stipulates that people who took posts as procuratorial personnel before the law took effect and do not have the qualifications as specified shall receive training and acquire the qualifications as specified in the law within the specified time limits. Following such training, their qualifications shall be judged according to the specific rules formulated by the Supreme People's Procuratorate.

Any person who has once been punished for criminal offence or has once been discharged from public service is not permitted to be a procurator.

3. Appointment and Removal of Procurators

A procurator must be appointed or removed in accordance with the procedure for appointment and removal as specified in the Constitution and other relevant laws.

The procurator-general of the Supreme People's Procuratorate is elected or removed by the National People's Congress, and its vice procurators-general, members of the procuratorial committee and procurators are appointed or removed by the Standing Committee of the National People's Congress upon the recommendation of the procurator-general.

The procurators-general of the local procuratorates at all levels are elected or removed by the local people's congresses at all levels, and their vice procurators-general, members of the procuratorial committees and procurators are appointed or removed by the standing committees of the people's congresses at the corresponding levels upon the recommendation of the procurators-general.

The appointment or removal of procurators-general of local procuratorates at all levels must be reported to the procurators-general of the next-higher procuratorates for approval by the standing committees of the people's congresses at the corresponding levels.

The procurators-general, deputy procurators-general, members of the procuratorial committees and procurators of the branch procuratorates established on the regional basis in the provinces and autonomous regions and those established in the municipalities directly under the central government shall be appointed or removed by the standing committees of the people's congresses at the provincial level upon the recommendation of the procurators-general of the procuratorates of the provinces, autonomous regions and municipalities directly under the central government.

The assistant procurators are appointed or removed by the procurators-general of the same procuratorates.

The procedure for the appointment or removal of procurators-general, deputy procurators-general, members of the procuratorial committees and procurators of the military procuratorates and other special procuratorates shall be specified separately by the Standing Committee of the National People's Congress.

Preliminary procurators and assistant procurators shall be nominated from among people with the best qualifications for procurators according to the criteria of combining political integrity and ability, after the nominees pass public examinations and strict assessment.

Candidates for procurators-general, deputy procurators-general and members of the procuratorial committees shall be selected from among the best of the procuratorial personnel with actual work experience.

In the case of a procurator who has lost the nationality of the People's Republic of China, who has moved to another job from a procuratorate, who has moved to another job and his or her post as a procurator shall not be kept, who is regarded as incompetent after assessment of his or her work, who is unable to perform his or her duties on account of poor health, who retires or resigns from his or her post or is dismissed, who is unable to continue to hold his or her post on account of violation of discipline or law or who must be removed for other reasons, the competent organ shall file a request to dismiss him or her from the post in accordance with the law.

If a procurator-general does not have the specified qualifications or is elected in violation of the legal procedure, the procurator-general of the higher procuratorate has the right to request the standing committee of the people's congress at the same level to withhold approval.

The procurators-general of the Supreme People's Procuratorate or of the procuratorate of a province, autonomous region or municipality directly under the central government may suggest to the standing committee of the people's congress at the corresponding levels for the replacement of a procurator-general, deputy procurator-general or member of the procuratorial committee of a lower procuratorate.

A procurator shall not be a member of the standing committee of a people's congress, nor take a post in an administrative organ, judicial organ, enterprise or institution, nor practice as a lawyer.

4. Avoidance by a Procurator

Procurators who have marital or affinal relations, or consanguineous relations within three generations shall not hold the following posts at the same time: procurator-general, deputy procurator-general and member of the procuratorial committee of the same procuratorate; procurator-general, deputy procurator-general, procurator and assistant procurator of the same procuratorate; procurator and assistant procurator of the same work department, and procurator-general and deputy procurator-general of procuratorates at two adjoining levels.

5. The Committee for the Evaluation of Procurators

A procuratorate shall establish a committee for the evaluation of procurators. The evaluation committee shall be composed of five to nine persons. The chairman of the committee shall be the procurator-general of the procuratorate.

The duty of the committee for the evaluation of procurators is to give guidance to the training, check-up and appraisal of the procurators.

The committee for the evaluation of procurators of the Supreme People's Procuratorate organizes nationwide uniform examinations for preliminary procurators and assistant procurators.

6. The Dismissal of, and Appeals and Accusations by Procurators

A procurator can be dismissed if he or she is ascertained to be unqualified for two years running in annual check-ups, is found to be incompetent for the present job and refuses to accept another job, is transferred to another job as a result of readjustment of procuratorial organs or staff reduction, or refuses to accept a new job, stays away from work without leave or exceeds leave without justified reason by 15 successive days or by a total of 30 days in a year, or fails to perform his or her duties as a procurator and refuses to correct his or her way of doing things after education.

The dismissal of a procurator shall follow the procedure as specified by law.

If a procurator refuses to accept the administrative action against himself or herself, he or she may apply to the original organ that takes the action for reconsideration within 30 days from the day he or she receives the decision on the action, or he or she has the right to appeal to the original organ's higher organ. The organ that accepts the appeal must handle it in accordance with the stipulations, but during the period of reconsideration and appeal, the execution of the decision will not be halted.

A procurator has the right to lodge lawsuit against any organ of the state and its staff for infringing on his or her rights. Any administrative organ, public organization or individual interfering with a procurator's performance of his or her procuratorial duty in accordance with the law shall be held responsible for the consequences.

A procurator shall be held responsible for any fabricated facts or false charges in any lawsuit or legal appeal he or she lodges.

If any action taken against a procurator is wrong, it shall be corrected in time. If the procurator's reputation is harmed, it shall be rehabilitated and an apology be made. If there is any economic loss, compensation shall be made. The responsibility of the person directly responsible for taking revenge shall be investigated in accordance with the law.

Section 4 The Operation of the Court and Procuratorate

I. How Does the Court Work?

1. The Collegiate System

The collegiate system is adopted for the trial of cases in court.

The form of the collegiate system is the collegiate bench. The collegiate bench is the organizational form of collective trial of cases by judges. The composition of a collegiate bench differs from case to case. The collegiate bench for a case of first instance must be composed of judges for hearing any case involving the roll of voters or major and difficult non-contentious cases. It may be composed of judges or composed of judges and people's assessors for hearing other cases. This is decided by the court depending on the circumstances. The collegiate bench for hearing any appeal or protest cases, namely, the court of second instance, is composed of judges only and no people's assessors. The collegiate bench shall be composed of three people or a larger odd number. The chief judge of the collegiate bench is the judge appointed by the president of the court or the president of the tribunal, and its members have equal rights. The principle of the minority being subordinate to the majority is adopted for the deliberation of and the judgment passed on a case.

The president of the court or the president of the tribunal appoints one of the judges as the chief judge of the collegiate bench. The president of the court or the president of the tribunal is the chief judge of the collegiate bench when either of them participates in hearing a case.

Apart from the collegiate bench, the single-judge form is also used in a few cases. It is usually limited to grassroots courts for hearing simple civil cases of first instance, and private prosecution and minor criminal cases. The intermediate and higher courts do not adopt this form in practice for hearing cases of both first and second instances. None of the courts use the single-judge system for hearing administrative cases.

2. The System of Final Judgment after Two Hearings

So far as the procedure for adjudication is concerned, the system of final judgment after two hearings is adopted in the trial of court cases.

The system of final judgment after two hearings is a system under which the final judgment is passed on a case after it is heard by courts at two adjoining levels. In other words, after a local court passes its judgment or delivers a verdict on a case of first instance within its jurisdiction, if the party concerned refuses to accept it, it may appeal to the next-higher court within the legal time limit. If the procuratorate at the same level refuses to accept the verdict, it may make a protest to the next-higher court within the legal time limit. This court has the right to accept the appeal or protest against the judgment or verdict made by the lower court on a case of first instance, and has the power to change or maintain the judgment or verdict made by the court of first instance after hearing the case again. The judgment or verdict made by the higher court is the final judgment or verdict. The party concerned is not permitted to appeal against the final judgment or verdict.

If a grassroots court is the court of first instance, the intermediate court is the court of final jurisdiction. If a party concerned refuses to accept the judgment passed by the intermediate court on a case of first instance, he or she may appeal to the next-higher court. At this stage, the next-higher court is the court of final jurisdiction. If a party refuses to accept the judgment passed by this court on a case of first instance, he or she may appeal to the Supreme People's Court, and then the Supreme People's Court is the court of final jurisdiction, and its judgment or verdict of the first and second instance is final.

Therefore, although there are courts at four levels, there are only two hearings for each case in a specific lawsuit. As large numbers of lawsuits are filed at the grassroots and intermediate courts — especially in an economic case or a civil suit, the final judgment after two hearings often ends at the intermediate or high court. The essence of the system of different stages of trial is to ensure a trial to proceed strictly according to the judicial procedure.

However, if the parties involved in a case do not appeal nor does the procuratorate make a protest against the judgment or verdict of a local court of first instance, the judgment or verdict of the court of first instance is a legally effective judgment or verdict.

Death sentences shall be reported to the Supreme People's Court for examination and approval, except for those passed by the Supreme People's Court itself. When necessary, the Supreme People's Court can authorize the provincial, autonomous regional and municipal high courts to exercise the power of examining and approving death sentences in cases of murder, rape, robbery, explosion and other crimes that seriously endanger public security and social order.

3. The Judicial Committee

The Organic Law of the People's Courts stipulates that judicial committees are established in the courts at all levels. The task of the judicial committee is to sum up the adjudicative experience, and discuss major or difficult cases, and other questions related to judicial work. The judicial committee is usually made up of the president of the court, vice-president(s) of the court, a few chief judges and senior judges. The judicial committee is the highest organ of power in the judicial work of the court. All major cases handled by a court should be discussed and the verdicts should be made after the judicial committee discusses them.

The members of the judicial committees of the local courts at all levels are appointed or removed by the standing committees of the people's congresses at the corresponding levels upon the recommendation of the presidents of the courts. The members of the judicial committee of the Supreme People's Court are appointed or removed by the Standing Committee of the National People's Congress.

The meetings of the judicial committees of the courts at all levels are presided over by the presidents of the courts, and the procurators-general of the procuratorates at the corresponding levels may attend the meetings as non-voting members.

Democratic centralism is practiced within the judicial committees.

4. Examination and Approval of Cases

Courts at all levels establish not only judicial committees, but also tribunals. Tribunal meetings are similar to those of judicial committees in function. They are, in fact, responsible for making decisions on the cases within the scope of the tribunals. A tribunal meeting, like that of a judicial committee, holds the actual power of adjudication over cases.

The courts in fact practice the system of examination and approval in the handling of cases. It is a system under which, after all cases are heard by a single-judge tribunal or collegiate bench and before the judgment is passed, the presiding judge must report the decision to the administrative and judicial leader in charge — the president or vice-president of the tribunal, or the president or vice-president of the court — for examination and approval. The president or vice-president should give concrete instructions and comments. If the president or the vice-president in charge thinks there is any problem, the judge or bench concerned shall hold another hearing of the case or make further investigations in accordance with the instructions of the president or the vice-president in charge. Once the decision is approved, the judge or bench in charge of the case shall prepare the legal documents in accordance with the instructions of the president or vice-president.

II. How Does the Procuratorate Work?

1. Investigation

When a procuratorate believes that a crime has been committed, it may start the investigation on its own or turns the case over to the relevant public security organ or state security organ for investigation. The procuratorate exercises supervision over the investigation conducted by the public security organ or state security organ of the case it hands over.

After the procuratorate concludes its investigation, it shall make a decision on whether to prosecute or not.

A public security organ or state security organ may also start investigations into cases on its own without approval from the local procuratorate. The procurator shall keep a record of and exercise supervision over the cases reported by a public security organ or state security organ for investigation on its own.

2. Approval of Arrest

At present, only the procuratorates and courts have the power to approve arrests. The arrest of any citizen is subject to approval from a relevant procuratorate except when it is decided by a court.

If a public security organ (state security organ) deems it necessary to arrest a person it has detained, it should apply to the relevant procuratorate for examination and approval within three days after the detention. In special circumstances, the time requested can be extended by one to four days. In the case of those who flee and commit crimes hither and thither, habitual criminals and members of criminal gangs, the time requested can be extended to 30 days.

The procuratorate shall make a decision on whether to approve the arrest or not to approve the arrest within seven days after it receives a written request for approval of arrest from a relevant public security organ (state security organ). If the procuratorate does not approve the arrest, the public security organ (state security organ) concerned shall immediately release the detainee after it receives the notice, and inform the procuratorate of the release in good time. A detainee for whom further investigation is deemed necessary and who meets the conditions for obtaining a guarantor pending trial and who lives at home under surveillance may obtain a guarantor pending trial or live at home under surveillance.

If the public security organ (state security organ) deems that the decision made by the procuratorate on not approving the arrest is wrong, it may request reconsideration, but must release the detainee immediately. If its request is refused, it may request reexamination by the next-higher procuratorate. The latter shall reexamine the case, and immediately make a decision on whether to make the change. It shall then inform the lower procuratorate and the relevant public security organ (state security organ) to implement its decision.

Any person a court or procuratorate decides to arrest or the public security organ (state security organ) arrests with the approval of the relevant procuratorate must be interrogated within 24 hours after the arrest. If the arrest is found to be wrong, the detained person must be released immediately, and issued a certificate of release. After an arrest is made, the organ that makes the arrest shall inform the family of the arrested person or the organization where he or she works of the cause of the arrest and the place of custody within 24 hours, unless such is impossible or would hinder the investigation.

The public security organ (state security organ) shall inform the procuratorate that has approved the arrest when it releases the arrested person or changes the conditions of arrest.

The procuratorate shall make a decision on arresting a person involved in a case it handles directly within 10 days if it deems it necessary to arrest him or her. In special circumstances, the time for making the decision can be extended by one to four days. If no grounds for arrest are found, the detained person must be released immediately. If further investigation is needed on a detainee who meets the conditions for obtaining a guarantor pending trial or let live at home under surveillance, he may be allowed to obtain a guarantor pending trial or to live at home under surveillance.

3. Public Prosecution

All cases that call for public prosecution are subject to examination and decision by the relevant procuratorate.

When a procuratorate deems that the criminal facts of a suspect have been verified with clear and full evidence, and criminal responsibility shall be investigated in accordance with the law, it shall make a decision on prosecution in a court in accordance with the rules for judicial jurisdiction.

A procuratorate shall make a decision within one month on any cases transferred to it by the public security organ (state security organ) for prosecution, and the time can be extended by 15 days for major and complex cases.

If a procuratorate requires additional investigation for a case it examines, it may return the case to the public security organ (state security organ) for additional investigation or make the investigation on its own. Such additional investigation shall be completed within one month. Only two additional investigations are allowed. After the additional investigation facts have been transferred to the procuratorate, the latter shall recalculate the time limit for the examination and prosecution. If the procuratorate still deems that the evidence is not sufficient and does not meet the requirements for prosecution after additional investigation, it can make a decision of non-prosecution.

When a procuratorate deems that the criminal facts of a suspect have been verified with clear and full evidence and that criminal responsibility shall be investigated in accordance with the law, it shall make a decision on prosecution, and prosecute the culprit in a court in accordance with the rules for judicial jurisdiction.

The procuratorate shall at the same time release all goods distressed or frozen during the investigation of a case it decides not to prosecute. If an administrative penalty or administrative sanction is to be given to a person who is not to be prosecuted for a criminal offense or illegal income is to be confiscated, the procuratorate shall make its procuratorial remarks and transfer the case to the competent organ for implementation. The competent organ shall inform the procuratorate of the result of the implementation in good time.

A decision of non-prosecution shall be made public, and sent to the person concerned and the organization where he or she works. The person who is still in custody shall be released immediately.

As for cases the public security organ (state security organ) transfers for prosecution, if the procuratorate decides not to prosecute, it shall send the decision of non-prosecution to the public security organ (state security organ). If the public security organ (state security organ) deems that the decision of non-prosecution made by the procuratorate is wrong, it may ask the procuratorate to reconsider. If its request is refused, it may request reexamination by the next-higher procuratorate.

If the procuratorate decides not to prosecute a case involving a victim, it shall send the decision of non-prosecution to the victim. If the victim refuses to accept the decision, he or she may appeal to the next-higher procuratorate within seven days after he or she receives the decision, and request public prosecution. The next-higher procuratorate shall inform the victim of the decision of reexamination. If the victim refuses to accept the next-higher procuratorate's decision to uphold the original decision, the victim may complain to a court. He or she may also make his or her complaint directly to a court without making an appeal for reexamination. After the court accepts the case, the procuratorate shall transfer the materials concerning the case to the court. If loss of state property or collective property is involved in a criminal suit, the procuratorate may bring in a supplementary civil action while making the public prosecution.

When a procuratorate pursues a public prosecution, the procurator-general or the procurator shall attend the court sessions in the capacity of the state prosecutor, support the public prosecution and exercise supervision over the legal proceedings.

In civil cases, the current law has not yet definitely delegated the procuratorate the power of bringing prosecution to a court.

4. Protest

When a local procuratorate at any level considers that a judgment or verdict of first instance made by a court at the corresponding level is erroneous, it shall make a protest to the next-higher court. If the victim and his or her legal agent refuses to accept a judgment of first instance made by a local court at any level, they have the right to request that the procuratorate at the same level make a protest. The procuratorate shall make a decision on whether to make a protest or not, and give a reply to the person(s) demanding the protest within five days after receiving the request. If a procuratorate makes a protest against a judgment or verdict of first instance made by a court at the same level, it shall send a written protest to the original court, and submit a copy to the next-higher procuratorate. The original court shall transfer the written protest together with the relevant files and evidence to the next-higher court and send duplicates to the parties concerned. The next-higher procuratorate may withdraw the protest from the court at the same level, and inform the lower procuratorate if it deems the protest inappropriate.

As for a case against which the procuratorate makes a protest or pursues a public prosecution in a court of second instance, the procuratorate at the same level shall have an officer present at the court session. The court of second instance must inform the procuratorate to examine the file ten days before it opens the session.

If the Supreme People's Procuratorate finds a legally effective judgment or verdict made by a court at any level to be erroneous, and a higher procuratorate finds a legally effective judgment or verdict made by a lower court to be erroneous, it shall make a protest in accordance with the procedure for judicial supervision. The scope of such protests includes when:

(1) the main evidence for the facts established in the original judgment or verdict is insufficient;

(2) the application of the law to the original judgment or verdict is wrong;

(3) a breach of legal procedure by a court may sway the judgment or verdict in a case; and

(4) judicial officials are accused of corruption, bribery, self-seeking misconduct or misuse of the law in judgment when hearing a case.

If a local procuratorate at any level finds circumstances as specified in any of the above clauses in a legally effective judgment or verdict made by a court at the same level, it shall request the next higher level procuratorate to make a protest in accordance with the procedure for judicial supervision.

A case against which a procuratorate has lodged a protest must be reheard.

If a procuratorate decides to make a protest against a judgment or verdict made by a court, it shall do so in writing.

When a court rehears a case against which a procuratorate has made a protest, it shall inform the procuratorate to have an official present at the court session.

5. Supervision

Judicial supervision exercised by a procuratorate runs through the whole process of litigation. When a public security organ (state security organ) decides to start investigation into a case, the procuratorate has the power to supervise the process. When a procuratorate deems that a public security organ (state security organ) does not start investigation into a case that should be investigated, or the victim in a case complains to the procuratorate that the public security organ (state security organ) does not start investigation into a case that should be investigated, the procuratorate shall ask the public security organ (state security organ) to state its reason(s) for not making the investigations. If the procuratorate deems that the reason(s) given by the public security organ (state security organ) is/are untenable, it shall order the public security organ (state security organ) to investigate the case, and the public security organ (state security organ) shall put the case on file and start the investigations after it receives the notice. When the public security organ (state security organ) exercises its power of investigation, the procuratorate is responsible for supervising the investigative activities of the public security organ (state security organ). When the procuratorate examines a case, if it deems that the investigation made by the public security organ (state security organ) should be re-examined, it shall ask the public security organ (state security organ) to make the re-examination, and send a procurator to take part in the process. If a procuratorate finds any violation of law in the investigative activities of the public security organ (state security organ) in examining a request for approval of arrest, it shall order the public security organ (state security organ) to correct the situation, and the public security organ (state security organ) shall inform the procuratorate of its corrective measures. When a procuratorate finds any violation of the proper procedure by a court in hearing a case, it shall order the court to make a correction. If a procuratorate finds any violation of law in the execution of criminal judgment or verdict made by a court, it shall order the executing authority to correct it. When a procuratorate finds that a court verdict on commutation and parole is inappropriate, it shall issue a notice for correction to the court within 20 days after it receives a copy of the written verdict. The procuratorate also exercises supervision to see to it that the execution of any criminal punishment is carried out by the related law-enforcing department in accordance with law. If it finds any violation of law, it shall inform the department to correct it.

6. Democratic Centralism

The procurators-general of the procuratorates at all levels direct the work of the procuratorates.

The procuratorates establish procuratorial committees, which practice democratic centralism. Each committee, presided over by the procurator-general, discusses and decides on major cases and other major matters. If the procurator-general does not agree with a decision made by the majority of the committee members on major questions, he or she may ask the standing committee of the people's congress at the corresponding level to make the decision.

Chapter Six

LOCAL GOVERNMENTS

Section 1 The Political and Administrative Status of Local Governments

Local governments are local organs of state power as well as the local organs of state administration the State establishes in local areas in accordance with the Constitution. In terms of the Constitution, a complete local government in the strict sense is composed of the local people's congress, local administrative organs, local courts and local procuratorates.

Besides the local governments as such, there are some other types of local governments in China. First, there are dispatched organs by the governments at higher levels to take charge of the overall improvement of given areas, of which the major part appears as administrative departments, and which may also include other departments (such as a liaison organ of the People's Congress). Such a setup, by nature, is no different from an ordinary local government in terms of its function of local administration of the State; it acts as a local organ of government. Second, there are the governments of special administrative regions, which are specially established by the National People's Congress through legislation, and which have a constitutional status and structure that are different from an ordinary local government. The area under the jurisdiction of such a government is also different from that under the jurisdiction of an ordinary local government. As China adopts a system of unitary centralization, the government of a special administrative region and the area under its jurisdiction are not definite in their nature and status. Such a government can be regarded as a local government in a sense. Third, there are organs of self-government of ethnic minority autonomous areas, which are political and administrative organs set up in ethnic minority autonomous areas, and which enjoy various degrees of autonomy besides exercising functions of local administration on behalf of the Central Government.

I. Impacts of the System of Unitary Centralization over the Local Governments

China adopts a system of unitary centralization.[1] The unitary system is a structure and pattern of relationship between the central and local governments in "a state in which the major institutions of government, legislature, executive and judiciary have power in all matters over the whole area and all persons within the territory of the state, ... power is delegated, not distributed, and technically, all belongs to the central government."[2] In this pattern, a local government is established by the central government, and its powers are granted by the central government. As all local governments are derived from the central government, the central government, therefore, can arrange the internal departments of the local government, and enhance or weaken the powers of the local governments. The central government also has the power to demand the local governments exercise and fulfil its own political and administrative intentions.

In China, unlike in some small states practicing unitary centralization, not all local governments are established by the central government. Some local governments are established by local governments at a higher level. But this fact does not change China's nature as a state of unitary centralization: As China is a very large country in terms of both geography and population, its local governments have to be hierarchical. Formally, not all Chinese local governments are set up by the central government, but as the government at the higher level that sets up a lower-level government has been set up by the central government, a local government not set up by the central government itself can be regarded as having been set up indirectly by the central government through one of its local organs.

The system of unitary centralization provides the central government with power and conditions for controlling and influencing the local governments, which, to a certain extent and in a certain sense, become local agencies and organs of the central government. This fact determines the basic status and standing of the local governments in local political and administrative affairs. In turn, the basic status and standing of the local governments affects the development of local politics and economy. Therefore, generally speaking, under the system of unitary centralization, a local government represents the standing and will of the central government more than those of the local politics and society. Restricted by the influence of agents of the central government, the growth of local politics and society will be on a relatively low level. On the other hand, a local government, being a political and administrative unit set up in a certain area, necessarily reflects to some extent the local characteristics. Therefore, the central government cannot set up a local government at will. It has to do this by taking into consideration of the local history and tradition, and by acknowledging the local characteristics. Thus, a local government, in turn, can generate some influence on the central government.

One other thing to be clarified is that a local government under the system of unitary centralization does not necessarily mean that the local government only exercises the political and administrative functions of the central government. As a matter of fact, in modern countries effective governing over local areas requires that the local governments play the political and administrative role on behalf of the central government. Meanwhile, the political symbolism of a local government as a local community is also very important. To realize the political symbolic function of a local government, it is necessary to confer onto the local government the status of local political representative. Therefore, even in a country with a system of unitary centralization, the local government is not simply a political and administrative organ of the central government, but also a local legislative and political organ.

II. Impact of the People's Congress System over the Status and Functions of the Local Governments

The People's Congress system is the basic political system of China. The people's congress is the source of the legality of state power. The National People's Congress is the one and only constitutional source of the legality of the power of the central government. However, under the system of unitary centralization, unlike the central government, the local governments has two sources for the legality of their power: That is, to the local government, while the local people's congress confers legality on the power of the local government as a political community, the legality of the power of the local government also comes from the authorization delegated by the central government to the local government. Since there exist two sources of legality of power, logically the local government is obviously in a conflicting and contradictory situation. However, under the system of democratic centralism, this superficial conflict can be solved by way of "local governments obeying the central government."

Therefore, basically there is only one source regarding the legality of power of a local government, i.e. the central government.

On the other hand, at the level of the central government, as the National People's Congress is the one and only constitutional source of power of the central government, there is no latitude for the local governments to exert any influence on the issue of the source of legality of the central government's power. Yet, the deputies to the National People's Congress are elected indirectly from lower to higher levels rather than through a nationwide general election. Therefore, from a microcosmic point of view, the National People's Congress is, in nature, composed of local deputies who have close connections with various local governments. The "national-ness" of the National People's Congress is predicated on the "local-ness" of the deputies. In other words, the National People's Congress *per se* is "national," but the deputies to it can in no way cut off all relations with the localities and only remain connected with the central government. So, the National People's Congress, which is able to delegate legality to the power of the central government, is "intrinsically" local. Moreover, during the election of deputies to the National people's Congress, the local politics and society as well as the local governments cannot but exert a decisive influence on the selection of deputies. Hence, the deputies they choose bound to reflect, to a certain extent, the standing and will of the local governments, which will, to a certain extent and in a certain sense, be able to exert influence on the central government through choosing the deputies. Such influence is indirect, in some cases ineffective, and is largely combined with reflecting the standing and will of the central government. Nevertheless, viewed institutionally, it still serves as a practical channel for the local governments to exert influence on the central government.

III. Impact of the System of Regional Autonomy of Ethnic Groups over the Local Governments

Regional autonomy of minority ethnic groups is a system instituted to handle the relationship between the central government and regions inhabited by ethnic minorities in compact communities, where, under a unitary system, autonomic organs are established, and ethnic minorities exercise their autonomic power. Under this system, the governments of the regions inhabited by the ethnic minorities in compact communities, like other regions of the country, are local organs of state power under the unified leadership of the central government. Yet, the central government exercises its leadership over these regions in a somewhat different way from the leadership it exercises over other localities. Considering factors such as the characters of the composition of ethnic groups in these regions, the local governments are vested with a certain level of autonomy, which an ordinary local government cannot enjoy. Therefore, the general nature of China's system of autonomy for regions inhabited by ethnic minorities in compact communities still remains a form of the system of unitary centralization.

Although the overall institutional framework remains to be the system of unitary centralization, the government of an ethnic-minority region enjoys a certain degree of autonomy that an ordinary local government has no right to. Therefore, the government of a region where the ethnic minority group(s) exercise(s) autonomy is different from the government of an ordinary region in the degree of self-government. Moreover, as exercise of autonomy is not only a question of legal system, but, more importantly, a question of practical operation — it is, in fact, a function of the degree of the political, legal and social development in an ethnic-minority region — autonomy is intrinsically variable, which makes the pattern of the relationship between the local government and the central government, as well as the status and influence of the local government in local political affairs, constantly changing. Of course, restricted by the fundamental unitary system, such changes, in many cases, may be unilaterally subject to the will of the central government. But, when the pressure of the change is great enough, the system of regional autonomy of ethnic groups itself, in certain conditions, will provide some institutional room for such pressure, making more salient the autonomy of the local government of an ethnic-minority autonomous region, even breaking through the framework of the existing system of ethnic-minority autonomy and presenting a new model for governing such regions.

IV. Impact of "One Country, Two Systems" Concept over the Local Government System

"One country, two systems" is a special concept regarding state structure. At present, it applies only to the former foreign colonies the sovereignty over which has been retrieved. It means that China recovers its sovereignty over the former foreign colonies without changing their existing social and political systems, which are completely different from those practiced throughout China's mainland. In other words, within the framework of one country's sovereignty, two different social and political systems coexist. Therefore, "one country, two systems" is a system of political arrangement rather than a system of state structure in the general sense: it is neither a unitary system nor a federal system. The government of a special administrative region is neither an ordinary local government nor an autonomic local government; it comes directly under the central government and enjoys complete autonomy (including the power of final adjudication), with its sovereignty coming under the central government. In state affairs, the chief executive of a special administrative region enjoys the status of a head of state. Therefore, the government of a special administrative region is different from an ordinary local government or the autonomous organ of an ethnic-minority autonomous region in terms of its relationship with the state and the central government, as well as in nature and status. The government of a special administrative region, in essence, is not an ordinary local government or autonomous local government. Moreover, although the government of a special administrative region enjoys a high degree of autonomy, and comes under the state and the central government in terms of sovereignty, the relationship between the central government and the government of a special administrative region based on the "one country, two systems" concept is also not a form of federal relationship, as there is no practical channel for the special administrative region to influence the state's political affairs or central government affairs. In a certain sense, a special administrative region is more like an enclave beyond the rule of the central government than a federal unit under the central government; only this "enclave" is under the sovereignty of the central government.

The system of special administrative region was established specially with the recovery of China's sovereignty over Hong Kong and Macao. It is a innovation in China's political system and in the form of state structure, which indicates the possibility that the current form of state structure that remains stable now can be changed or adjusted. Such change and adjustment may occur in two directions: First, when the range of application of the special administrative region system becomes larger and larger, such as after reunification with Taiwan, and as the proportion of special administrative regions reaches a certain scope throughout the country, will they be satisfied with being only "enclaves" with a high degree of autonomy and not seek a say and influence in state political affairs? That is to say, when the system of special administrative region further develops, will there be any possibility of adopting a federal system between the central government and the governments of the special administrative regions? If the special administrative regions are able to play a more important role and exert greater influence in state political affairs, the basic pattern of relationship between the central government and the local governments will inevitably change. The second direction is the possibility to extend the application of the system of special administrative regions beyond regions independent of actual control by the central government to those which are under the actual control of the central government but, due to their special nature, are difficult to fit appropriately in the existing pattern of relationship between the central and local governments. Such regions include, for instance, some ethnic-minority autonomous regions and those of which the economic development is of special significance. If a system similar to that of special administrative regions is adopted in today's ordinary local areas and ethnic-minority autonomous regions, the current long-stable system of local governments will inevitably undergo far-reaching change.

V. Impact of the System of Rural Villagers' Self-Government over the Grassroots Governments in Rural Areas

Autonomy for villagers is a system for people in rural areas to achieve self-management. It was established to organize and govern the rural population, and link the state power with individual rural residents after the disintegration of the people's commune system, and when the rural population had gained a certain level of independence in production following the adoption of the contract system with remuneration linked to output. As the rural residents basically exist as individuals in society, after the disintegration of people's communes the former basic political organization that the state power depended on to rule the rural areas and rural population ceased to exist, so allowing individual rural residents to depend solely on the town or township powers established on the basis of the people's commune system was an inadequate solution to the problem of governing in the rural areas. It was a choice in line with the state interest to establish self-government organizations capable to organize and govern the individual rural residents. Autonomy for rural villagers can effectively assist the state power to perform its governing function, and at the same time facilitates the development of self-government in the rural areas and the development of democracy. The system of self-government for rural villagers has been gradually established and developed with the promotion of the state power. In a certain sense, the system of self-government for rural villagers was established to fill the gap in rural grassroots society left by the disappearance of production teams after the disintegration of the people's communes, which town or township governments are unable to fill. The basic motive for its establishment was to enable the state power to better govern rural areas and the rural population.

Although the basic motive for establishing the system of self-government for rural villagers was to realize more efficiently the target of governing by the state power, as the practice of the system *per se* provides rural residents with a certain right to participate in rural affairs, this system also has some influence on the actions taken by town or township governments. The main manifestations are as follows: As the government at the lowest level, the town or township government has to perform wide-reaching functions of governing the rural areas and rural residents, which, in many cases, exceeds its limits in terms of organization and resources. It has to depend on assistance and support from villagers' organizations. Therefore, what is crucial for a town or township government to realize its functions is whether the self-government organizations of the villagers, set up through their direct participation, are able to form a situation together with the town or township governments in which they work in coordination and share responsibilities with governments at higher levels, including the central government. Therefore, with effective self-government for rural villagers, the town or township governments, which previously only represented the policies and will of the central government and governments at higher levels, now have to integrate rural residents' interests and demands into their policy-making and administration. This intermediate position of the town or township governments, to a certain degree, modifies and breaks the traditional pattern of relationship between grassroots governments and members of society.

Moreover, as the system of self-government for rural villagers has developed under the guidance of the state power, and the latter exerts important influence in the building of the latter, the "autonomous" nature and degree of "autonomy" of the rural villagers is obviously limited. The state power is able to successfully influence the self-government organizations of the rural villagers in major aspects, mainly through the town or township governments. When the rural residents enjoy certain rights to decide their own affairs, the town or township governments shall take into consideration the rural residents' degree of acceptance while trying to interfere with the self-government of the rural villagers. This limitation, to a certain degree, will change the traditional political and operational methods of town or township governments that are deprived from the people's commune system, although such a change may take a long time.[3]

Section 2   Levels and Types of Administrative Areas

In accordance with the Constitution, China's administrative divisions are as follows:

1. The entire country is divided into provinces, autonomous regions and municipalities directly under the central government;

2. The provinces and autonomous regions are divided into autonomous prefectures, counties, autonomous counties and cities;

3. The counties and autonomous counties are divided into townships, townships of ethnic groups, and towns;

4. The municipalities directly under the central government and large cities are divided into districts and counties;

5. The autonomous prefectures are divided into counties, autonomous counties and cities.

In addition, the central government may also establish special administrative regions.

The actual administrative divisions of China are much more complicated than that prescribed in the Constitution. Besides the administrative units clearly prescribed in the Constitution, there are prefectures, subdistricts in cities, jurisdiction zones in counties, and other administrative organs in special areas, such as those in the special economic zones, development zones, mining areas, nature reserves, etc.

I. Hierarchy of Administrative Divisions

In China, the local administrative divisions are different in terms of administrative levels of the grassroots governments from the central government. In some of them, the number of levels is fewer. For example, the district governments — grassroots governments in Beijing and Shanghai, are only two levels from the central government. They are districts directly under municipalities directly under the central government. Some grassroots governments are four or five levels from the central government. For instance, the townships, ethnic townships and towns in counties under cities (or prefectural administrative offices). Generally, governments of municipalities directly under the central government (with the exception of Chongqing) have the least number of administrative levels, only two or three, under them. Governments of the autonomous regions and provincial governments with administrative prefectures (leagues) have under them four or five levels of local governments. In general, there are now the following forms of hierarchy of local governments:

The two-level system: municipality directly under the central government — district;

The three-level system: municipality directly under the central government — county and autonomous county — township, ethnic township and town;

The four-level system: province or autonomous region and municipality directly under the central government — city with districts (prefectural administrative office), and autonomous prefecture (league) — county, autonomous county, banner and city — township, ethnic township and town;

The five-level system: province and municipality directly under the central government — city at sub-provincial level — city with districts (prefectural administrative office) — county and city — township, ethnic township and town; and

Province, autonomous region and municipality directly under the central government — autonomous prefecture — prefectural administrative office — county and city — township, ethnic township and town (now, this system only exists in Yili, Xinjiang Uygur Autonomous Region).

II. Types of Administrative Divisions

As a country with the system of unitary centralization, China does not have uniform types of administrative divisions, however. In terms of their functions and nature, local governments can be classified into those of ordinary administrative areas and those of cities. In terms of ethnic constitutions of local governments, there are ordinary local governments and governments of autonomous areas for ethnic minorities. Therefore, there are mainly three types of administrative divisions: ordinary administrative divisions, cities and autonomous administrative divisions of ethnic minorities.

1. Ordinary Administrative Divisions

An ordinary administrative division is established in a local area that includes both rural and urban areas. This type of administrative division, when it was first established, mainly exercised jurisdiction over the rural areas (including a few underdeveloped towns), as urbanization in most areas of China was relatively low. However, along with economic and social development, as well as urbanization, there have been more and more cities under such administrative divisions and, correspondingly, the functions of local governments have changed to certain extent. For instance, a local government formerly exercising jurisdiction mainly over rural areas now has extended their jurisdiction over both rural areas and cities. In addition, with the change of government functions, some local governments have also undergone some changes in form. For example, some prefectures have changed into cities with counties under them. Such gradual changes in function and form have blurred the nature of an ordinary administrative division (i.e. as to whether it exercises jurisdiction mainly over the rural areas or cities).

Ordinary administrative divisions mainly include provinces, prefectures, counties and townships.

(1) Provinces

A province is a top-level administrative division in China. There are now 23 provinces.

Provinces, as top-level administrative divisions, emerged first in the Yuán Dynasty (1206-1368). Since then, some partial changes had taken place, including changes made during the revolution led by the Communist Party of China. But only a small part of the changes remains now. The present provinces basically embrace the areas they covered in history. To a certain extent, this reflects the historical and cultural stability of each province.

Generally speaking, a province is not only a basic local political and administrative unit of the state, but also cultural and secondary territorial unit, with local identification as well as the status and influence as necessary for local governments as against the central government in the central-local relationship system. The provinces have an important status and great significance in the political and administrative life of the nation.

The significance of the provinces is also expressed in their nature as ordinary local governments. Unlike the other types of local governments, the provinces are basically governmental branches in a local territory, with little relation to ethnic, economic, military or supervisory factors. In other words, they simply function to govern the territory and its residents. Therefore, the administrative area of a province usually includes both rural and urban areas. But when an urban area becomes sufficiently developed, it will exceed the administrative structure and range of the province, sometimes even growing into a local government unit with a similar administrative standing as the province. This is fully evinced by the development of governments of municipalities directly under the central government, sub-provincial cities and special economic zones.

Due to the nature of the system of unitary centralization, the status of a province as a top-level administrative division gives it great importance in China's political and administrative activities. A province is usually the direct object of administration of the central government, and the only channel via which all the other local government units are connected to the central government.

(2) Prefectures

A prefecture is a local government unit within an area of provincial-level administration. An administrative organ dispatched by the provincial administrative authority, a prefecture does not constitute a level of administrative division in the two-level system of administration, that is, province and county. Prefectures were first established in the Ming Dynasty (1368-1644), and have basically retained their form till today. Unlike a province, a prefecture can be changed greatly from time to time, and its function and power are unstable.

Since 1949, the setup and legal status of prefectures have undergone great changes. Before 1966, the system of the prefectural commissioner's office was adopted; from 1966 to 1978 there was the prefectural revolutionary committee system, which acted as an independent local organ of state power, and the prefecture was not an organ dispatched by the provincial administrative authority. Since 1978, with the establishment of prefectural administrative offices, a prefecture has again become an administrative organ dispatched by the provincial administrative authority. The general trend of development of the prefecture system is that there are more and more departments in the prefectural administrative offices playing more administrative functions. As a result, the prefectural administrative offices are becoming more and more similar to ordinary local government units, although, legally, they are not independent local government units.[4]

At present, there are 79 prefectures throughout China.

(3) Counties

As a local administrative unit, the county first appeared in the early Spring and Autumn Period (722-481 BC). The Qin Shi Huang, First Emperor (246-209 BC) of the Qin Dynasty, adopted the system of prefectures and counties, thus making the county an important local administrative unit. The county system immediately proved to be stable after its establishment, and hence has lasted till today.

The county is a basic and important local government unit, and throughout China's long history it has remained stable in terms of system and boundaries.

The county system is linked to the agricultural nature of Chinese society. Since 1949, with the adoption of the system of separate governing of urban and suburban areas, the county has become more important in China's political and administrative activities: It is the main administrative unit directly governing rural residents; it manages immense amounts of land and resources, and production of agricultural materials; and it is the main unit responsible for contributing financial resources for the industrialization of the nation. At present, although the market economy system has been introduced, the long-stagnant agricultural situation determines that the modernization and development of the agricultural society will be slow and lengthy. Therefore, it is still one of the major tasks of the state power to govern rural residents and areas under the system of separate governing of urban and suburban areas, and the county still has the important functions of political and administrative government, especially political government.

(4) Townships

Townships first appeared in the Western Zhou Dynasty (1046-771 BC) as governmental organizations under the central power of "state" and

ranked above the prefectures and counties. The status of township has
been greatly changed since its first establishment: From the Qin Dynasty
to the 15th year of the reign of Emperor Wen of Sui Dynasty (221
BC-AD 595), the township was a component part of the system of state
power. From the 16th year of Emperor Wen's reign (596) to the Qing
Dynasty (1644-1911), the township was changed into a self-government
organization in grassroots rural society. And at the end of the Qing Dynasty,
the township again became a state administrative organ under the county.[5]

Since 1949, the township system has undergone some major changes:
From 1949 to 1953, townships and administrative villages coexisted as
grassroots rural administrative units. From 1954 to 1958, the administrative village system was dismantled, and the township became the
grassroots rural administrative unit. In the latter half of 1958, the people's
commune system was adopted, and the township system was abolished.
And after 1983, the people's commune system was dismantled, and the
township system was restored on the basis of the people's commune, becoming again the grassroots rural administrative unit.

The people's commune combined political, economic and social
functions, comprehensively governing rural areas and rural residents. After the contract system with remuneration linked to output was adopted in
rural areas, the people's communes basically lost their function of managing production and the local rural economy, and were transformed into
townships, state organs which completely inherited the political, administrative and social management functions of the people's communes.
Thus the township is by nature a grassroots organization of state power in
the rural society. Today's township, with its extensive functions, is intrinsically different from the township set up after the founding of the
Republic of China in 1912. The latter was a grassroots self-government
organization and state administrative organ as well, while the township
now is only an organ of state administration without the nature of a
grassroots self-government organization.

(5) Ethnic Townships

Ethnic townships were first established in 1955. Their predecessors
were township-level autonomous regions, as provided by the Common
Program adopted by the Chinese People's Political Consultative Confer-
ence and the Outline for the Implementation of Regional Autonomy of
Ethnic Minorities of the People's Republic of China, promulgated by the
Central People's Government in 1952.

An ethnic township is a grassroots administrative unit established in a town-level area inhabited by one or more ethnic groups in compact communities, or by ethnic minorities mainly. In such an area, the population of ethnic minorities is generally 30 percent or a little bit lower in the total local population. The name of the ethnic township usually contains the name(s) of the ethnic minority or minorities and of the local area.

Although it has some residents of ethnic minorities, an ethnic township does not have the legal status of an autonomous area of ethnic minorities, but is an ordinary administrative division. The head of an ethnic township shall be a member of the ethnic minority that constitutes the township, and the appointment and election of officials of the government shall take into consideration all the ethnic minorities in the area. The language of the local ethnic minority can be used as an official language of the township government. While performing its functions, the government can take into consideration the characteristics of the ethnic minorities. The government above the ethnic township also needs to consider the characteristics of the ethnic minorities while working with the township leaders.

2. Cities

The city is a new type of political, administrative and economic center, which emerged with the growth of the commodity economy and social contacts. It is not a concept of natural geography, but an ever-changing and developing place related to the degree of social political and economic development. Nor is it a relatively stable concept with a long history. In China, except for a few political and administrative centers, cities basically have been the product of development of the commodity economy since the beginning of the 20th century, and the result of the transformation of economic composition when the rural commodity economy developed to a certain level. Therefore, in a strict sense, a city is not by nature an ordinary local administrative unit. It exists mainly as an economic or political and administrative center, and its ability to survive and develop depends on its economic and political attraction and ability to radiate, unlike an ordinary local administrative unit, which mainly depends on the state power to keep control of the area under its jurisdiction.

Though different from a hierarchical ordinary local administration intrinsically, at present China's cities are still established based on an administrative hierarchy. A major characteristic of China's city system is that a city is regarded as an ordinary local administration instead of a socio-economic structure with an intrinsic integration ability. The state relies on the governing function of the city more than it brings out its intrinsic "service" function.

City administrations include municipalities directly under the central government, sub-province-level cities, prefecture-level cities, county-level cities, city districts and towns.

(1) Municipalities Directly under the Central Government

A municipality directly under the central government (MDUCG) is a top-level administrative unit. There are four MDUCGs.

The legal status of the MDUCG first appeared in relevant provisions of the "System of Autonomy of Cities" promulgated by the Beijing Government in 1921. In 1926, the government of the Republic of China established a "special municipality government" in Hankou. In 1927, Shanghai and Nanjing became special municipalities directly under the central government.

The MDUCG system of the People's Republic of China was first established in the early years of government construction, and there were two MDUCGs and 11 municipalities directly under major regions. In June 1954, the major regions were dissolved, and so was the system of municipalities directly under them. The only MDUCGs remained were Beijing, Shanghai and Tianjin. The Constitution of 1954 provided for the constitutional status of the system of MDUCGs.[6]

An MDUCG is a top-level administrative division. It is different from a province in that it is artificial, and the area under its jurisdiction subject to constant changes, while a province is formed as a result of historical and cultural continuance, and consequently has a stable status and a relatively fixed administrative area. The MDUCGs are mainly established in areas with political and regional significance, which are important to the administration or certain strategic arrangements of the central government (for example, the establishment of the Chongqing MDUCG was directly related to the Three Gorges Dam Project on the Yangtze River), while a province is basically a natural territorial administrative division, with no special administrative significance for the central government; an MDUCG is mainly a city government, while a province is a government with cities and rural areas under its jurisdiction; an MDUCG is basically the one and only local government with complete functions in its own administrative area, while a province has several lower-level local governments with complete functions in its administrative area; an MDUCG, compared with a province, is "closer" to the citizens, while a province has no direct administrative function in its own administrative area; an MDUCG has relatively fewer levels and numbers of local governments units under it, while a province has more.

In spite of the differences between an MDUCG and a province, from the perspective of constitutional status, they are similar: they are both local governing divisions of the central government under the system of unitary centralization, except that an MDUCG is established in an urban area. But, generally speaking, an MDUCG has more political, economic, cultural, and human resources advantages than a province. Perhaps this is the reason why an MDUCG is established: Its advantages in resources and efficiency determine that a city developed to this level need not be put under the jurisdiction of a higher local government. If it were put under the jurisdiction of a province, the additional unnecessary administrative level would impede the performance of its functions. Secondly, as an MDUCG has far more important resources and radiating ability than an ordinary city, if it were not put under direct jurisdiction of the central government, on the one hand, its capabilities would be hindered by extension of administrative depth, and, on the other, it would add strength to a certain local government and disturb the balance of strength, which is indirectly detrimental to the capabilities of the central government and its control over local areas. Viewed from the internal reasons for the establishment of MDUCGs, the MDUCG system may become an effective tool for adjusting the relationship between the central government and local governments in the future, as there could be more and more important cities emerging with super strength and radiating capabilities, which will demand to become MDUCGs to enhance their own status and their officials' ranks and influence. In such cases, the strength and interests of the relevant provinces will be directly impaired. On the other hand, as the MDUCG system is by its nature a certain way of handling the relationship between the central government and local governments under the system of unitary centralization, when a local government's strength becomes great to a certain degree, the central government reduces its power by establishing a MDUCG. Therefore, as long as the system of unitary centralization is unchanged, more and more cities will inevitably become MDUCGs. In fact, this trend has already appeared more or less.

(2) Sub-provincial Cities

Sub-provincial cities are developed on the basis of cities that draft their own plan for economic and social development. In the 1980s, to facilitate the development of some large cities with special status and conditions in the course of the reform and opening-up, some cities were made to draw up their own plans for economic and social development. Although their administrative status changed, such cities gained equal power and status with the relevant provincial administrative units in many matters under the old planned economy. So, compared with other cities, a city with its own plan for economic and social development enjoyed more preferential conditions.

Starting in 1993, the central government gradually readjusted these cities' relationship with the provinces where they belong. In 1994, the central government resolved to upgrade the 14 cities that were made to draw up their own economic and social development plans, together with Hangzhou and Jinan, to sub-provincial cities. Now, there are 15 sub-provincial cities, namely, Shenyang, Dalian, Changchun, Harbin, Jinan, Qingdao, Nanjing, Ningbo, Hangzhou, Xiamen, Wuhan, Guangzhou, Shenzhen, Xi'an and Chengdu (Chongqing has become a municipality directly under the central government).

As the sub-provincial city does not enjoy clearly defined constitutional status, nor even is there a clear political and administrative standard for it, the legal and political basis for setting up a sub-provincial city is absent. Mainly, it is a product of a technical compromise between the central government and relevant departments of local governments.[7]

At present, sub-provincial cities are still under the leadership of the province they belong to, do not form an independent level of administration, and are not much different in form from other prefecture-level cities. However, since their upgrading to the sub-provincial level has opened more channels for them to approach the central government, and the administrative ranks of the government officials has been enhanced with it, more sub-provincial cities are expected to appear in the near future. After all, there is no clearly laid legal basis for establishing a sub-provincial city, so when the number of such cities is high enough, there will come the question of how to change the administrative division system.

(3) Prefecture-level Cities

A prefecture-level city is a large or medium-sized city, smaller than an MDUCG and sub-provincial city. It generally has an urban, non-agricultural population of over 250,000, which includes over 200,000 in the seat of the city government; a total industrial output value of over 2 billion yuan; developed tertiary industry with an output value exceeding that of primary industry and accounting for over 35 percent of the GDP; over 200 million yuan of budgetary revenue at the local level; and has become a central city among several cities and counties. By the end of 1997, there were 222 prefecture-level cities around China.

Due to various factors, prefecture-level cities are vastly different in size and condition, and, as a result, enjoy different degrees of power. Cities where governments of provinces and autonomous regions are located, as well as larger cities, with the approval of the State Council, have the power to make their own administrative rules.

Prefecture-level cities are local administrative divisions under provinces and autonomous regions. They have districts, counties and county-level cities under them.

Since the system of cities exercising jurisdiction over counties has become the major way to handle the relations between province-level administrative organs and county-level ones (the system has been adopted throughout Liaoning, Guangdong and Jiangsu provinces), prefecture-level cities have gradually developed into an administrative level under that of provinces and autonomous regions with jurisdiction over the counties; their importance is growing in the whole administrative system. In fact, a prefecture-level city has become a local administrative unit with the characteristics of both ordinary local administrative divisions and local city divisions.

(4) County-level Cities

A county-level city is established in a relatively small area that meets the state standards for a city.

Generally speaking, a county-level city is a small city, and is basically a city not divided into districts.

The models of such cities are a few small commodity economy centers with long histories and obvious local characteristics. They are basically towns with a relatively developed urban economy and culture.

Another type of county-level cities are developed on the basis of counties. As the economy and society of many counties have not developed enough for urbanization of the entire area under their jurisdiction, such county-level cities still have rural areas. Only some of their government organs and functions related to the management of urban affairs are expanded. This type of county-level city is, in fact, an ordinary administrative division with jurisdiction over both rural and urban areas.

Although under the Constitution a county-level city is an grassroots urban administrative division not being divided into districts, most county-level cities developed out of the former counties still have townships and towns in their rural areas.

Generally speaking, a county-level city is developed from a county with a relatively high level of economic and social development. Except for a few directly under provincial or autonomous regional governments, most of the county-level cities are under the jurisdiction of prefecture administrative offices or prefecture-level cities. There are generally three types of county-level cities in the organizational setup of state administration: 1) County-level cities where there are prefecture administrative offices — these cities are under the direct leadership of provincial or autonomous regional governments and subject to supervision from the prefecture administrative offices. 2) County-level cities in places where there are no prefecture administrative offices — these cities are under the direct leadership of the provincial or autonomous regional governments. 3) County-level cities in places where the system of prefecture-level cities exercise jurisdiction over the counties and county-level cities, and county-level cities in places where autonomy of ethnic minorities is practiced — these cities are under the leadership of the governments of the prefecture-level cities or autonomous prefectures, or prefecture administrative offices.

Under a county-level city there are governments of townships, ethnic townships, towns, and in some cases subdistrict offices.

(5) Districts

A district is a functional local government within a city.

District governments are established in MDUCGs, sub-provincial cities and prefecture-level cities. A handful of prefecture-level cities have no districts under them.

The main reason for establishing districts in cities is to increase efficiency of administration.

A city is an economic and social unit with a relatively high degree of concentration and unity, and therefore it has a highly unified administration. This nature of a city limits the relative independence of its districts. Although the districts are independent administrative units, not dispatched organs of city governments, their powers and functions are limited by the government of the respective MDUCG, sub-provincial city or prefecture-level city, so as to keep consistency of city administration and social development. Therefore a district is an administrative unit with relatively incomplete functions.

The district government, in accordance with the nature of the area under its jurisdiction, can be divided into urban and suburban administrations. The suburbs are rural areas far from the city center, which are without any characteristics or development degree of a city. With vast lands and source of non-staple food supply for the city, the suburban areas are significant for further development of the city and the life of the urban residents.

An urban district government, located in the city proper, is a grassroots urban government. It can set up dispatched organs, known as neighborhood (sub-district) offices. Under a suburban district government there are governments of townships, ethnic townships, towns, and/or sub-district offices.

(6) Towns

In China, towns in the modern sense first appeared in the "Regulations of Autonomy of Towns and Townships"[8] of the Qing Dynasty. A town is a local administrative unit with the characteristics of a city, while a township is rural. The 1954 Constitution of China provided that a town is a grassroots administrative unit under a county, and at the same level as a township and ethnic township. Despite the several changes that occurred later, towns have always existed as administrative units under counties in areas with a certain level of industrial and commercial development. At present, towns as grassroots administrative units can be basically divided into sub-county-level towns, district-level towns and township-level towns.

A town is an administrative division under a county with jurisdiction over an area with a relatively high level of industrial and commercial development, a relatively dense population and fairly complete public facilities. Under the system of separate residence registration for urban and rural areas, a town is by nature a local administrative unit with both rural and urban features, or a city at the lowest level. Viewed from the perspective of social and economic development, a town has the features and functions of a city. But as the growth of China's cities is more a result of planning and administrative arrangement than a product of natural social and economic development, a town cannot obtain the status of city naturally and its development is limited.

3. Ethnic Regional Autonomy

Regional autonomous governments of ethnic minorities are local administrative units with autonomous rights and status established in places where regional autonomy for ethnic minorities is practiced.

China's current system of regional autonomy for ethnic minorities is a unique type of autonomy. It is "an appropriate combination of ethnic autonomy and regional autonomy, and of economic and political factors.... This system is an unprecedented creation."[9] It basic characteristics are as follows: Regional autonomy for ethnic minorities is not autonomy for each individual ethnic group, but is practiced in areas inhabited by ethnic minorities in compact communities; it does not mean autonomy for all ethnic groups living in the autonomous area, but that of the ethnic group enjoying regional autonomy in the autonomous area.[10] Therefore, it is neither ethnic autonomy nor regional autonomy. Rather, it is regional autonomy for certain ethnic minorities in the area they inhabit.

There are four types of ethnic autonomous areas: 1) autonomous areas established mainly for one ethnic minority group, such as the Liangshan Yi Autonomous Prefecture in Sichuan; 2) autonomous areas established mainly for one large ethnic minority group, but are inhabited by one or more other ethnic minority groups with smaller populations, such as the Guangxi Zhuang Autonomous Region and Xinjiang Uygur Autonomous Region; 3) autonomous areas based on places inhabited by two or more ethnic minority groups, such as the Jishishan Bonan, Dongxiang and Salar Autonomous County; 4) autonomous areas established for ethnic minorities where the Han population makes the overwhelming part, such as the Inner Mongolia Autonomous Region. To a certain extent, autonomous areas for ethnic minorities reflect the distribution of ethnic minority groups.

An ethnic-minority autonomous government is more like an ordinary local administration than a city administration. In accordance with the current laws and policies on regional autonomy for ethnic minorities, a province-level ethnic-minority autonomous area is called autonomous region, the one between the province and the county is an autonomous prefecture, and the one at the county level is an autonomous county. Only autonomous regions, prefectures and counties are autonomous areas for ethnic minorities; districts of the cities and ethnic townships in the counties are not. Although "the people's congresses of ethnic townships may, within the limits of their authority as prescribed by law, take specific measures suited to the characteristics of the ethnic groups concerned,"[11] in legal sense, they are only a subsidiary administrative divisions in areas where certain ethnic minorities live in relatively compact communities.

(1) Autonomous Regions

An autonomous region is an ethnic regional autonomous area at the level of a province. There are now five autonomous regions in China, the first to be set up being the Inner Mongolia Autonomous Region, and the most recent being the Tibet Autonomous Region.

Autonomous sub-divisions of other ethnic minority groups can be set up within an autonomous region. For example, in the Xinjiang Uygur Autonomous Region there is the Mongolian Autonomous Prefecture of Bayingolin.

An autonomous region can also have ordinary local administrative sub-divisions.

(2) Autonomous Prefectures

An autonomous prefecture is an ethnic regional autonomous division in-between the province and county. It is generally at the same level as a prefecture (except for the Kazak Autonomous Prefecture of Ili in Xinjiang, which is above the prefectural level and below that of an autonomous region).

Apart from the five in Xinjiang, all the other autonomous prefectures are set up in the various provinces, such as Jilin, Hunan, Hubei, Yunnan, Guizhou, Sichuan and Gansu. Sichuan Province has the most autonomous prefectures.

Autonomous prefectures have jurisdiction over counties, autonomous counties, cities and, in the case of the Kazak Autonomous Prefecture of Ili in Xinjiang, prefectures.

There are 30 autonomous prefectures in China.

(3) Autonomous Counties (Banners)

An autonomous county is a county-level ethnic autonomous division catering to one or more ethnic minorities, and it is the lowest autonomous division.

An autonomous county (banner) can be set up within an ordinary administrative division or an autonomous division for ethnic minorities. The provinces with autonomous counties (banners) are: Heilongjiang, Jilin, Liaoning, Qinghai, Gansu, Hebei, Hubei, Hunan, Zhejiang, Yunnan,

Guizhou, Sichuan, Guangdong, and Hainan. Yunnan has the most autonomous counties. The autonomous regions with autonomous counties (banners) under them are: Guangxi, Inner Mongolia, and Xinjiang. Guangxi has the most autonomous counties.

There are 124 autonomous counties (banners) in China.

Section 3 Local People's Governments

I. Legal and Administrative Status of Local Governments

1. Legal and Administrative Status of Local Governments

Local governments at various levels are the executive bodies of state power as well as local organs of state administration at the corresponding levels.

Local governments are responsible and report on their work to the people's congresses at the corresponding levels. Local governments at and above the county level are responsible and report on their work to the standing committees of the people's congresses at the corresponding levels when the people's congresses at the corresponding levels are not in session.

Local governments are responsible and report on their work to the state administrative organs at the next-higher level. Local people's governments at various levels throughout the country are state administrative organs under the unified leadership of the State Council and are subordinate to it.

Local governments at and above the county level direct the work of their subordinate departments and of the governments at lower levels. They have the power to alter or annul inappropriate decisions of their subordinate departments and of governments at lower levels. Local governments at or above the county level establish auditing departments. Local auditing departments at various levels independently exercise the power of supervision through auditing in accordance with the law and are responsible to the governments at the corresponding levels and to auditing bodies at the next higher level.

2. Functions and Powers of Local Governments

Local governments at and above the county level have the following functions and powers: executing resolutions of the people's congress at

the corresponding levels and their standing committees, and decisions
and mandates of state administrative organs at a higher level; taking administrative actions, and issuing decisions and issuing mandates; directing
the work of their subordinate departments and governments at lower levels; altering or annulling inappropriate decisions, mandates and instructions
of the subordinate departments and the people's governments at lower
levels; appointing and removing administrative functionaries, training
them, appraising their performance, and rewarding or punishing them;
carrying out national economic and social development plans and budgets; conducting administrative work concerning the economy, education,
science, culture, health, physical culture, environment and resources
protection, urban and rural development, finance, civil affairs, public
security, ethnic affairs, judicial administration, supervision and family
planning in their respective administrative areas; protecting public and
collective-owned properties, and citizens' legal private property; maintaining social order; ensuring citizens' right of the person, democratic
rights and other rights; protecting the legal rights and interests of various
economic organizations; guaranteeing the rights of ethnic minorities and
respecting their traditions and customs; helping with regional autonomy
in places inhabited by ethic minorities in compact communities within
their administrative areas in accordance with the Constitution and law;
helping ethnic minorities with political, economic and cultural development; guaranteeing the constitutional and legal rights of women, including
equality between men and women, equal pay for equal work, and voluntary marriage; and handling tasks assigned by state administrative organs
at higher levels.

The governments of provinces, autonomous regions and MDUCGs
have the authority to enact, in accordance with the law, local laws and
regulations of the provinces, autonomous regions and MDUCGs, and report them to the State Council and the standing committees of the
people's congress at the same level for the record. People's governments
of cities where the provincial or autonomous regional governments are
located, and those of large cities designated by the State Council have the
authority to, in accordance with the law, enact local laws and regulations,
and report them to the State Council, standing committee of the provincial or autonomous regional people's congresses, people's governments
of the provinces or autonomous regions, and the standing committee of
the people's congress at the same levels for the record. But all the regula-

tions to be enacted must be discussed and decided on by meetings of the standing committees or plenary meetings of the governments at the corresponding levels.

Governments of provinces and autonomous regions have the right to decide on the establishment and geographic division of townships, ethnic townships and towns.

The functions and powers of governments of townships, ethnic townships and towns are as follows: executing the resolutions of the people's congresses at the corresponding level, and decisions and orders of the state administrative organs at the next-higher level; issuing decisions and mandates; carrying out local economic and social development plans and budgets; conducting administrative work in economy, education, science, culture, health, physical culture, environment and resources protection, urban and rural development, finance, civil affairs, public security, ethnic affairs, judicial administration, and family planning in their respective administrative areas; protecting public and collective-owned properties, and citizens' legal private property; maintaining social order; ensuring citizens' right of the person, democratic rights and other rights; protecting the legal rights and interests of various economic organizations; guaranteeing the rights of ethnic minorities and respecting their traditions and customs; helping with regional autonomy in areas inhabited by ethic minorities within its administrative area in accordance with the Constitution and law; helping ethnic minorities with political, economic and cultural development; guaranteeing the constitutional and legal rights of women, including equality between men and women, equal pay for equal work, and voluntary marriage; and handling tasks assigned by state administrative organs at higher levels.

People's governments of provinces, autonomous regions, MDUCGs, autonomous prefectures, counties, autonomous counties, cities and districts shall provide assistance to state organs, enterprises and institutions which are located in their administrative areas but not under their jurisdiction, and exercise supervision over them in the sphere of abiding by or enforcing laws and policies.

Functional departments of provincial, autonomous regional and MDUCG governments are under the unified leadership of the governments, and under the guidance or leadership of the authorities of the State Council in their work in accordance with the law or administrative regulations. Departments of governments of autonomous prefectures, counties, autonomous counties, cities and districts are under the unified leadership of the governments, and under the guidance or leadership of the authorities of the governments above them.

II. Composition and Terms of Office of Local Governments

1. Composition of Local Governments

Governments of the provinces, autonomous regions, MDUCGs, autonomous prefectures, and cities divided into districts are respectively headed by the governor and vice-governor of the relevant province, chairman and vice-chairman of the autonomous region, mayor and vice-mayor of the MDUCG, and head and deputy head of the prefecture. The other members of the governments are: secretaries, heads of departments, heads of bureaus and chairmen of committees. People's governments of counties, autonomous counties, cities not divided into districts, and districts are respectively headed by the magistrate and vice-magistrate of the county, mayor and vice-mayor of the city, and head and deputy head of the district. The other members of the governments are: heads of bureaus and heads of divisions. People's governments of townships and ethnic townships are led by the head and deputy head. The head of an ethnic township shall be a member of the relevant ethnic minority group or one of the relevant ethnic minority groups in the township. People's governments of towns are led by the head and deputy head.

Governors, mayors and heads of counties, districts, townships and towns assume overall responsibility for and preside over the work of local people's governments at the respective levels.

Within two months after their election by the people's congresses at the corresponding levels, the leaders of the new local governments shall submit to the standing committees of the people's congress at the corresponding levels for appointments of the secretaries, heads of departments, bureaus and divisions, and chairmen of committees.

Departments, bureaus, committees and divisions are led by their respective heads, and, if necessary, have deputy heads. General offices are led by their directors, and, if necessary, have deputy directors.

Each of the governments of provinces, autonomous regions, MDUCGs, autonomous prefectures and cities divided into districts shall have a secretary-general and deputy secretaries-general.

2. Terms of Office of Local Governments

The term of office of the governments of provinces, autonomous regions, MDUCGs, autonomous prefectures, counties, autonomous counties, cities and municipal districts is five years. The term of office of the governments of townships, ethnic townships and towns is three years.

III. Working Departments of Local Governments

The local governments at any level can establish their own working departments, which include component and non-component departments.

1. Component and Non-Component Departments of Local Governments

Component departments of local governments are those that form parts of the local governments. There are departments at various levels and of various types in a local government. Besides the component departments, the local governments also have various non-component departments, such as organizations directly affiliated to them, working organs, temporary organizations, institutions, and even offices established by governments at higher levels. Except for the last, all others are under the leadership of the local governments.

Organs under the leadership of local governments have different statuses in local politics and administration. Some organs are more independent, with independent administrative and legal status, while others have no legal subject status. Some are mainly in charge of certain aspects of social affairs on behalf of the local governments, while others mainly provide services to the heads of the local government and other departments. The heads of some organs must be appointed or removed by the local people's congresses, while those of some organs are appointed or removed by the local governments. In general, as there is no legislation on local government organs — with only vague principles guiding the establishment of working organs of local governments, in practice the continuity of previous methods of administration, instructions of departments at higher levels and specific policies on certain organs all affect the establishment of the organs of local governments. As a result, local governments differ in the establishment of their organs.

At present, there is no clear standard, or no direct and clear standard, so to speak, with which to judge whether a local government organization is a component part of the local government. In accordance with the Organic Law of the People's Republic of China on Local People's Congresses and Local People's Governments at Various Levels, local governments at or above the county level shall get approval from the government at the next-higher level for establishing, adding, reducing or merging their working organs, such as departments, bureaus and committees, and report such to the people's congresses at the corresponding levels for the record. In practice, the standard for determining a component department of the local government is deduced from the above provision, that is, a component department of a local government is a working organ established with the approval of the government at the next-higher level, in the records with the people's congress at the corresponding level, and with its head appointed or removed by the people's congress at the corresponding level. Besides this indirect provision, there are provisions in some laws concerning the qualification of a few organizations as component departments of local governments. In accordance with the Organic Law of the People's Republic of China on Local People's Congresses and Local People's Governments at Various Levels, local governments at or above the county level shall establish auditing departments. In accordance with the Law of Supervision, local governments at or above the county level shall establish supervision departments. So these two departments are naturally component departments of the local governments.

Except for the auditing and supervision departments, the qualification of an organization as a component department of the local government is determined by approval of the administrative organ at the next-higher level, and the people's congress at the corresponding level, based on this approval, decides the staff of the local government, in order to exercise its power of appointing and removing officials of administrative organizations. So it is the administrative organ at the next-higher level that has the power to decide whether an organization is a component department of a local government. Thus, the administrative organ at the next-higher level and the people's congress at the corresponding level have a certain influence on the structure, size and staff composition of the local government. Moreover, as the administrative organ at the next-higher level and the people's congress at the corresponding level have no power over the non-component departments of the local government, the local government has almost unlimited power to appoint the heads of these departments. This is obviously a legal, political and administrative blind spot in the present local government system.

2. Establishment of Local Government Departments

Local governments at all levels have more than one departments. The system of unitary centralization determines that the establishment of local government departments basically follows the same pattern. There is seldom an obvious difference between local governments at different levels or of different types in the establishment of their departments. Moreover, the low degree of separation between government and society, between government and enterprises, and between government and individuals has resulted in the dominant position of government in today's society, and the large number and scale of government organizations. In accordance with the current regulations on the establishment of government organizations, there are 40 to 50 government organizations under a provincial or autonomous regional government, around 60 under a municipal government directly under the central government or a sub-provincial city government, 40 to 50 under a prefecture-level city government or a prefecture administrative office, and 20 to 30 under a county or a county-level city government.

Organizations under townships, ethnic townships and towns vary in different areas. There are offices, committees or divisions directly under a township, ethnic township and town government; offices dispatched by the government at the next-higher level, which are under the leadership of both town or township government and the government that dispatches it; and offices of enterprises and institutions from the county or city government. In accordance with the 1993 plan on reform· of town and township organizations, the staff of a township, ethnic-minority township and town government numbers between 15 and 45.

Township or town government, the grassroots government in rural areas, has important political and administrative functions. Its organizations are essentially the same as those of local governments at different levels, corresponding to those of the government at the next-higher level. Since a township or town has a relatively small population, a less-developed economy and fewer resources, its government organizations are different from those of governments at higher levels in terms of administrative subordination and scale. For example, Chenliu Town, under Kaifeng City, Henan Province, has a General Office, Family Planning

Office, Civil Administration Office, Land Management Office, Rural Cooperative Economy and Operation Station, Agricultural Technology Station, Water Resources Station, Animal Husbandry Station, Forestry Station, Culture and Broadcasting Station, Administration Office of Industry and Commerce, Office of Finance, Office of Justice, Police Station, and Power Station. Among them, the General Office, Family Planning Office, Civil Administration Office, Office of Land Management, Rural Cooperative Economy and Operation Station, Agricultural Technology Station, Water Resources Station, Animal Husbandry Station, Forestry Station, and Culture and Broadcasting Station are under the leadership of the town government. The rest are under the dual leadership of both the town and county governments. That is, the relevant departments of the county government are in charge of the personnel, financial affairs and property of the organizations, while the town government is in charge of their CPC groups.

Notes:

[1] Some scholars suggest the term "unitary democratic centralism." This classification takes into consideration China's political principle of democratic centralism, but seems to shed little additional light on the issue. Also see *Form of State Structure* by Tong Zhiwei, pp.221-222. Wuhan: Wuhan University Press, 1997.

[2] *The Oxford Companion to Law*, by David M. Walker. Oxford: Oxford University Press, New York, 1980.

[3] See "Administration of Townships and Towns Needs a Breakthrough in the System" by Yang Fengchun, *Consultation on Decision Making*, Vol. 10, 2001, pp.10-11.

[4] See "Status Quo of China's Administrative Division System and the Plan for Reform" by Gong Guizhi, *Political Studies*, Issue No. 2, 2000, p.63.

[5] See *Essentials of Local State Organizations of China*, compiled by Diao Tianding, p.307. Beijing: Law Press, 1989.

[6] See *Essentials of Local State Organizations of China*, compiled by Diao Tianding, pp. 175-176. Beijing: Law Press, 1989.

[7] See "Economists Fan Hengshan, Hu An'gang and Others Discuss Whether the Cities Working Out Their Own Economic and Social Development Plans Shall Be Upgraded to the Sub-provincial Level," *Domestic Trends*, July 25, 1996.

[8] See *Essentials of Local State Organizations of China*, by Diao Tianding, chief ed., p.341. Beijing: Law Press, 1989.

[9] "Some Questions about China's Ethnic Policy" by Zhou Enlai (August 4, 1957), *Selected Works of Zhou Enlai on United Front Work.* Beijing: People's Publishing House, December 1984.

[10] *Survey of China's Ethnic Policies*, compiled by Zhang Youjun and Xu Jieshun, pp.286-287. Nanning: Guangxi Education Press, 1992.

[11] Article 99, *Constitution of the People's Republic of China.* Beijing: Foreign Languages Press, fourth edition (with Chinese text), 1999, p. 46.

Chapter Seven

THE PRESIDENT

I. Status and Functions of the President

The president of the People's Republic of China is the head of the state, representing the People's Republic of China.

Like the National People's Congress, the State Council, the Supreme People's Court, the Supreme People's Procuratorate and the Central Military Commission, the president of the People's Republic of China is an important state organ.

According to the Constitution, the president of the PRC is mainly a ceremonial organ and post: the president does not decide on any state affairs independently, but exercises relevant functions and powers in pursuance of the decisions of the National People's Congress and its Standing Committee. Together with the Standing Committee of the National People's Congress, the president exercise functions and powers as the highest representative of the state both in domestic and foreign affairs.

II. Qualifications, Election, Term of Office and Succession of the President

1. Qualifications of the President

According to Article 79 of the Constitution of the PRC, "Citizens of the People's Republic of China who have the right to vote and to stand for election and who have reached the age of 45 are eligible for election as President or Vice-President of the People's Republic of China."[1]

Compared with constitutions of other countries, the Constitution of the PRC gives relatively liberal provisions on the qualifications of the president. It does not include such elements as party affiliation, political belief, experience, achievements, or social or economic status. A comparatively large number of PRC citizens are eligible.

2. Election, Resignation and Dismissal of the President

The president of the PRC is the head of the PRC, and represents the PRC. But the method of election of the president does not give prominence to this high position. The president, the head of state, and the vice-president are elected through the same procedure and at the same time.

The presidium of the National People's Congress puts forward the candidates for the president and vice-president, and the congress elects them through a single-candidate election.

The presidium has the power to put forward the candidates for the president and vice-president. No deputy, delegation, group of deputies, group of delegations, or the Standing Committee has power as such.

For election, the candidates for the president and vice-president should win over half the votes of all the deputies.

The usual procedure is as follows: The presidium of the new National People's Congress puts forward an initial list of candidates for the president and vice-president at the first meeting of the NPC for "study and discussion" by all the delegations; then the presidium of the NPC decides the final candidates for the president and vice-president in accordance with the majority opinion of the delegations, and officially submits them to the NPC for vote.

If the president or vice-president resigns during a session of the National People's Congress, the presidium will submit his or her resignation to the delegations for discussion, and then submit it to a plenary meeting of the congress for decision. If the president or vice-president resigns while the National People's Congress is not in session, the council of Chairmen of the Standing Committee will submit the resignation to the Standing Committee of the NPC for discussion and decision. If the Standing Committee of the NPC accepts the resignation, it will be submitted to the next NPC for confirmation.

The NPC has the power to remove the president. The procedure is as follows: More than three delegations or over one tenth of the deputies of the NPC jointly put forward a proposal for removing the president or vice-president, and the presidium submits it to the National People's Congress for discussion and voting.[2]

3. Term of Office of the President

The term of office of the president and vice-president is the same as that of the National People's Congress, and they may serve no more than two consecutive terms.

The president exercises his or her functions and powers until the new president the next NPC has elected assumes office.

4. Succession to the Post of the President

The office of the president or vice-president is considered to be vacant when the president or vice-president is unable to attend to his or her duties because of illness or death. According to Article 84 of the Constitution, "In the event that the office of the President of the People's Republic of China falls vacant, the Vice-President succeeds to the office of the President. In the event that the office of the Vice-President of the People's Republic of China falls vacant, the national People's Congress shall elect a new Vice-President to fill the vacancy. In the event that the offices of both the President and Vice-President of the People's Republic of China fall vacant, the National People's Congress shall elect a new President and a new Vice-President. Prior to such election, the Chairman of the Standing Committee of the National People's Congress shall temporarily act as the President of the People's Republic of China."[3]

When the office of the vice-president falls vacant, the National People's Congress shall elect a new vice-president.

III. Basic Functions and Powers of the President

The basic functions of the president are: promulgating statutes, issuing decrees and officiating at ceremonies.

1. Domestic Functions and Powers of the President

(1) Promulgating Statutes

Statutes adopted by the NPC and its Standing Committee go into effect upon promulgation by the president of the PRC. The president of the PRC has no power to veto statutes, and shall promulgate any statute adopted by the NPC and its Standing Committee.

No statute shall become effective without promulgation by the president of the PRC.

(2) Appointing and Removing Officials

The president of the PRC, in pursuance of the decisions of the NPC and its Standing Committee, promulgates the appointment or removal of the premier, vice-premiers, state councilors, ministers in charge of ministries or commissions, the auditor-general and the secretary general of the State Council.

(3) Issue Decrees

The president issues orders granting special pardons; proclaims martial law; proclaims a state of war; and issues mobilization orders.

(4) Officiating at Ceremonies

The president confers state medals and titles of honor in pursuance of the decisions of the NPC and its Standing Committee.

Medals and titles of honor conferred by the president are the highest honors granted by the PRC.

2. External Functions and Powers of the President

(1) Receiving foreign diplomatic representatives on behalf of the PRC;

(2) Appointing and recalling plenipotentiary representatives abroad in pursuance of the decisions of the NPC Standing Committee;

(3) Ratifying and abrogating treaties and important agreements concluded with foreign states in pursuance of decisions made by the NPC or its Standing Committee.

The president of the PRC shall promulgate the treaties and agreements concluded by the State Council or its relevant departments with foreign countries, which have been ratified by the NPC or its Standing Committee. The president of the PRC shall abrogate treaties and agreements in pursuance of decisions made by the NPC or its Standing Committee.

IV. Changes in the Presidential System

1. The Organization of the Office of the President

The office of the president is in nature a state organization. Before the Eighth National People's Congress, there was no working organization for the president. After taking office as the president, Jiang Zemin appointed special aides for the president and established the Presidential Office. The organization of the president has been set up because the power and authority of the post of the president are obviously and strongly linked to the individual acting as the president.

2. Development of the Functions and Powers of the President

Since the Eighth National People's Congress, the president's functions and powers have developed significantly. The most striking development is in the president's diplomatic power. According to the current Constitution and laws, the premier of the State Council and the foreign minister, as the major executives of the diplomatic power, engage in essential diplomatic activities. But with the promotion of China's strategy of great-nation diplomacy, "head-of-state diplomacy" has become more and more important, and the president is becoming more and more involved in and assuming some of the powers of diplomacy.

Notes

[1] *Constitution of the People's Republic of China*, Fourth edition (with Chinese text), p. 37. Beijing: Foreign Languages Press, 1999.

[2] Article 15 of the "Organic Law of the National People's Congress of the People's Republic of China," and Article 39 of the "Rules of Procedures of the National People's Congress of the People's Republic of China."

[3] *Constitution of the People's Republic of China*, Fourth edition (with Chinese text), p. 38. Beijing: Foreign Languages Press, 1999.

图书在版编目（CIP）数据

中国政府 / 杨凤春著.
－北京：外文出版社，2004
ISBN 7－119－03285－2
I. 中…　II. 杨…　III. 国家行政机关－简介－中国－英文
IV. D630.1

中国版本图书馆 CIP 数据核字（2004）第 009445 号

英文翻译	章挺权　王宗引	**责任编辑**	贾先锋
	王增芬　张韶宁	**装帧设计**	蔡　荣
英文审定	李振国	**印刷监制**	韩少乙

中　国　政　府

杨凤春　著

*

©外文出版社
外文出版社出版
（中国北京百万庄大街 24 号）
邮政编码　100037
外文出版社网址 http://www.flp.com.cn
外文出版社电子信箱: info@flp.com.cn
sales@flp.com.cn

三河市汇鑫印务有限公司印刷
中国国际图书贸易总公司发行
（中国北京车公庄西路 35 号）
北京邮政信箱第 399 号　邮政编码　100044
2004 年(小 16 开)第 1 版
2004 年第 1 版第 1 次印刷
（英）
ISBN 7－119－03285－2
06800
3－E－3542 S